The Brexit Policy Fiasco

This volume attempts to examine the many possible causes of Brexit. The conceptual 'peg' on which the volume hangs is that, irrespective of one's views on whether Britain's exit from the EU was a good or a bad thing, Brexit can justifiably be seen as yet another example of a British policy fiasco. Put simply, the British political elite was not at its best.

The collective concern of this volume is twofold. First, it advances possible explanations of how the Brexit issue arose. Why was Britain's membership of the EU thought to be so problematic for so many members of the British political elite and ultimately for a majority of voters? How did we get to June 2016 and the Brexit Referendum? Second, the volume examines how the issue was managed (or mismanaged) following the referendum result up until the Withdrawal Agreement in March 2019. The contributions to this volume explore these questions by looking at Brexit from different analytical angles. Some authors explore the long-term causes of Brexit by disentangling the fraught relationship between the UK and the EU, which had provided the Brexit train with steam; others explore the highly conflictual domestic political dynamics in the run-up to the referendum and in the negotiations of a Brexit deal.

The chapters in this book were originally published as a special issue of *Journal of European Public Policy.*

Jeremy Richardson is Emeritus Fellow at Nuffield College at the University of Oxford, UK, and an Adjunct Professor at the University of Canterbury, Christchurch, New Zealand. His most recent book is *British Policy-making and The Need for a Post-BREXIT Policy Style,* Palgrave, 2018. Previous titles include *European Union. Power and policy-making,* Fourth Edition, edited with Sonia Mazey, Routledge, and *Constructing a Policy-Making State? Policy Dynamics in the EU* (Ed.), 2012, Oxford University Press.

Berthold Rittberger is Professor of International Relations at the University of Munich, Germany. His research focuses on EU integration, political representation, and regulatory-policy-making.

Journal of European Public Policy Series

Series Editors

Jeremy Richardson *is Emeritus Fellow at Nuffield College, Oxford University, UK, and an Adjunct Professor in the National Centre for Research on Europe, University of Canterbury, New Zealand.*

Berthold Rittberger *is Professor and Chair of International Relations at the Geschwister-Scholl-Institute of Political Science at the University of Munich, Germany.*

This series seeks to bring together some of the finest edited works on European Public Policy. Reprinting from Special Issues of the *Journal of European Public Policy*, the focus is on using a wide range of social sciences approaches, both qualitative and quantitative, to gain a comprehensive and definitive understanding of Public Policy in Europe

The Politics and Economics of Brexit
Edited by Simon Bulmer and Lucia Quaglia

Free Movement and Non-discrimination in an Unequal Union
Edited by Susanne K. Schmidt, Michael Blauberger and Dorte Sindbjerg Martinsen

The Political Economy of Pension Financialisation
Edited by Anke Hassel and Tobias Wiß

The European Union Beyond the Polycrisis?
Integration and Politicization in an Age of Shifting Cleavages
Edited by Jonathan Zeitlin and Francesco Nicoli

Ideologies and the European Union
Edited by Carlo Invernizzi Accetti and Jonathan White

Strategic Responses to Domestic Contestation
The EU Between Politicisation and Depoliticisation
Edited by Edoardo Bressanelli, Christel Koop and Christine Reh

The Brexit Policy Fiasco
Edited by Jeremy Richardson and Berthold Rittberger

Domestic Contestation of the European Union
Edited by Sara B. Hobolt and Toni Rodon

For more information about this series, please visit: https://www.routledge.com/Journal-of-European-Public-Policy-Special-Issues-as-Books/book-series/JEPPSPIBS

The Brexit Policy Fiasco

Edited by
Jeremy Richardson
and Berthold Rittberger

Routledge
Taylor & Francis Group
LONDON AND NEW YORK

First published 2021
by Routledge
2 Park Square, Milton Park, Abingdon, Oxon, OX14 4RN

and by Routledge
605 Third Avenue, New York, NY 10158

Routledge is an imprint of the Taylor & Francis Group, an informa business

British Library Cataloguing-in-Publication Data
A catalogue record for this book is available from the British Library

ISBN13: 978-0-367-74890-6 (hbk)
ISBN13: 978-0-367-74894-4 (pbk)
ISBN13: 978-1-003-16010-6 (ebk)

Typeset in Myriad Pro
by codeMantra

Publisher's Note
The publisher accepts responsibility for any inconsistencies that may have arisen during the conversion of this book from journal articles to book chapters, namely the inclusion of journal terminology.

Contents

Citation Information

The chapters in this book were originally published in the *Journal of European Public Policy*, volume 27, issue 5 (April 2020). When citing this material, please use the original page numbering for each article, as follows:

Introduction
Brexit: simply an omnishambles or a major policy fiasco?
Jeremy Richardson and Berthold Rittberger
Journal of European Public Policy, volume 27, issue 5 (April 2020) pp. 649–665

Chapter 1
Narrative genres of Brexit: the Leave campaign and the success of romance
Alexander Spencer and Kai Oppermann
Journal of European Public Policy, volume 27, issue 5 (April 2020) pp. 666–684

Chapter 2
Explanations for the Brexit policy fiasco: near-impossible challenge, leadership failure or Westminster pathology?
Allan McConnell and Simon Tormey
Journal of European Public Policy, volume 27, issue 5 (April 2020) pp. 685–702

Chapter 3
Can't get no learning: the Brexit fiasco through the lens of policy learning
Claire A. Dunlop, Scott James and Claudio M. Radaelli
Journal of European Public Policy, volume 27, issue 5 (April 2020) pp. 703–722

Chapter 4
Divided they fail: the politics of wedge issues and Brexit
Tim Heinkelmann-Wild, Lisa Kriegmair, Berthold Rittberger and Bernhard Zangl
Journal of European Public Policy, volume 27, issue 5 (April 2020) pp. 723–741

Chapter 5

Political, process and programme failures in the Brexit fiasco: exploring the role of policy deception
Darrin Baines, Sharron Brewer and Adrian Kay
Journal of European Public Policy, volume 27, issue 5 (April 2020) pp. 742–760

Chapter 6

The Brexit car crash: using E.H. Carr to explain Britain's choice to leave the European Union in 2016
Justin O. Frosini and Mark F. Gilbert
Journal of European Public Policy, volume 27, issue 5 (April 2020) pp. 761–778

Chapter 7

No match made in heaven. Parliamentary sovereignty, EU over-constitutionalization and Brexit
Susanne K. Schmidt
Journal of European Public Policy, volume 27, issue 5 (April 2020) pp. 779–794

Contributors

Darrin Baines is Professor of Health Economics at Bournemouth University, UK. He has an active research interest in deception, politics and disinformation.

Sharron Brewer is independent researcher who contributed to this paper whilst working at Birmingham University, UK. Her work focuses on Brexit, deception and the moral foundations of voter beliefs.

Claire A. Dunlop is Professor of Politics and Public Policy at the University of Exeter, UK.

Justin O. Frosini is Associate Professor of Comparative Public Law at Bocconi University, Milan, Italy, and Adjunct Professor of Constitutional Law at The Johns Hopkins University SAIS Europe, Bologna, Italy.

Mark F. Gilbert is Resident Professor of History and International Studies at The Johns Hopkins University SAIS Europe, Bologna, Italy.

Tim Heinkelmann-Wild is researcher and doctoral candidate at the Department of Political Science at the University of Munich, Germany.

Scott James is reader in Political Economy at King's College London, UK.

Adrian Kay is Honorary Professor in the Crawford School of Public Policy at Australian National University, Cranberra, Australia.

Lisa Kriegmair is researcher and doctoral candidate at the Department of Political Science at the University of Munich, Germany.

Allan McConnell is Professor in the Department of Government and International Relations at the University of Sydney, Australia.

Kai Oppermann is Professor of International Politics at the Chemnitz University of Technology, Germany.

Claudio M. Radaelli is Professor of Public Policy at University College London, UK.

Jeremy Richardson is Emeritus Fellow at Nuffield College at the University of Oxford, UK, and Adjunct Professor at the University of Canterbury, Christchurch, New Zealand.

Berthold Rittberger is Professor of International Relations at the Department of Political Science at the University of Munich, Germany.

Susanne K. Schmidt is Professor at the University of Bremen, Germany.

Alexander Spencer is Professor of International Relations at Otto von Guericke University Magdeburg, Germany.

Simon Tormey is Professor and Dean, Faculty of Social Sciences and Law at the University of Bristol, UK.

Bernhard Zangl is Professor of Global Governance and Public Policy at the Department of Political Science at the University of Munich, Germany.

INTRODUCTION

Brexit: simply an omnishambles or a major policy fiasco?

Jeremy Richardson and Berthold Rittberger

ABSTRACT
The collective concerns of this Special Issue are twofold. First, it advances possible explanations of how the Brexit issue arose. Why was Britain's membership of the EU thought to be so problematic for so many members of the British political elite and ultimately for a majority of voters? In a nutshell, how did we get to June 2016 and the Brexit Referendum? Secondly, the Special Issue examines how the issue was managed (or mismanaged) following the referendum result up until the Withdrawal Agreement in March 2019. Drawing on the varied contributions in the Special Issue, this introduction contains our own overview of the Brexit saga, distinguishing idiosyncratic processes from the more general trends that to led to Brexit and its aftermath.

Brexit and the merging of satire and political reality?

Political satire and the reality of politics have been hand in glove in Britain for a very long period. For example, the 1980s TV series *Yes Minister* captured ministerial/civil service relations better than any academic article. Similarly, the more recent political satire TV series, *The Thick of It* encapsulated perfectly the seemingly serial chaos of elite politics in Britain. Each episode depicted a truly shambolic system of decision-making. The first episode of the third series, broadcast in 2009, featured the Minister for the (fictional) Department of Social Affairs and Citizenship being involved in a series of disasters, prompting the now famous rebuke from the Government's Director of Communications, as follows: 'Jesus Christ, you are a fucking *omnishambles*, that's what you are. You're like that coffee machine, you know: From bean to cup, you fuck up'. The term omnishambles, meaning *a situation which is shambolic from every angle*, became so established that it was awarded the word of the year prize by the Oxford Dictionary in 2012, the judges saying that it had crossed over into real life in that year. Whatever happened in Britain in 2012, it pales in comparison with the Brexit omnishambles enacted in Britain's House of Commons during 2019. Real life policy-making made the fictional shambles depicted in *The Thick of It* seem quite mundane. One of the lasting images of 2019 was of Speaker John Bercow repeatedly yelling, *Order, Order, Order* amidst scenes of what can only be describe as total *disorder*. The British political elite most certainly presided over a *policy process* that was an omnishambles of monumental proportions. The process lurched from one shambles to the next, totally undermining images of Britain as having a well-oiled, smooth running policy-making machine. Each stage of the process fitted the dictionary definition of shambles perfectly, namely *'a state of confusion, bad organisation'*. This led to a situation where office holders lost the ability to steer, let alone control, the policy process, with little or no understanding of what the short-term or long-term outcome would be. Our use of the term omnishambles is rather similar to the definition of fiasco used by Baines et al. in this volume who see fiasco as meaning to 'suffer a complete breakdown of performance' (Baines et al., 2020, p. 743).

However, rather like a play in which the rehearsals go badly but the play turns out fine on the night, it is at least possible that an omnishambles does not turn out to be a policy fiasco or blunder in the generally accepted sense (of ending in policy failure). Policy fiascos and blunders might be rather different to an omnishambles, although 'policy fiasco' is a commonly used term which has a considerable degree of elasticity. For the purposes of this Special Issue, we have consciously avoided binding our contributors to a strict definition of policy fiasco (and, on reflection, we had better used the term omnishambles, as this has no implications regarding actual policy outcomes).

Indeed, there appears to be no clear, robust, and agreed definition of what a policy fiasco is. As Oppermann and Spencer argue '... there is, however, very little agreement on the precise conceptualization of *fiasco*, with many authors referring to alternative concepts such as failure, mistake, crisis, disaster or blunder as synonyms' (Oppermann & Spencer, 2016, p. 644). For example, Jennings et al. use 'blunder', 'failure', 'fiasco', 'breakdown', and 'disaster' interchangeably (Jennings et al., 2018, p. 2). In their seminal study of policy-making in Britain, King and Crewe prefer to use the term 'blunder'. Starting with the dictionary definition of the verb 'to blunder', namely *'to move blindly, flounder, or stumble'* they go on to define a blunder as follows:

> ... an episode in which a government adopts a specific course of action in order to achieve one or more objectives and, as a result largely or wholly of its own mistakes, either fails completely to achieve those objectives, or does achieve some or all of them but contrives at the same time to cause a significant amount of "collateral damage" in the form of unintended and undesired consequences. (King & Crewe, 2014, p. 4)

This definition is an important reminder that much of the literature on policy fiascos etc. is actually about *policy outcomes,* where policy-makers' objectives (good or ill) were not actually achieved. The cases under study are usually about where a policy did not achieve its stated aims or even made the problem much worse, as King and Crewe suggest. However, with Brexit, we do not know whether Britain's exit from the EU will be a success or failure. The Brexiteers are convinced that it will be a huge success – and many already consider Britain's actual exit from the EU on 31 January 2020 as such a success –, but the Remainers are just as convinced that it will be a massive failure. We will probably not know for at least a decade. As Jenkins-Smith et al. argue, 'policy processes are ongoing, without a beginning or an end' (Jenkins-Smith et al., 2018, p. 142). 31 January 2020 is not the end of the Brexit policy process by any means, as the post-Brexit policy process will be characterised by at least two key features. First, Britain's trading relationship with the EU and the rest of the world will have to be hammered out in tortuous trade negotiations. Secondly, Britain will have to decide what to do about a huge raft of 'domestic' public policy which emanated from the EU over decades (Richardson, 2018a, p. 120). Being absolutely 'free' of EU legislation (itself only possible under a hard Brexit), does not suddenly replace EU legislation with new 'home made' legislation overnight. The 'Brexit game', at the time of writing (February 2020) is just beginning. If it is a game of two halves, we are not yet at half time. As Bovens et al. point out, 'assessments of success and failure in government are ... dependent upon temporal, spatial, cultural, and political factors' (Bovens et al., 2001, p. 20). They cite the example of the Sydney Opera House, which has featured in many studies of 'planning disasters', but where the dominant assessment has evolved over time. How many people think of this iconic building as a planning disaster now? Thus, the passage of time can change perceptions of policy success and failure quite radically. Currently, however, the Brexit process appears to meet one of the criteria for the use of the term 'blunder' suggested by King and Crewe, namely 'a really serious blunder is also likely to be widely – possibly universally – acknowledged to have been such; there is usually generally agreement on the point' (King & Crewe, 2014, p. 4). Focusing on the *process* at least, there is little doubt that, to put it mildly, the Brexit process was not a pretty sight. This characterisation of the general perception of the Brexit process comes quite close to one set of indicators of political failure or success suggested by Bovens et al. nearly two decades ago, as follows:

> Indicators of political failure or success are political upheaval (press coverage, parliamentary investigations, political fatalities, litigation) or lack of it, and changes in general patterns of political legitimacy (public satisfaction with policy or confidence in authorities and public institutions. (Bovens et al., 2001, p. 21)

The Brexit process appears to match this list fairly well, but one particular problem in analysing fiascos etc. is that policy fiascos are not neutral events. As Bovens and 't Hart argue '… "success" and "failure" are not attributes of policy, but rather labels applied by stakeholders and observers' (Bovens & 't Hart, 2016, p. 654). One person's policy success might be seen as another person's policy fiasco. For example, what President Donald Trump might see as succeeding 'bigly' (sic), might be seen by the many of us in a somewhat different light. All of the contributions in this Special Issue inevitably reflect the authors' own perceptions of Brexit, with perhaps a collective bias from all of us that the Brexit process has not been a pretty sight, whatever label is attached to it. Our collective task is to suggest a range of (not mutually exclusive) possible explanations of how this saga came about. Thus, the contributions highlight different causal mechanisms, although in truth, there is not going to be one main explanation for the Brexit (process) fiasco.

We also need to note that Brexit, though certainly a mega-policy, is in principle not fundamentally different to any major policy change. In trying to address the question 'how did this happen?' it is useful to remember Kingdon's warning that it is almost impossible to trace the origin of a policy proposal. He cited a US respondent as follows, 'This is not like a river. There is no point of origin' (Kingdon, 1984, p. 77). At a superficial level, one might argue that Brexit is an exception to this generalisation in that the Referendum in 2016 was the origin of the process. However, there is a huge amount of historical context to the Referendum as a key event, one example being the lack of goodness of fit between the EU and UK legal systems as suggested by Schmidt (Schmidt, 2020). One even might argue that there is a significant element of path dependency at work in the Brexit story. Brexit did not happen simply due to the Referendum. The Brexit story is more likely a story of slow tectonic forces at work, leading to the spectacular eruptions, first in 2016, then throughout 2019. Thus, we first discuss the idea that Britain never quite 'fitted' the EU and might have been destined to leave at some point. We then explore the possibility that the EU itself contributed to the Brexit fiasco and might have been engaged in some kind of 'slow burn' blunder itself. We then conclude with some reflections on Brexit as a purely domestic policy problem.

Britain as always an 'awkward partner': destined to walk out eventually?

One obvious starting point for explaining Brexit is, of course, Britain as an 'awkward partner' in Europe (George, 1990). In George's seminal work, he began his Introduction with a statement that has by now become conventional wisdom. Thus, he wrote:

> On 1 January 1973 Britain became a member of the European Communities, twenty-two years after the first of those Communities was created without British participation. Within a year of achieving membership, Britain was already regarded as something of an awkward partner, a reputation that has remained through to the time of writing. (George, 1990, p. 1)

The thirty years since George made that observation may have cemented that image throughout the EU, with Brexit probably adding the epithet 'incompetent partner' to 'awkward partner'! It should be no surprise, then, that at some point, the marriage would end in divorce or, as Frosini and Gilbert put it, 'Brexit was an accident waiting to happen' (Frosini & Gilbert, 2020, p. 761). The narrative might be that Britain joined for the wrong reasons (a marriage made in Hell not in Heaven), the EU as a partner developed more and more habits that Britain did not like at all, and, finally, Britain thought it could find better partners outside the marriage. No more explanation needed, 'the origin of the river' is clear enough. Yet this narrative is, surely, just too simple. First, we have no robust measure (or indeed definition) of 'awkwardness'. For example, how do we know that Britain has been more 'awkward' than, say France, still remembered for the 'empty chair' episode in 1965? Was Mrs Thatcher any more 'awkward' in her 1988 "Bruges Speech" than President De Gaulle in 1965? However awkward Britain may have been, it was never threatened with the Article 7 procedure (the so-called nuclear option) as is the case with Hungary and Poland today. Thus, the Polish President argues that Poland has the right to regulate its internal legal order, notwithstanding the Treaty obligations to obey EU law and respect EU rulings.

Equally importantly, does 'awkwardness' as a concept distinguish between being awkward at the policy-*making* stage in the EU and being awkward at the stage of *implementing* EU policy? If we focus on EU policy-*making*, might it be that Britain has often articulated concerns that other member states shared but were reluctant to raise so clearly and publicly? As George himself notes, when discussing the Thatcher period after 1984:

> … Britain was not quite as isolated as may have appeared from the headlines in its doubts about some of the developments within the EC which the Delors Commission was promoting. The main reason for Britain appearing as an awkward partner was the willingness of the British Prime Minister to speak out forcibly on these issues while others kept diplomatic silence. (George, 1990, p. 208)

This passage suggests that one should be cautious in accepting the notion that the Brexit problem is purely a British problem due to a long history of Britain being 'awkward'. As Daddow and Oliver point out, the title of George's book was *an* awkward partner, not *the* awkward partner. Indeed, they argue that Britain, whilst certainly being awkward at times, has actually been a constructive and influential partner much of the time, most notably regarding the Single European Act, economic reform, but also in other policy areas such as deregulation, privatisation, climate change, and even animal welfare legislation (Daddow & Oliver, 2016). Britain was initially a reluctant partner, but having joined late it adjusted quickly to the European Communities' 'ways of doing things'. As Spence noted in 1993 '… British arrangements for the co-ordination of European policy are generally reckoned to be the most effective of any of the Member States' (Spence, 1993, p. 53). In some respects, Britain became the model of how to co-ordinate EU policy at the domestic level. Similarly, British pressure groups were quick to learn the Brussels game and became effective lobbyists within the European policy process (Mazey & Richardson, 1992). They were at the same time pro-European and were well used to (indeed, liked) the type of bureaucratic politics practiced by the Commission. The UK government also seems to be rather successful when it comes to achieving its policy objectives at the EU level. Analysing data from 125 pieces of EU legislation in the period between 1996 and 2008, Hix finds that rather than being marginalised in the EU's legislative process 'the UK government has been closer to final policy outcomes than most governments' (Hix, 2015). Hence, 'awkward' surely cannot mean that Britain is losing, rather that it is winning!

Some might correctly posit that Britain used to be a main driver behind policy differentiation, i.e., the demand for treaty-based opt-outs and EU secondary law exemptions or special provisions. The UK was hardly alone in its quest to ask for treaty as well as secondary law differentiation. Duttle et al. (2017) show that EU secondary law differentiation is most pronounced in EU member states in which there is a strong principled opposition to the integration of core state powers. Yet, Britain is not alone in this regard. Together with other 'Northern' member states (such as Denmark, Sweden, but also Ireland), Britain negotiated wide-ranging primary as well secondary law exemptions from the integration of core state powers, such as monetary policy and justice and home affairs. Differentiated integration has become a permanent feature of the EU and EU policy-making, reflecting the EU's growing heterogeneity from enlargement and strong opposition in some member states against the integration of core state powers (Leuffen et al., 2013; Rittberger et al., 2014). It is thus simply impossible to characterise Britain as *an* awkward partner, let alone *the* awkward partner.

The same holds if we look at the *implementation* of EU policy. As Schmidt points out (though believing that 'the UK has always been a difficult member of the EU', Schmidt, 2020, p. 781), Britain's common-law tradition 'implies that the UK's administration is more attuned to implementing case law alongside legislation' (Schmidt, 2020, p. 783). Indeed, the research on compliance with EU law conducted by Börzel et al. has Britain bracketed with Denmark, the Netherlands, and Luxemburg '... whose compliance records are exemplary' (Börzel et al., 2010, p. 1364). Along with the Netherlands, the UK seldom violates EU law (2010, p. 1366). Their research findings point to a huge puzzle, namely 'why EU-skeptical countries such as the United Kingdom and Denmark comply much better with European Law than states that are highly supportive of European Integration such as Italy, Portugal, and Belgium' (2010, p. 1367). Finally, their findings contain a possible clue to the UK having acquired the awkward partner tag. They see the UK as scoring high on the *capacity* to implement EU law. France and Italy score much less well. Thus, 'although the United Kingdom is as powerful as France and Italy, it complies better with European Law thanks to its bureaucratic efficiency' (2010, p. 1382). To be sure, Britain is justifiably known for fighting its corner in the EU. This might be defined as 'awkwardness' perhaps but this behaviour might simply be rooted in a strong cultural belief by British negotiators that, whatever becomes EU law, Britain will do its level best (including 'gold plating') to implement it. As Börzel et al. point out, countries such as France and Italy '... are less sensitive to enforcement costs' (Börzel et al., 2010, p. 1381). If one is going to be relaxed about actually implementing a policy, one can be equally relaxed about agreeing to it!

It is, therefore, at least possible to turn the 'awkward partner' narrative on its head. History will judge, but it might just be that Britain was actually quite a good member of the EU, contributing constructively (and sometimes playing a leading role) in EU policy-making, fighting hard when it felt the need to (just like every other Member State), and not regarding laws properly passed by the EU as simply 'cheap talk' to be ignored in practice.

Moreover, if we take British policy actors as a *whole* (i.e., the British Government, British civil servants, British interest groups, and British implementing agencies), it might be more accurate to characterise Britain as a quite *professional, co-operative and successful* European partner rather than typecasting Britain simply as *the* awkward partner. From this perspective, it might therefore be argued that it was not *inevitable* that Britain would leave the European family at some point, as Britain's policy-making elite was rather well integrated into European policy-making, and the EU and the UK had learned to live together rather well.

As indicated above, we are not suggesting that the processes by which Brexit was achieved were not an omnishambles or, indeed, a total fiasco, but in terms of how that shambles came about in the first place, we wonder if the 'awkward partner' narrative has very much to contribute by way of explanation. Thus, we now turn to a very different explanation, namely the *exogenous* contribution that the EU possibly made to the setting of the Brexit agenda in the first place.

It takes two to tango: has the EU been itself engaged in a slow-burn blunder?

It is easy to blame British governments (particularly under David Cameron, but also under Theresa May, and Boris Johnson), together with the British electorate for the Britain's exit from the EU. However, was the Brexit fiasco a purely *British* fiasco? This seem implausible. Thus, the long-term role of European elites, and the EU institutions which they created and expanded surely played some part in the emergence of the Brexit fiasco and, indeed, in the more general (rather long-running) crisis within the EU. Might it be that the seemingly inexorable expansion of EU public policy and of supranational authority laid the bedrock of Brexit? Those of us who are confessed Europhiles might find the argument hard to swallow, but is it possible that the EU itself has been engaged in a 'slow-burn' omnishambles caused by task expansion and centralization? For example, Leuffen et al. argue that:

> the EU covers all policy fields. Having started as an economic organization, it has expanded into all areas of public policy including foreign policy, internal and external security, and the protection of civil and social rights. Although its competences vary from issue-area to issue-area, *there is hardly a field of policy-making that is not shaped in some way by the EU.* (Leuffen et al., 2013, p. 4, emphasis added)

So great has been the EU's expansion into policy areas traditionally the reserve of nation states, that academic debate has developed on how best to characterise the EU, a state or an international organisation? For example, Leuffen et al. argue that' the EU '… is like an international organization in some respects but more akin to a state in others' (Leuffen et al., 2013, p. 2). Somewhat similarly, Richardson argues that the EU is in fact a 'policy-making state' as '… the range of policy areas in which the EU has at least some remit is now quite vast …' (Richardson, 2012, p. 14). Not only has the EU encroached on national policy-making, including core state powers (see Genschel & Jachtenfuchs, 2015), it has moved '… towards a more coercive top-down policy style' (Richardson, 2018a, p. 124). This steady task expansion combined with a reliance on regulation has extended well beyond the EU's own borders. For example, Bradford argues that 'EU regulations penetrate numerous aspects of people's everyday lives around the world. The Brussels Effect affects the food they eat, the air that they breath, and the products they produce and consume' (Bradford, 2020, p. xv). Her empirical analysis demonstrates that the EU is what she terms a ' global regulatory hegemon' (Bradford, 2020, p. 3; see also Young, 2015).

Whatever type of 'beast' the EU has become over time, there now is much talk (again!) about 'Europe in Crisis'. However, (like Brexit) the EU's own crisis did not suddenly fall out of the sky. Indeed, nearly a quarter of a century ago Jack Hayward captured perfectly the problem which is now at the heart of the EU's current crisis. Thus he wrote:

> Monnet-style European integration relied upon behind-the-scenes influence of a few self-conscious agents of change. The negotiating skills of technocrats and the political skills of statesmen secured inconspicuous compromises without arousing public fears. By the 1990s, unification by stealth became increasingly difficult to sustain, as elite concertation was less able to achieve consensus and *public acquiescence in the complex processes of EU decision-making risked turning into public alienation*. (Hayward, 1996, emphasis added)

What Hayward saw in 1996 has, surely, come to haunt the European elites today. The main causes of Europe's current crisis are probably twofold. First is the general phenomenon of European integration itself. Though one could argue about characterising the EU as a 'policy-making state', there is no dispute that the EU has created a huge panoply of European legislation which has plenty of bite at the national level, as we have argued above (and as Bradford argues, also at the global level). Secondly, the integration of core state powers in general, and the specific policy area of immigration in particular, have had a disproportionate effect on the attitudes of national electorates towards EU membership. As Hooghe and Marks argue, political competition in the EU is profoundly affected by the emergence of 'a transnational cleavage, which has as its core a political reaction against European integration and immigration' (Hooghe & Marks, 2018, p. 109). Drawing on Lipset and Rokkan's cleavage theory, they note:

> Lipset and Rokkan had no idea that the containers of the (then) main cleavage, nation states, were going to be transformed around the turn of the twenty-first century. Territorial identity as a motive for conflict was thought to be a thing of the past. Nationalism was viewed as the dead-end result of inter-war fascism, never to be repeated … but they were unable to see that *national sovereignty might be deconsolidated in authoritative design*. (Hooghe & Marks, 2018, p. 113, emphasis added)

According to Hooghe and Marks (2009), it is the growing mis-match between supranational integration, and the political communities people identify with, which has become a root cause of the current discontent with the EU. EU integration has become politicised and contested in the political mass arena, where identity politics assume a prominent role. In a telling passage they go a long way to explaining how Brexit came about. Thus:

> Nationalism has long been the refuge of those who are insecure, who sense they are losing status, and who seek standing by identifying with the group. The

> promise of transnationalism has been gains for all, but the experience of the past two decades is that it hurts many. Hence, opposition to transnationlism is for many a populist reaction against élites who have little sympathy for national borders. (Hooghe & Marks, 2018, pp. 114–5)

The Brexit referendum vote was clearly a vote against the political ruling class in Britain, but it was also a vote against the European-level elite. As Bogdanor has put it, 'the referendum was a genuine grass roots insurgency, *a revolt from below*' (Bogdanor, 2016, p. 350, emphasis added). In fact, the revolt is a rare example of authoritarian populism breaking into 'normal' politics in Britain. As Crewe argues

> authoritarian populism has always had a place in British political life. But its impact on elections, parties and government action has been – at least until the Brexit Referendum – remarkably limited, a case study in the capacity of the UK political institutions to impede the conversion of a significant and strongly held block of opinion into public policy. (Crewe, 2020, p. 17)

From the perspective of European elites, it might be comforting to present Brexit as just the most recent example of British exceptionalism within the EU, yet Hobolt warns otherwise. She argues that:

> although the attitudinal data show that Britain is something of an outlier in terms of Euro-scepticism, there is a growing divide within the EU both economically and culturally between those who feel left behind by the forces of globalization and those who have benefitted from it. The former group favours a "drawbridge up" policy of *less European integration*, closed borders, and fewer immigrants, whereas the latter group are in favour of greater openness and international co-operation. (Hobolt, 2016, p. 1272, emphasis added)

Thus, there is at least a case to be answered by the EU in terms of the causes of Brexit. As Schmidt notes '… *Brexit can also be read as a warning about fundamental problems in the EU integration process* … constitutionalising policy choices, accepting case law rather than political preferences, implies the danger of shifting political contestation to another level' (Schmidt, 2020, p.790, emphasis added). Edema and Kelemen, somewhat earlier, also warned of the effects of the judicialization of EU policy-making, arguing that the tendency to produce detailed inflexible regulations was deeply rooted in the EU's political system, with a predilection for 'judicial enforcement of strict legal norms' (Idema & Kelemen, 2006, p. 116). Hobolt and Rodon point to the possible consequences of the 'Europeanization' of domestic *electoral politics*. Thus, 'Europeanization' has not, they argue,

> … provided a panacea to democratic politics in the Union. On the contrary, the domestic contestation of the EU presents a new kind of challenge to the European policy-makers, not least when public opinion and populist politicians turn against European solutions to collective problems. (Hobolt & Rodon, 2020, p. 161)

Thus, the EU itself might have been involved in two kinds of blunder perhaps? First, has it been partaking in some kind of 'slow burn' blunder, with political elites pushing integration generally too far and too fast for its peoples to swallow? Many scholars speak in favour of this interpretation. As the political mainstream pressed on with integration to address transnational policy challenges, it helped unleash the forces of popular anti-European opposition that policy-makers actually sought to contain. Integration by depoliticisation was a time-honoured recipe for mainstream political elites: It allowed policy-makers to combine functional and technocratic problem-solving at the EU-level without facing opposition and contestation about Europe at home. Van der Eijk and Franklin (2004) characterised the EU as a "sleeping giant" waiting to be awakened, and the political mainstream sought to prolong its slumber by keeping the giant 'deliberately sedated' (Mair, 2007, p. 13). Now, the sedative has worn off and the sleeping giant has unleashed the forces of politicisation and anti-EU opposition. Short of alternative sedatives, the pro-European political mainstream is struggling to come to grips with its new interlocutor. Brexit is merely one of many possible consequences of the giant's awakening and hence of a fundamental transformation of political competition in the EU.

Secondly, did the *specific policy* of free movement of workers (a principle which we ourselves support) turn out to be a policy disaster of considerable proportions because of its serious unintended consequences for the support of the integration project as whole? Had the free movement policy been much more constrained in the first place, and had the ECJ not been so active in developing the free movement regime (Schmidt, 2020), would the EU have been in so much trouble now? The lesson from Brexit for liberals is, as Crewe argues, '... to recognise that throughout Europe, rapid and large waves of migration across national borders are followed by the electoral advance, sometimes into government, of radical-right parties that threaten liberal values and, usually, democratic institutions' (Crewe, 2020, p. 29). In the Brexit case, the British discovered that the single market also meant freedom of movement of and for people. And they could not do anything about flows of people without 'taking back control' (Frosini & Gilbert, 2020, p. 764).

The domestic policy problem

King and Crewe suggest, 'in previous generations, foreign observers of British politics viewed the British political system with something like awe. Government in Britain was not only highly democratic: *it was astonishingly competent. It combined effectiveness with efficiency*' (King & Crewe, 2014, p. ix, emphasis added). However, they go on to observe, '[s]adly, the British system is no longer held up as a model, and we suspect that one reason is that today's

British governments screw up so often' (King & Crewe, 2014, p. ix). King and Crewe's seminal volume is replete with examples of British governments screwing up. We, therefore, need to be careful in seeing the Brexit omnishambles as something especially unusual. It is possible to argue that it was business as usual! To be sure, Brexit was a rather spectacular and long drawn- out omnishambles, but it was certainly not a unique example of the British policy-making process not running smoothly. Indeed, it is possible to fit the Brexit case into a quite different narrative about the British policy process, which might lead one argue that the real puzzle would have arisen if Britain had managed the Brexit process well. Certainly, for much of the post-war period, British policy-making could be accurately characterised as emphasising '... the importance of bargaining and consensus, leading to a more consensual policy style via a process of power sharing between government and interest groups, so called *governance*' (Richardson, 2018b, p. 215). The process emphasised fact based, deliberative policy-making. However, the post-1979 period (beginning with the election of Margaret Thatcher) has seen major changes in the British policy style, notably a considerable weakening of the civil service, the increasing role of political advisers in government, the arrival of ministers who are deeply committed to a particular set of ideas, and a considerable weakening of interest group influence (for a fuller discussion of long-term changes in the British policy style, see Richardson, 2018b, and for a discussion of government by 'permanent campaign' and the weakening of civil service influence see Diamond, 2019). One of the strangest aspects of the Brexit saga is the lack of interest group influence during the whole process. The lack of business influence (which appears to be continuing post-Brexit) is especially odd, but it was difficult to find any well-established interest group clearly in the leave camp. It is not that the interest groups did not bark. They certainly did (and are still doing so). It is that their bark no longer had any bite. Those interests who knew where the post-Brexit shoe might pinch were simply ignored. Having played a significant role in getting the UK *into* Europe, and having played a major role in the UK's long period *within* Europe, interest groups played little or no role in the UK's *exit* from Europe. Also, they appear to be struggling to gain any influence over the UK Government's negotiations with the EU post-Brexit, particularly regarding the possibility that the UK will not align itself with EU rules after 31 December 2020.

As King and Crewe put it, one component of a policy-making system that emphasises careful *deliberation* is '... conferring and taking council, of reaching out' (King & Crewe, 2014, pp. 386–7). An overriding feature of the Brexit saga was the determination of politicians to ignore civil service advice (and advice from the Bank of England), ignore warnings from interest groups, and to regard 'expert' as a pejorative term. Indeed, this shift from what used to be standard operating procedures in British policy-making seem to have facilitated outright *deceit* in the Referendum. Thus, Bains et al. argue that 'if conventional, instrumental politics led by experts and analysts had played a bigger part in designing the complexities of leaving the EU, then the straw casing of deceit may have been removed … ' (Baines et al., 2020, p. 757). Dunlop et al. also point to policy *process* problems playing a major part in the Brexit fiasco. They argue that 'the policy setting was well-suited to *reflexive and epistemic learning* following the referendum' (Dunlop et al., 2020, p. 703, emphasis added), but 'learning shifted to the realm of hierarchy as the Article 50 negotiations got underway' (Dunlop et al., 2020, p. 705).

Thus, it is not that the Brexit problem of itself was impossible to solve, as McConnell and Tormey argue. To them, ' … the narrative that Brexit was a near impossible challenge, does not stand up to close scrutiny' (McConnell & Tormey, 2020, p. 692). Instead of a rational debate between experts, the policy dispute ended up more like a religious war, with both sides utterly convinced that they were right. The policy dispute was between two rival advocacy coalitions where strongly-held belief systems played a crucial role. As Jenkins-Smith et al. note, ' … policy actors have a three-tiered belief system structure. *Deep core beliefs* are fundamental normative values and ontological axioms … which are not policy specific' (2018, p. 140). They also note that:

> … people are motivated instrumentally by goals but are often unclear how to achieve those goals, and they are limited in their cognitive abilities to process stimuli such as information and experience … Additionally, given limited cognitive abilities, individuals simplify the world through their belief systems and are, therefore, prone to biased assimilation of stimuli. (Jenkins-Smith et al., 2018, p. 140)

For the role of 'limited cognitive abilities' in the Brexit saga, one need look no further than the thinking of the International Trade Secretary (no less!) in July 2017 who believed that a Brexit agreement would be 'one of the easiest in human history' (quoted by McConnell & Tormey, 2020).

Now, as McConnell and Tormey point out, even long standing and deeply entrenched religious disputes, as in Northern Ireland, can be resolved (McConnell & Tormey, 2020, p. 685). However, Brexit, whilst having the obvious overtones of a religious divide, such as in Northern Ireland, is different in at least one respect, namely that one side could (and, in the end, did) have an outright win. The Brexit policy game was a winnable game and both side new it, unlike in Northern Ireland where, after a long period of terrible conflict, both sides came to realise that neither could have a clear win. Thus, Brexit was an *especially* 'wicked' policy problem as a key condition for a solution was absent because the two camps had little interest in compromise. In practical policy terms, there were endless compromises that could be made in terms of Britain's relationship with the EU (as history had shown, many times) but each side had an unshakable belief that it could win. However, perhaps the leave camp was more single minded or at least had the more coherent narrative? As

Spencer and Oppermann put it, '... the power and resonance of the Leave story in the 2016 Brexit referendum was enhanced by the relative consistency of its romantic narrative, while the Remain story was weakened by its inconsistent mix of narrative genres' (Spencer & Oppermann, 2020, p. 679).

The problem presented by the existence of two competing advocacy coalitions with irreconcilable belief systems was, of course, hugely compounded by the fact that the two advocacy coalitions crossed traditional party lines, thus turning Brexit into a 'wedge issue' which provoked bitter intra-party divisions (Heinkelmann-Wild et al., 2020, p. 723). Put simply, Brexit appears the type of cleavage which Lipset and Rokkan's classic study suggested appear in fully mobilised polities. Such cleavages, in one way or another, 'all express deeply felt convictions about the destiny and mission of the nation, some quit incohate, others highly systematized ...' (Lipset & Rokkan, 1967, p. 23). The combination of this deep cleavage and the tactics employed by the two camps, namely 'opting for a politics of intransigence' (Heinkelmann-Wild et al., 2020, p. 723) produced a situation which, as it turned out, could be resolved only by an election result in which one side had a clear and emphatic win.

In the event, the omnishambles trundled on in parliament month after month (and, in that sense, the Westminster Model had re-asserted itself over policy community policy-making). Indeed, it is possible that the endless omnishambles actually strengthened support for the Conservatives in the 2019 General Election. The main Conservative Election slogan, 'Get Brexit done, Unleash Britain's Potential', seems to have chimed with many voters weary of the long Brexit saga who possibly felt 'Please get this over with'!

Perhaps the ultimate irony of the 2019 election is that the Conservatives were very successful both in convincing voters that they could clean up a mess which the Conservatives themselves had created (starting, of course, with Cameron's fateful decision to hold a referendum in June 2016), and managing to avoid any serious discussion of the huge policy problems that would need to be solved in the period after Brexit. In a sense, therefore, the *finale* to three years of Conservative omnishambles ended with a rather polished last act by someone, Boris Johnson, generally thought to be a bit of a buffoon. The team might have appeared to be a bunch of total amateurs, but we all need to remember that they won the game by a good margin!

So, how *did* this all happen? As we suggest, there are many possible causes, but we conclude with a pithy but wise observation from a committed European, the late Ralf Dahrendorf. He was introducing a conference at Oxford University on the theme of 'European elites and their peoples'. The title of his Introduction perhaps solves, in a mere six words, the Brexit puzzle. The title was *Mediocre Élites Elected by Mediocre Peoples'* (Dahrendorf, 1996, p. 1).

Disclosure statement

No potential conflict of interest was reported by the author(s).

References

Baines, D., Brewer, S., & Kay, A. (2020). Political, process and programme failures in the Brexit fiasco: Exploring the role of policy deception. *Journal of European Public Policy, 27*(5), 742–760. https://doi.org/10.1080/13501763.2020.1722203

Bogdanor, V. (2016). Europe and the sovereignty of the people. *The Political Quarterly, 87*(3), 348–351. https://doi.org/10.1111/1467-923X.12297

Börzel, T., Hofmann, T., Panke, D., & Sprungk, D. (2010). Obstinate or inefficient? Why member states do not comply with European law. *Comparative Political Studies, 43* (11), 1363–1390. https://doi.org/10.1177/0010414010376910

Bovens, M., & 't Hart, P. (2016). Revisiting the study of policy failures. *Journal of European Public Policy, 23*(5), 653–666. https://doi.org/10.1080/13501763.2015.1127273

Bovens, M., 't Hart, P., & Peters, G. (2001). Analysing governance success and failure in six European States. In M. Bovens, P. 't Hart, & G. Peters (Eds.), *Success and failure in public governance: A comparative analysis* (pp. 12–29). Edward Elgar.

Bradford, A. (2020). *The Brussels effect: How the European Union rules the world*. Oxford University Press.

Crewe, I. (2020). Authoritarian populism and Brexit in the UK in historical perspective. In I. Crewe & D. Sanders (Eds.), *Authoritarian populism and liberal democracy* (pp. 15–31). Palgrave.

Daddow, O., & Oliver, T. (2016). A not so awkward partner: The UK has been a champion on many causes in the EU [Blog article]. https://blogs.lse.ac.uk/brexit/2016/04/15/a-not-so-awkward-partner-the-uk-has-been-a-champion-of-many-causes-in-the-eu/

Dahrendorf, R. (1996). Introduction: Mediocre elites elected by mediocre peoples. In J. Hayward (Ed.), *The populist challenge to elitist democracy in Europe* (pp. 1–9). Oxford Clarendon Press.

Diamond, P. (2019). *The end of Whitehall: Government by permanent campaign*. Palgrave.

Dunlop, C. A., James, S., & Radaelli, C. M. (2020). Can't get no learning: The Brexit fiasco through the lens of policy learning. *Journal of European Public Policy, 27*(5), 703–722. https://doi.org/10.1080/13501763.2019.1667415

Duttle, T., Holzinger, K., Malang, T., Schäubli, T., Schimmelfennig, F., & Winzen, T. (2017). Opting out from the European Union legislation: The differentiation of secondary law. *Journal of European Public Policy, 24*(3), 406–428. https://doi.org/10.1080/13501763.2016.1149206

Frosini, J., & Gilbert, M. (2020). The Brexit car crash: Using E.H. Carr to explain Britain's choice to leave the European Union in 2016. *Journal of European Public Policy, 27*(5), 761–778. https://doi.org/10.1080/13501763.2019.1676820.

Genschel, P., & Jachtenfuchs, M. (2015). More integration, less federation: The European integration of core state powers. *Journal of European Public Policy, 23*(4), 42–59. https://doi.org/10.1080/13501763.2015.1055782

George, S. (1990). *An awkward partner: Britain in the European Community*. Oxford University Press.

Hayward, J. (1996). The populist challenge to elitist democracy in Europe. In J. Hayward (Ed.), *Elitism, populism and European politics* (pp. 10–32). Oxford Clarendon Press.

Heinkelmann-Wild, T., Kriegmair, L., Rittberger, B., & Zangl, B. (2020). Divided they fail: The politics of wedge issues and Brexit. *Journal of European Public Policy, 27*(5), 723–741. https://doi.org/10.1080/13501763.2019.1683058

Hix, S. (2015). Is the UK marginalised in the EU? [Blog article]. https://blogs.lse.ac.uk/europpblog/2015/10/20/is-the-uk-marginalised-in-the-eu/

Hobolt, S. (2016). The Brexit vote: A divided nation, a divided continent. *Journal of European Public Policy, 23*(9), 1259–1277. https://doi.org/10.1080/13501763.2016.1225785

Hobolt, S., & Rodon, T. (2020). Domestic contestation of the European Union. *Journal of European Public Policy, 27*(2), 161–167. https://doi.org/10.1080/13501763.2019.1701066

Hooghe, L., & Marks, G. (2009). A postfunctionalist theory of European integration: From permissive consensus to constraining dissensus. *British Journal of Political Science, 39* (1), 1–23. https://doi.org/10.1017/S0007123408000409

Hooghe, L., & Marks, G. (2018). Cleavage theory meets Europe's crisis: Lipset, Rokkan, and the transnational cleavage. *Journal of European Public Policy, 25*(1), 109–135. https://doi.org/10.1080/13501763.2017.1310279

Idema, T., & Kelemen, D. (2006). New modes of governance, the open method of co-ordination and other fashionable red herring. *Perspectives on European Politics and Society, 7*(1), 108–123. https://doi.org/10.1080/15705850600839637

Jenkins-Smith, H. C., Nohrstedt, D., Weible, C. M., & Ingold, K. (2018). The advocacy coalition framework: An overview of the research program. In C. M. Weible & P. A. Sabatier (Eds.), *Theories of the policy process* (pp. 135–171). Westview Press.

Jennings, W., Lodge, M., & Ryan, M. (2018). Comparing blunders in government. *European Journal of Political Research, 57*(1), 238–258. https://doi.org/10.1111/1475-6765.12230

King, A., & Crewe, I. (2014). *The blunders of our governments*. Oneworld.

Kingdon, J. (1984). *Agendas, alternatives and public policies*. Harper Collins.

Leuffen, D., Rittberger, B., & Schimmelfennig, F. (2013). *Differentiated integration: Explaining variation in the EU*. Palgrave.

Lipset, M., & Rokkan, S. (1967). Cleavage structures, party systems, and voter alignments: An introduction. In M. Lipset & S. Rokkan (Eds.), *Party systems and voter alignments: Cross-national perspectives* (pp. 1–64). The Free Press.

Mair, P. (2007). Political opposition and the European Union. *Government and Opposition, 42*(1), 1–17. https://doi.org/10.1111/j.1477-7053.2007.00209.x

Mazey, S., & Richardson, J. (1992). British pressure groups and the challenge of Brussels. *Parliamentary Affairs, 45*(1), 92–107. https://doi.org/10.1093/oxfordjournals.pa.a052914

McConnell, A., & Tormey, S. (2020). Explanations for the Brexit policy fiasco: Near-impossible challenge, leadership failure or Westminster pathology? *Journal of European Public Policy, 27*(5), 685– 702. https://doi.org/10.1080/13501763.2019.1657485

Oppermann, K., & Spencer, A. (2016). Studying fiascos: Bringing public and foreign policy together. *Journal of European Public Policy, 23*(5), 643–652. https://doi.org/10.1080/13501763.2015.1128228

Richardson, J. (2012). Supranational state building in the European Union. In J. Richardson (Ed.), *Constructing a policy-making state? Policy dynamics in the EU* (pp. 3–28). Oxford University Press.

Richardson, J. (2018a). Brexit: The EU policy-making state hits the populist buffers. *The Political Quarterly*, *89*(1), 118–126. https://doi.org/10.1111/1467-923X.12453

Richardson, J. (2018b). The changing British policy style: From governance to government. *British Politics*, *13*(2), 215–233. https://doi.org/10.1057/s41293-017-0051-y

Rittberger, B., Leuffen, D., & Schimmelfennig, F. (2014). Differentiated integration of core state powers. In P. Genschel & M. Jachtenfuchs (Eds.), *Beyond the regulatory polity? The European integration of core state powers* (pp. 189–210). Oxford University Press.

Schmidt, S. (2020). The odd one out? Institutional mismatch with an over-constitutionalized EU as a cause of Brexit. *Journal of European Public Policy*, *27*(5), 779–794. https://doi.org/10.1080/13501763.2020.1733635

Spence, D. (1993). The role of the national civil service in European lobbying: The British case. In S. Mazey & J. Richardson (Eds.), *Lobbying in the European community* (pp. 47–81). Oxford University Press.

Spencer, A., & Oppermann, K. (2020). Narrative genres of Brexit. The leave campaign and the success of romance. *Journal of European Public Policy*, *27*(5), 666–684. https://doi.org/10.1080/13501763.2019.1662828

Van der Eijk, C., & Franklin, M. N. (2004). Potential for contestation on European matters at national elections in Europe. In G. Marks & M. Steenbergen (Eds.), *European integration and political conflict* (pp. 32–50). Cambridge University Press.

Young, A. (2015). The European Union as a global regulator? Context and comparison. *Journal of European Public Policy*, *22*(9), 1233–1252. https://doi.org/10.1080/13501763.2015.1046902

Narrative genres of Brexit: the Leave campaign and the success of romance

Alexander Spencer and Kai Oppermann

ABSTRACT

This article argues that the Leave narrative was successful in the 2016 referendum in part because it conformed to one of the well-established narrative genres of tragedy, comedy, satire and romance. These genres are story telling conventions that orientate audiences and guide the interpretation of the story being told. Specifically, the article shows that the Leave campaign constructed a largely consistent romantic narrative, while the Remain campaign mixed narrative genres. This difference in 'genre consistency' contributed to the success of Leave and the failure of Remain in the referendum. The investigation into the role of genre consistency adds to theoretical scholarship on narrative dominance in political discourse which has so far focused on the narrator, the structure and content of the story or the audience. The analysis points to structural similarities between the romantic genre and populist narratives more generally which enables populism to tap into the power of romance.

It is well established that narratives are of upmost importance in politics and international relations (e.g., Krebs 2015; Miskimmon, O'Loughlin and Roselle 2017; Spencer 2016). Not only are they critical for any form of community in which stories of the self in the past and future are the building blocks of national, regional or local identities, narratives are also a means of making sense of the social world around us. It is the struggle over narratives which is a defining feature of democratic politics where one encounters often dichotomous stories of government and opposition. This political struggle over narratives is about success and failure on two levels. Firstly, it involves the success and failure of certain narratives to gain discursive dominance. Secondly, in this struggle political actors try to achieve dominance by telling stories of success of the self and failure of the other.

These dynamics were exemplified in the Brexit debate in which the Leave campaign, in order to prevail and gain narrative dominance, told a story of the

European Union's (EU) failure and the foreseeable success of Britain outside of the EU. This article will be concerned with the success of the Leave campaign by reflecting on one potential reason for why the Leave narrative was able to 'win' in the 2016 referendum: genre consistency. It brings together and contributes to two strands of literature. Firstly, the article complements empirical research on the reasons behind the success of Leave in the Brexit referendum (see Cummings 2017; Grant 2016; Hobolt 2016). This research has identified a range of long- and short-term factors that may have contributed to the referendum result, including the long-standing dominance of eurosceptic narratives in British political discourse, the impact of the financial crisis and austerity, anti-establishment sentiments of voters who felt 'left behind' by liberal elites and globalisation, the failure of David Cameron's renegotiations of Britain's terms of EU membership, the high salience of the immigration issue, as well as the ambivalent position of the Labour party, the role of the media, the popularity of key figures on the Leave side and strategic mistakes and weaknesses of the Remain campaign, such as its dysfunctional organisation and focus on the economic risks of Brexit.

Secondly, the article adds to the theoretical literature on the reasons for narrative dominance which have so far focused on the role of the narrator, the story structure and content as well as the audience (see Krebs 2015; Oppermann and Spencer 2018; Van Ham 2002). We hold that narrative success is linked to genre consistency in the sense that this consistency with previously known story telling conventions in genres such as tragedy, satire, comedy and romance makes for a simple and easily understandable story (see White 1973). This does not mean that simple will always win over more complex stories, but that they do have an advantage as they are easier to follow and need less critical engagement to be understood by an audience with limited knowledge on the issue at hand. While a number of scholars have made valuable contributions to the strategic use of narratives by political actors (Miskimmon, O'Loughlin and Roselle 2017) this article is not so much concerned with the question of whether actors employed specific narrative genres strategically in order to win. Rather the focus is on showing how the Leave campaign constructed a largely consistent narrative which includes important features of a romance.

In pursuit of this aim the article will proceed as follows. Part one elaborates our understanding of narratives and outlines the main narrative genres, focusing in particular on typical features of the romantic genre. Part two attends to genre inconsistencies in both the Remain and Leave narratives and illustrates that especially the Remain narrative did not predominantly conform to one of the narrative genres but included a mix of different genre elements. This serves as a counterpoint to our main empirical analysis in the third part of the article, in which we apply a method of narrative analysis to show how the story told by the Leave campaign was largely consistent with the romantic genre.

Narratives and genres

While the social sciences have recently seen an increase in the use of the concept of 'narrative', there is little agreement on definition as many use the concept as a synonym for discourse, rhetoric or argument (see Ruback 2010). Based on the insights in narratology, however, we hold that narratives all rely on similar structural elements (Van Peer and Chatman 2001: 2). This includes a *setting*, the *characterisation* of the main actors involved and the *emplotment* of events.

The setting refers to the background or location in front of which the story unfolds (Bruner 1991: 7). It is not only a passive background picture (Toolan 2001: 91), but can become part of the action and provide an indication of why the story develops the way it does. Settings offer insights into the characters and the reasons or justifications for actions as they set the limits of appropriate behaviour in a given context. The narrative element of setting provides the essential discursive anchorage needed for the construction of social reality. It gives clues on the context of the story and involves guidelines for how the audience is supposed to interpret behaviour.

In addition, a narrative has to involve some sort of actor who is characterised in a certain way. 'Narrative roots itself in the lived, felt experience of human or human-like agents interacting in an ongoing way with their cohorts and surrounding environment' (Herman 2009: 21). Characterisation proceeds in a number of ways, including giving agents a name or label, describing their appearance, placing them in relationship to others, reporting direct speech or prescribing attributes and behaviour. 'The actors are provided with distinct traits. In this manner they are individualized and transformed into characters' (Toolan 2001: 41), with whom one is able to emotionally identify or not.

A final key ingredient of narratives is an event, as narratives involve 'someone telling someone else that something *happened*' (Herrenstein Smith 1981: 228, emphasis added). Moreover, there has to be some sort of order to and connection between the events within the setting (Genette 1982: 127). This is provided by the emplotment which makes events, characters and their behaviour coherent and intelligible. It is by emplotting actors in settings that actions become meaningful as it illustrates how the elements of a narrative hang together (Ewick and Silbey 1995: 200).

Consisting of these three structural elements, narratives can be understood as 'cognitive schemes' (Rimmon-Kenan 2006: 14) that are essential for the human cognitive process in the everyday and for any form of identity formation. The assumptions are that narrative comprehension is one of the first abilities of the mind to appear in a child and that humans have a natural tendency to organise complex experiences in narratives (Bruner 1991: 9). Narratives are thus an essentially human activity and a fundamental instrument of thought which is needed to make sense of the world in which one lives (Turner 1996). This holds true not only on the individual level, but also on the level of groups in which there is a desire to create a common identity. Therefore, '[n]arratives do political work' (Kohler Riessman 2008: 8) as they play an important role in the constitution of norms, identities and ideologies and are fundamental to the construction of not only the individual and past historical but also the current political world (Ewick and Silbey 1995).

Moreover, narratives do not stand on their own, as they usually conform to and are embedded in some form of genre. Genre here is understood as a story telling convention or narrative style. As Baumann (1999: 84) holds, a genre is 'a constellation of systematically related, co-occurrent formal features and structures that serves as a conventionalized orienting framework for the production and reception of a particular kind of text'. In other words, it is a framework, code or a set of expectations of how a story goes (Chandler 1997: 1–15). This is based on the assumption that audiences of narratives within a genre are already familiar with the basic elements of the genre from previous encounters with other texts. Genre therefore is 'an intertextual concept' (Wales 1989: 259) as it can be considered 'a practical device for helping any mass medium to produce consistently and efficiently and to relate its production to the expectations of its customers' (McQuail 1987: 200) from their previous readings. Genres influence the interpretation of narratives as they 'offer an important way of framing texts which assists comprehension. Genre knowledge orientates competent readers of the genre towards appropriate attitudes, assumptions and expectations about a text which are useful in making sense of it' (Chandler 1997: 8).

Based on the work by Northrop Frye (1957, 1963), Hayden White argues that there are a number of different ways of telling narratives, including the genres of tragedy, comedy, satire and romance (White 1973). These ideal types of genres include a number of specific elements identified in literary studies (see Frye 1957, 1963). It is important to point out that these genres often overlap, and it is by no mean fully settled which elements are the most important or whether they should be considered more part of the setting, characterisation or emplotment. The following paragraphs serve only as a rough, incomplete guide to some of the features which we extracted from the theoretical literature on the different genres. Importantly, this does not imply that all of these features will be found in the narratives of the Leave or Remain campaigns.

The setting in a *tragedy* is commonly considered to be composed of a dark background, including an atmosphere of dread and inevitable failure. It is based on attitudes and emotions such as cynicism and sadness and while the audience of such a narrative is not content with the tragedy being acted out, it does provide a form of emotional catharsis. The characters are considered to have clear roles and the tragic hero is characterised as uncompromising and dangerously absolute with excessive and vehement behaviour. He or she cannot be helped nor will he/she turn. Yet an emotional attachment of empathy of the audience to the hero remains. Key events commonly take the form of a violent disruption and a fight for a doomed cause. Throughout there is a feeling of inevitable failure culminating in the ultimate demise and a sad ending which results in the resigned acceptance of the degeneration of the human race (Frye 1957: 206–222; Golden 1976; Lebow 2003; Kuuisisto 2018).

While the setting in a *satire* is largely shaped by indeterminacy it is commonly chaotic, negative and destructive. There is an atmosphere of scepticism and pessimism as it emphasises the hypocrisy and absurdity of the situation as a form of cynical and subversive critique. The main characters are incoherent, untrustworthy and incompetent. Their behaviour appears nightmarish or lunatic and there is a disparity of awareness between the character in the narrative and the observer. He or she is mocked, ridiculed or shamed as there is a lack of identification and a feeling of superiority of the audience. With regard to emplotment we find a continuation of incomprehensible processes or events involving violent clashes and total havoc which however remain fragmentary and unfinished. We encounter attacks against conventions by outsiders where the surface meaning and the underlying meaning are not the same. The emplotment does not provide for a positive meaning to human existence nor does it formulate constructive suggestions (Frye 1957: 223–241; Griffin 1994; Hall 2014; Kuusisto 2018).

The setting of a *comedy* embraces indeterminacy and is considered less aggressive and more fun than satire. It is not as spectacular or deeply moving but nevertheless makes us happy. The atmosphere as well as the main characters are enthusiastic. They are less black/white as they have faults and make silly mistakes we can laugh at. They misunderstand each other and stumble into embarrassing situations. In contrast to satire or tragedy we encounter self-criticism and humility as their behaviour is constructive, conciliatory, inventive and resourceful. Events are emplotted to culminate in an inevitable happy or satisfactory ending and final celebration which is to restore our faith in life. Actions are positive and constructive and offer novel and compromising solutions as they are, similar to romance, working for a better future. There is a belief in progress as events are emplotted as replacing the old with a new and better society (Frye 1957: 163–185; Stott 2005; Kuusisto 2009; Holm 2017).

With regard to the *setting* of the romantic narrative, 'the romance concentrates on far-away, foreign and exotic settings' (Fischer 1991: 25). This offers the light background for the characteristic adventure or quest in a romantic narrative which involves some sort of conflict involving two antagonistic sides. While a romantic narrative is generally an exciting and entertaining story involving conflict and adventure, it is above all a story of sentimentality and exciting emotions. The main characters are said to be strong, brave and courageous and, more importantly, truthful, upright, proud and honourable in following certain ideals. They are often considered heroes engaged in a dialectic conflict in which they are characterised into the underdog position, struggling against the odds and facing opponents in a materially stronger yet morally weaker position. Through the humanness of the characters we are able to identify with them. In a romance the characters become likable and there is a strong identification between the audience and the hero. As for the emplotment, the romantic story, is about a sequential adventure or quest. A romantic narrative commonly involves some sort of asymmetrical conflict between two antagonistic sides in which the hero is facing an uphill struggle against the odds. They have to overcome a more powerful opponent and thereby resist and challenge the existing order. The hero is fighting for some kind of ideal or sacred value such as liberation, justice, freedom, democracy or love. 'The romance is nearest of all literary forms to the wish-fulfilment dream' (Frye 1957: 186) as there is a certain level of idealism in the emplotment in which the hero is seeking a kind of utopian future (Frye 1957: 186–205; 1963: 16; Fischer 1991; Jameson 1975; Spencer 2016).

Genre inconsistencies in the Brexit campaign

Political narratives are never fully consistent. They generally overlap and feature a number of different literary genre elements. For one thing, this is due to the fact that political narratives found in debates, media reports or speeches are not complete, fully articulated narratives like those found in literary novels or films. They are far more fragmented and retold by bringing segments together from different speakers/authors, times and locations. Furthermore, this inconsistency and fussiness is a consequence of the fact that different genres share some of the same elements. Genres cannot be distinguished by way of an inventory of individual elements alone, but come from a particular combination and weighting of these elements.

With these caveats in mind, the empirical question becomes whether or not the bundle of observable elements in a narrative points to the predominance of a certain literary genre to which the narrative can be attributed. While narratives with low genre consistency do not display a discernible pattern of individual elements and can therefore not be seen to conform to a particular literary genre, narratives with high genre consistency are told in a way that clearly foregrounds a particular genre.

Judged against this benchmark, the Remain story in the Brexit campaign was marked by low genre consistency and did not conform to one particular genre. Rather, in the speeches of the main protagonists of the

Remain campaign, including David Cameron, George Osborne and Jeremy Corbyn (Moore and Ramsay 2017: 32–33), we encounter a mix of tragedy, romance, comedy and satire at the same time, with none of the genres standing out.

In the case of tragedy this involved the inevitable downfall of the UK following the departure from the EU which 'will have profound consequences for our economy, for living standards and for Britain's role in the world' (Osborne 2016a). Here '[l]eaving the EU is a one way ticket to a poorer country' (Osborne 2016b) as '[a] vote to leave could see family incomes fall, growth hit, and borrowing cost rise' (Osborne 2016b). Not only would the tragedy of leaving the EU mean 'uncertainty' and 'a leap in the dark' (Cameron 2016a) but it 'would be a disaster for the British economy' (Osborne 2016b).

Next to the narrative genre of tragedy, the Remain narrative contains elements of comedy and satire in the form of engagement with stereotypes of the self:

> People from all 4 corners of the earth watch our films, dance to our music, flock to our galleries and theatres, cheer on our football teams and cherish our institutions. These days, even our food is admired the world over. (Cameron 2016a)

Similarly, the Leave side is made fun of with regard to their disregard for widespread expert advice:

> They say it's all a massive conspiracy. [...] The next thing we know the Leave camp will be accusing us all of faking the moon landings, kidnapping Shergar, and covering up the existence of the Loch Ness monster. (Osborne 2016b)

Finally, the Remain campaign also attempts to engage with romantic genre elements when highlighting the benefits of the 'imperfect' European Union (Cameron 2016b) which 'needs to change' (Corbyn 2016a). However, the focus is on fairly unemotional technical and future economic advantages of EU membership:

> But there's a positive future for Britain on offer if we stay in the EU. Our economy is expected to keep growing, businesses will keep creating jobs and families will benefit from rising wages and living standards. (Osborne 2016c)

Beyond the purely economic benefits we can also encounter more normatively engaging arguments for the EU as a means to 'protect social and human rights, tackle climate change' (Corbyn 2016b) and spread peace:

> The European Union has helped reconcile countries which were once at each others' throats for decades. (Cameron 2016a)

The closest the Remain campaign gets to a romantic narrative is in its attempt to constitute the Remain vote as a question of identity and as a 'big, bold patriotic case' (Cameron 2016a).

> For me, in the end, it's not just about the economics, It's about who we are as a country. The Britain I love is open, confident in its values and ready to shape the future of our world. […] Strong. Proud. Prosperous. Stronger, safer and better off in the European Union. (Osborne 2016a)

While the campaign makes the case that 'Britain has always been a European power, and we always will be' (Cameron 2016a), the focus remains on the romantic elaboration of the self:

> We love this country, and we want the best future for it. Ours is a great country. Not just a great country in the history books, although it surely is that. But a great country right now, with the promise of becoming even greater tomorrow. (Cameron 2016a)

Although romantic genre elements of emotions, identification, the asymmetrical conflict and the pursuit of an ideal are visible in the Remain narrative, it is inconsistent as the EU is not part of the romance. It is merely seen as a 'tool': 'We have always seen the European Union as a means to an end – the way to boost our prosperity and help anchor peace and stability across the European continent – but we don't see it as an end in itself' (Cameron 2016a). 'Taking advantage of the single market is one of the ways this country has made itself great. As I've said before, I don't love Brussels; I love Britain – and my mission is to make it greater still' (Cameron 2016c).

The Remain narrative can thus best be described as an eclectic mix and match of genre elements which makes it impossible to attribute the narrative to one dominant literary genre. This serves as the counterpoint for our narrative analysis of the Leave story in the next section, which shows that the narrative put forward by the Leave campaign largely conforms to the romantic genre. It is important to note, however, that the Leave narrative, perhaps inevitably, also displays some genre inconsistencies, albeit to a much lesser extent than the Remain narrative.

In particular, the Leave narrative brings in some elements of tragedy, most notably when speakers paint a picture of inevitable failure of the EU and of Britain in the EU. For example, the Leave story is sometimes embedded in a setting that describes the EU as a 'disaster zone' that is haunted by multiple crises which are 'utterly out of control […] causing human misery on a shocking scale' (Farage 2016a). The Remain protagonists, in turn, are characterised as actors who cannot be helped to see the damage done by the EU because of their 'faith in its failing institutions' (Patel 2016a) and 'desperation to remain part of the Brussels club' (Duncan Smith 2016a). If Britain voted to remain in the EU, it 'will be swept up in a United States of Europe with open borders' (Farage 2016a) 'kissing goodbye permanently to control of immigration' (Johnson 2016a), and the 'inevitable result will be worsening overcrowding' (Fox 2016). The sad ending of remaining in the EU is that Britain will 'give away more power and control to unaccountable EU institutions this year and every year […] and send about another £200 billion to Brussels over the next decade' (Gove 2016a).

Moreover, the Leave narrative is interspersed by elements of satire and comedy, but these are few and far in between and can only be found in speeches of Boris Johnson and Michael Gove. We encounter elements of satire, for example, when Michael Gove (2016b) ridicules the EU bureaucracy for rules that 'dictate everything from the maximum size of containers in which olive oil may be sold (five litres) to the distance houses have to be from heathland to prevent cats chasing birds (five kilometres)'. The cynical critique of Boris Johnson (2016b) that big business was only in favour of Remain because 'they are able to use [the EU system] to their advantage [and] are personally getting richer and richer' is another case in point. Elements of comedy come into play when the Leave narratives mocks the Remain campaign for suggesting that leaving the EU would turn Britain into 'some sort of hermit kingdom, a North Atlantic North Korea only without that country's fund of international good will' (Gove 2016a). Another rare example for comedy elements in the Leave narrative is Boris Johnson's humorous account of himself being insulted as a 'liberal cosmopolitan [who] had no right to vote Leave […] in terms that were redolent of 1920s Soviet Russia' (Johnson 2016c). These examples of tragedy, satire and comedy elements in the Leave narrative, however, are dwarfed by the predominance of romantic genre elements. In contrast to the Remain narrative, the Leave narrative, as a bundle of (partly overlapping) genre elements, displays a relatively high genre consistency and largely conforms to the romantic genre. This argument is substantiated in the next section which illustrates the romantic Leave narrative that was put forward by leading advocates of Brexit on the three narrative dimensions of *setting*, *characterisation* and *emplotment*.

The romantic success of Leave

The data for the following narrative analysis come from selected contributions from the most prominent voices for the Leave side in the timespan between mid-February 2016, when Prime Minister David Cameron formally announced the referendum, and 23 June 2016, when the vote was held. As a first cut, the analysis relies on statements from members of the official 'Vote Leave' campaign that are accessible on the campaign website.[1] This material was complemented by additional LexisNexis searches that were targeted at those Leave campaigners who received most media coverage (Moore and Ramsay 2017: 32–33). Importantly, this includes Nigel Farage who was not affiliated with the 'Vote Leave' campaign and whose speeches are therefore not listed on the campaign website, but who was still among the most visible pro-Brexit campaigners in the referendum. Altogether, the analysis rests on more than 30 public interventions of Leave campaigners, including speeches, interviews, op-eds and public letters. The main speakers of the Leave narrative covered in the analysis are Boris Johnson, Michael Gove, Nigel Farage and Gisela Stuart, but also include, for example, Iain Duncan Smith, Priti Patel and Dominic Raab.

Our narrative analysis was guided by a coding frame that distinguishes the main features of romantic narratives along the narrative elements of setting, characterisation and emplotment. We used the MAXQDA data analysis software to code our material and to interpret our findings. The analysis shows that the Leave narrative weaves together key elements of romantic narratives on all three dimensions. In other words, the case for Brexit was made in the form of a romantic narrative.

Setting

The Leave narrative was situated in a romantic setting that provided the stage for telling a story about an exciting and emotional quest to exit the EU. As others have pointed out, speakers for the Leave campaign routinely employed highly emotional language (Cummings 2017; Grant 2016). Specifically, they conjured up a sense of excitement in depicting the referendum as a unique opportunity to effectuate positive change that must not be missed. The Leave narrative constructed the background against which voters had to decide about Britain's EU membership as a 'once-in-a-generation chance' (Stuart 2016a). 'We must seize this chance' (Farage 2016a) as '[t]his is a once-in-a-lifetime moment' (Farage 2016a). In the Leave narrative, the referendum was a 'defining moment in the history of our country' (Farage 2016b) at which voters had to 'take the most important decision for the future of our country in our lifetimes' (Lawson 2016).

Furthermore, the Leave campaign embedded the narrative in a far-away yet vague historical setting which does not give a clear indication of where the UK is travelling to. For example, the Leave campaign drew parallels between the EU and 'Austria-Hungary under the Habsburgs, the Russian Empire under Nicholas the Second, Rome under its later Emperors or the Ottoman Empire in its final years' (Gove 2016a) as well as the 'failing Soviet system' (Gove 2016b) or the battle between Greeks and Persians at Marathon in 490 BC (Johnson 2016c). The Leave narrative constructed a setting using historical analogies to the First World War (Farage 2016a), anti-colonial struggles for independence (Gove 2016a, 2016c) or the British Empire and Commonwealth (see Kenny and Pearce 2018). In the setting outside the EU, Britain would be able to re-engage with 'our kith and kin in the Commonwealth' (Farage 2016b). More broadly, membership to the EU is negatively contrasted with the setting of Britain's history as a great power:

> We have become so used to Nanny in Brussels that we have become infantilised, incapable of imagining an independent future. We used to run the biggest empire the world has ever seen [...]. Are we really unable to do trade deals? (Johnson 2016d)

Characterisation

Against the backdrop of an exciting and emotional setting, the Leave narrative characterised the main protagonists of the campaign to exit the EU as honourable, upright and courageous underdogs who take on powerful opponents to fight for a just cause. The speakers of the Leave campaign are cast as characters who did not take their decisions lightly, but made hard choices to do the right thing for the greater good. For example, Michael Gove has been 'wrestling with the most difficult decision of my political life' and supports the Leave campaign to honour the 'big responsibilities' that being a government minister brings (Gove 2016c). Recounting her family history, Gisela Stuart explains her position to argue for Leave as 'the culmination of a sometimes difficult journey [...] from the recovery and optimism of my parents' generation to my disillusionment today' (Stuart 2016b). Similarly, Dominic Raab 'feel[s] the emotional tug of Europe' as a son of a refugee from Czechoslovakia, but still 'want[s] to leave the anti-competitive and undemocratic EU club' (Raab 2016). In these ways, the characters of the Leave narrative give expression to internal struggles and contradictions with which audiences can identify and which make them human and likeable.

In fighting for their cause, the protagonists of the Leave narrative are pictured as underdogs who have the courage and determination to take on the 'wealthy establishment' (Farage 2016a). They have chosen 'the route of freedom and democracy in the certain knowledge of an almighty battle ahead with [the] 'Establishment'' (Leadsom 2016). In the Leave narrative, the referendum was an uneven struggle between might and right:

> [T]hough they are many, and though they are well-funded, and though we know that they can call on unlimited taxpayer funds for their leaflets, it is we few who have the inestimable advantage of believing strongly in our cause, and that we will be vindicated by history. (Johnson 2016c)

In that struggle, the characters of the Leave narrative were cast in the 'tradition of the liberal cosmopolitan European enlightenment' (Johnson 2016c), speaking for 'a free people' (Gove 2016c) and appealing to the 'compassionate instincts of the British people' (Duncan Smith 2016b). They were depicted as honourable characters who 'play it straight' (Duncan Smith 2016c) and argue their case 'in a spirit of the utmost cordiality' (Johnson 2016c). This was contrasted with the Remain side that 'would stop at nothing to frighten voters into submission' (Leadsom 2016) and to 'scare the public' (Duncan Smith 2016c). For the Leave narrative, the Remain argument rested on a 'great, grotesque patronising and preposterous [...] conceit' that 'treats people like children, unfit to be trusted and easily scared by ghost stories' (Gove 2016a). It was high-time to 'give this cabal the kick in the pants they deserve' (Johnson 2016b). Drawing parallels to the heroism of Winston Churchill (Johnson 2016e), the 'brave' (Johnson 2016d) characters of the Leave narrative confront the 'defeatists' (Johnson 2016e) on the Remain side. For the main protagonists of the Leave campaign, the referendum was a moment to 'show leadership' (Gove 2016c) and 'believe in Britain again' (Johnson 2016e), rather than to 'just throw up our hands' (Stuart 2016c) and 'hug the skirts of Nurse in Brussels' (Johnson 2016d).

Emplotment

The emplotment of the Leave narrative displays a number of key romantic elements that are deeply intertwined with the setting and characterisation. As upright and courageous underdogs, the Leave campaign is involved in an asymmetrical conflict with the establishment in Whitehall and Brussels and fights against the odds to resist the unjust order of the EU and to defend their ideals of freedom and democracy. Against the backdrop of its exciting and emotional setting, the narrative emplots the struggle of the Leave campaign as an adventurous quest:

> For Britain, voting to leave will be a galvanising, liberating, empowering moment of patriotic renewal. (Gove 2016a)

In the Leave narrative, the campaign to exit the EU was fighting uneven battles on two fronts. In Britain, it was up against the political and economic elites and a 'stifling establishment consensus' (Stuart 2016a). The Leave campaign took on 'fat cat lobbyists and fat cat businesses' (Johnson 2016b) who benefit from the unjust EU system as well as the Whitehall establishment that was 'setting out to bully and harangue [voters] from the bubble in Westminster' (Duncan Smith 2016c). Leavers had to prevail against a 'remorseless torrent of propaganda' (Farage 2016c) from the Remain camp who 'shamefully sought to trick the British people' (Farage 2016a).

On the European level, the Leave campaign fought against a 'Brussels army of bureaucrats' (Duncan Smith 2016b) and 'powerful international civil servants, lobbyists and business people' (Johnson 2016b). More broadly, the Leave campaign confronted a European order that was rigged against British interests and in which Britain was 'powerless to act' (Patel 2016a). Britain was 'so uninfluential' (Duncan Smith 2016b) in this European order that it only ever got 'short shrift' (Raab 2016) and 'crumbs from the top table' (Duncan Smith 2016a). Ultimately, the struggle of the campaign to exit the EU was against a mighty and anonymous 'ratchet hauling us ever further into a federal structure' (Johnson 2016c). As an EU member, Britain was like 'a hostage, locked in the boot of a car driven by others to a place and at a pace that we have no control over' (Gove 2016a; see also: Gove 2016d).

According to the Leave narrative, Leave campaigners were forced into this uneven fight by the unjust and illegitimate nature of the European system of governance. That system is 'deeply anti-democratic' (Johnson 2016e) and becoming 'ever more centralizing, interfering and anti-democratic' (Johnson 2016c). The EU 'is built to keep power and control with the elites' (Gove 2016c) and shows a 'mule-like refusal to listen to democratic concerns (Stuart 2016b). It is run by 'a bunch of unelected old men in Brussels' (Farage 2016b), 'unaccountable and unelected bureaucrats' (Patel 2016a) in the European Commission (Patel 2016b) and 'unaccountable EU judges' (Stuart 2016c) in the 'rogue European Court of Justice' (Gove 2016e, see also: Johnson 2016a). The 'EU straightjacket' (Longworth 2016) has 'become a force for social injustice' (Duncan Smith 2016b) and an 'over-centralising, over-regulating job-destroying machine' (Johnson 2016f) that 'is playing Russian roulette with peoples' livelihoods' (Patel 2016a). 'The system has spun out of control [and] is exploited by some big companies' (Johnson 2016a). In this system, Britain's 'generosity has been abused' (Johnson 2016a) and its 'independence [...] is being seriously compromised' (Johnson 2016c). The fight of the Leave campaign is no less than to liberate Britain from an EU that 'stifle[s] democracy [in Britain] (Johnson 2016e), 'trample[s] over the rule of law' (Gove 2016f), 'has become an economic sink-hole' (Gove 2016b) and is 'hell bent on further, deeper centralisation' (Farage 2016a).

Beyond the fight against an unjust European order, the Leave narrative emplots the Brexit campaign in a struggle for the ideals of democracy and freedom while bringing back memories of British greatness and heroism. For the Leave campaign, the fight to 'take back control' from the EU was about the same values of freedom and democracy as 'those who came before us argued for, fought for and died for' (Howard 2016). Similarly, Nigel Farage put the referendum in the context of the Battle of the Somme 100 years ago: 'We should never forget just how much generations have sacrificed. Our democracy is precious and our right to self-determination is one which has been given away by the political class to the EU and bureaucrats such as Jean-Claude Juncker' (Farage 2016a).

Rejecting the 'depressing and pessimistic vision' of the Remain campaign, 'the case for leaving is positive and optimistic' (Gove 2016a). Brexit is portrayed as 'the great project of European liberalism' to overcome the 'ancient regime' represented by the EU (Johnson 2016c). Leavers 'stand resolute for freedom' (Gove 2016f) and 'speak for freedom in Britain and around the whole of the EU (Johnson 2016f). They 'believe in democracy' (Gove 2016f) and struggle to 'revitalise our democracy' (Farage 2016b) in Britain. For Boris Johnson (2016c), 'it is this fundamental democratic problem – the erosion of democracy – that brings me into this fight'. Outside the EU, Britain will be 'standing tall as a free, independent and sovereign country' (Patel 2016a). 'We will win for exactly the same reason that the Greeks beat the Persians at Marathon – because they are fighting for an outdated absolutist ideology, and we are fighting for freedom' (Johnson 2016c).

The Leave narrative envisions a rather vague utopian future outside the EU which remains unspecific about the future situation and where the UK is travelling to. 'Unshackled from the past [as an EU member]' (Gove 2016a), Britain 'would become once again a self-governing democracy' (Lawson 2016). Rather than a 'leap in the dark' as the Remain side would have it, leaving the EU 'is jumping from darkness into light' (Stuart 2016b). 'We can see the sunlit meadows beyond' (Johnson 2016a) as the UK is ready 'to embark upon an exciting future as an independent nation' (Farage 2016a). In the Leave narrative, Britain 'has tremendous untapped potential which independence would unleash' (Gove 2016a). Therefore, we should 'embrace a better future' (Gove 2016c) as 'Britain's best days lie ahead' (Gove 2016a). 'If we vote to leave it will be a glorious day' (Duncan Smith 2016c), it would be 'the great dawn of Britain's independence' (Duncan Smith 2016c) and the beginning of 'the democratic liberation of a whole continent' (Gove 2016a). The reward for leaving the EU would be no less than taking 'control of our destiny' (Patel 2016a).

Conclusion

The main theoretical contribution of the article is that narratives will more likely achieve dominance and be wide spread, adopted and accepted as plausible in political discourse if they conform to one of the established narrative genres of comedy, satire, tragedy or romance. In the empirical analysis, the article finds that the power and resonance of the Leave story in the 2016 Brexit referendum was enhanced by the relative consistency of its romantic narrative, while the Remain story was weakened by its inconsistent mix of narrative genres. The success of the Leave campaign thus attests to the appeal and discursive power of consistent romantic narratives.

Moreover, while the populism of Brexit and the Leave campaign have often been commented on (see Browning 2018; Iakhnis et al. 2018), a corollary of our analysis that has not so far been explored points to structural similarities between the narrative genre of romance and populist mobilisation more generally and the potentially strategic use of romantic narratives by populists. While the precise meaning and definition of the concept of populism is contested, understood as a thin ideology it essentially posits an antagonistic and asymmetrical struggle between 'the pure people' and 'corrupt elites' (Mudde 2004: 543). Populist narratives critically rely on a romantic emplotment in which the moral people resist an unjust order and stand up to fight for a better world against powerful adversaries (Stanley 2008: 102–106). Through their characterisation populist narratives give agency to the virtuous people who are constructed as the underdog (Laclau 2005: 47). Their setting, in turn, is highly emotional in that they invoke myths of popular sovereignty and quasi-religious promises of redemption (Taggart 2019: 83–85). It would be promising for further research to examine more fully the close 'fit' between populist and romantic narratives and how this enables populism to tap into the power of romance. If only in this sense, the upsurge in populism around the world speaks to a revival and the dangers of romantic storytelling in political discourse.

Note

1. The statements are listed on the 'Vote Leave' website: http://www.voteleavetakecontrol.org/key_speeches_interviews_and_op_eds.html (accessed 26 April 2019).

Disclosure statement

No potential conflict of interest was reported by the authors.

ORCID

Alexander Spencer http://orcid.org/0000-0001-9235-353X
Kai Oppermann http://orcid.org/0000-0002-5336-5930

References

Baumann, R. (1999) 'Genre', *Journal of Linguistic Anthropology* 9 (1/2): 84–7.

Browning, C. (2018) 'Brexit populism and fantasies of fulfilment', *Cambridge Review of International Affairs*. doi:10.1080/09557571.2019.1567461.

Bruner, J. (1991) 'The narrative construction of reality', *Critical Inquiry* 18 (1): 1–21.

Cameron, D. (2016a) 'PM Speech on the UK's Strength and Security in the EU', 9 May, available at https://www.gov.uk/government/speeches/pm-speech-on-the-uks-strength-and-security-in-the-eu-9-may-2016 (accessed 3 May 2019).

Cameron, D. (2016b) 'PM Speech at Caterpillar on the EU Referendum', 28 April, available at https://www.gov.uk/government/speeches/pm-speech-at-caterpillar-on-the-eu-referendum-28-april-2016 (accessed 3 May 2019).

Cameron, D. (2016c) 'PM speech at Vauxhall on the EU referendum', 10 March, available at https://www.gov.uk/government/speeches/pm-speech-at-vauxhall-on-the-eu-referendum-10-march-2016 (accessed 3 May 2019).
Chandler, D. (1997) 'Introduction to genre theory', available at http://faculty.washington.edu/farkas/HCDE510-Fall2012/Chandler_genre_theoryDFAnn.pdf (accessed 8 May 2019).
Corbyn, J. (2016a) 'Speech in South Yorkshire on the EU', 16 June, available at http://jeremycorbyn.org.uk/articles/jeremy-corbyn-my-speech-on-the-labour-case-to-vote-remain-in-the-eu-in-south-yorkshire/ (accessed 3 May 2019).
Corbyn, J. (2016b) 'Europe needs to change ... but I am voting to stay', 14 April, available at https://labourlist.org/2016/04/europe-needs-to-change-but-i-am-voting-to-stay-corbyns-full-speech-on-the-eu/ (accessed 3 May 2019).
Cummings, D. (2017) 'How the Brexit referendum was won', *The Spectator*, 9 January, available at https://blogs.spectator.co.uk/2017/01/dominic-cummings-brexit-referendum-won (accessed 12 April 2019).
Duncan Smith, I. (2016a) 'Why I fear a fresh stampede', *Daily Mail*, 23 April, available at https://www.dailymail.co.uk/debate/article-3554760/IAIN-DUNCAN-SMITH-says-desperation-stay-Brussels-means-government-rowing-pledge-cut-migration.html (accessed 26 April 2019).
Duncan Smith, I. (2016b) 'Are we in this together?', 10 May, available at http://www.voteleavetakecontrol.org/iain_duncan_smith_are_we_in_this_together.html (accessed 25 April 2019).
Duncan Smith, I. (2016c) 'Tory veteran says vote to leave on June 23 will make Britain Great Again', *Telegraph*, 30 April, available at https://www.telegraph.co.uk/news/2016/04/30/eu-referendum-iain-duncan-smith-interview–a-vote-to-leave-on-ju/ (accessed 25 April 2019).
Ewick, P. and Silbey, S. (1995) 'Subversive stories and hegemonic tales: toward a sociology of narrative', *Law and Society Review* 29 (2): 197–226.
Farage, N. (2016a) 'Why we must vote LEAVE in the EU referendum', *Express*, 21 June, available at https://www.express.co.uk/comment/expresscomment/681776/nigel-farage-eu-referendum-brexit-vote-leave-independence-ukip (accessed 25 April 2019).
Farage, N. (2016b) 'Why you should vote for Brexit this Thursday', *Independent*, 20 June, available at https://www.independent.co.uk/voices/eu-referendum-brexit-nigel-farage-on-why-you-should-vote-to-leave-a7091021.html (accessed 15 April 2019).
Farage, N. (2016c) 'EU referendum: Nigel Farage tells leave campaigners to focus on migration', *Sun*, 29 April, available at https://www.thesun.co.uk/archives/news/1152183/nigel-farage-tells-leave-campaigners-to-focus-on-migration/ (accessed 26 April 2019).
Fischer, H. (1991) *Romantic Verse Narrative*, Cambridge: Cambridge University Press.
Fox, L. (2016) 'Memories of green? The cost of uncontrolled migration', available at http://www.voteleavetakecontrol.org/rt_hon_liam_fox_mp_memories_of_green_the_cost_of_uncontrolled_migration.html (accessed 18 June 2019).
Frye, N. (1957) *Anatomy of Criticism. Four Essays*, Princeton, NJ: Princeton University Press.
Frye, N. (1963) *Romanticism Reconsidered: English Institute Essays*, New York: Columbia University Press.
Genette, G. (1982) *Figures of Literary Discourse*, New York: Columbia University Press.
Golden, L. (1976) 'Towards a definition of tragedy', *The Classical Journal* 72 (1): 21–33.

Gove, M. (2016a) 'The facts of life say leave: why Britain and Europe will be better off after we vote leave', available at http://www.voteleavetakecontrol.org/michael_gove_the_facts_of_life_say_leave.html (accessed 25 April 2019).

Gove, M. (2016b) 'Michael Gove's full statement on why he is backing Brexit', *Independent*, 20 February, available at https://www.independent.co.uk/news/uk/politics/eu-referendum-michael-goves-full-statement-on-why-he-is-backing-brexit-a6886221.html (accessed 25 April 2019).

Gove, M. (2016c) 'Soviet-style control freaks are a threat to our independence', *Times*, available at https://www.thetimes.co.uk/article/soviet-style-control-freaks-will-worsen-migration-free-for-all-m3rfb6vmb (accessed 25 April 2019).

Gove, M. (2016d) 'Why it is safer to take back control', 19 April, available at http://www.voteleavetakecontrol.org/michael_gove_s_oped_for_bbc_radio_4_today_programme.html (accessed 26 April 2016).

Gove, M. (2016e) 'The risks of remain – security', 6 June, available at http://www.voteleavetakecontrol.org/voting_to_stay_in_the_eu_is_the_risky_option.html (accessed 26 April 2019).

Gove, M. (2016f) 'Secure in our values: why an unreformed EU Weakens us in fighting for liberal democracy', 8 June, available at http://www.voteleavetakecontrol.org/gove_and_raab_eu_membership_makes_us_less_safe.html (accessed 26 April 2019).

Grant, C. (2016) 'How leave outgunned remain: the battle of the "Five Ms"', *Centre for European Reform*, 25 June, available at https://www.cer.eu/insights/how-leave-outgunned-remain-battle-five-ms (accessed 6 May 2019).

Griffin, D.H. (1994) *Satire: A Critical Reintroduction*, Lexington: University Press of Kentucky.

Hall, I. (2014) 'The satiric vision of politics: ethics, interests and disorders', *European Journal of International Relations* 20 (1): 217–36.

Herman, D. (2009) *Basic Elements of Narrative*, Chichester: Wiley-Blackwell.

Herrenstein Smith, B. (1981) 'Narrative versions, narrative theories', in W. Mitchell (ed), *On Narrative*, Chicago: University of Chicago Press, pp. 209–32.

Hobolt, S. (2016) 'The Brexit vote: a divided nation, a divided continent', *Journal of European Public Policy* 23 (9): 1259–77.

Holm, N. (2017) *Humour as Politics. The Political Aesthetics of Contemporary Comedy*, Basingstoke: Palgrave.

Howard, M. (2016) 'The lack of democracy in the EU is hurting business, speech to the confederation of British industry', 18 May, available at http://www.voteleavetakecontrol.org/lord_howard_to_the_cbi_the_lack_of_democracy_in_the_eu_is_hurting_business.html (accessed 25 April 2019).

Iakhnis, E., Rathbun, B., Reifler, J. and Scotto, T. (2018) 'Populist referendum: Was 'Brexit' an expression of nativist and anti-elitist sentiment?', *Research and Politics* 5 (2): 1–7.

Jameson, F. (1975) 'Magical narratives: romance as genre', *New Literary History* 7 (1): 135–63.

Johnson, B. (2016a) 'The only way to take back control of immigration is to vote leave on 23 June', 26 Mai, available at http://www.voteleavetakecontrol.org/boris_johnson_the_only_way_to_take_back_control_of_immigration_is_to_vote_leave_on_23_june.html (accessed 26 April 2019).

Johnson, B. (2016b) 'Of course our city fat cats love the EU – It's why they earn so much', *Telegraph*, 15 May, available at https://www.telegraph.co.uk/news/2016/05/15/of-course-our-city-fat-cats-love-the-eu–its-why-they-earn-so-mu/ (accessed 25 April 2019).

Johnson, B. (2016c) 'The liberal cosmopolitan case to vote leave', 9 May, available at https://www.conservativehome.com/parliament/2016/05/boris-johnsons-speech-on-the-eu-referendum-full-text.html (accessed 25 April 2019).

Johnson, B. (2016d) 'There is only one way to get the change we want – vote to leave the EU', *Telegraph*, 16 March, available at https://www.telegraph.co.uk/opinion/2016/03/16/boris-johnson-exclusive-there-is-only-one-way-to-get-the-change (accessed 25 April 2019).

Johnson, B. (2016e) 'For U.S. It's: Do as I Say Not as I Do', *Sun*, 22 April, p.10.

Johnson, B. (2016f) 'The risks of remain – democracy', 6 June, available at http://www.voteleavetakecontrol.org/voting_to_stay_in_the_eu_is_the_risky_option.html (accessed 26 April 2019).

Kenny, M. and Pearce, N. (2018) *Shadows of Empire: The Anglosphere in British Politics*, Cambridge: Polity Press.

Kohler Riessman, C. (2008) *Narrative Methods for the Human Sciences*, London: Sage.

Krebs, R. (2015) *Narrative and the Making of US National Security*, Cambridge: Cambridge University Press.

Kuusisto, R. (2009) 'Comic plots as conflict resolution strategy', *European Journal of International Relations* 15 (4): 601–26.

Kuusisto, R. (2018) 'Comparing IR plots: dismal tragedies, exuberant romances, hopeful comedies and cynical satires', *International Politics* 55 (2): 160–76.

Laclau, E. (2005) 'Populism: What's in a name?', in F. Panizza (ed), *Populism and the Mirror of Democracy*, London: Verso, pp. 32–49.

Lawson, N. (2016) 'Britain outside the EU would stand tall as a free and prosperous nation', *Telegraph*, 17 February, available at https://www.telegraph.co.uk/news/newstopics/eureferendum/12162009/Britain-outside-the-EU-would-stand-tall-as-a-free-and-prosperous-nation.html (accessed 25 April 2019).

Leadsom, A. (2016) 'The choice the UK now faces is to accept a largely unreformed EU, or choose the route of freedom and democracy, speech at vote leave', 17 May, available at http://www.voteleavetakecontrol.org/andrea_leadsom_the_choice_the_uk_now_faces_is_to_accept_a_largely_unreformed_eu_or_choose_the_route_of_freedom_and_democracy.html (accessed 25 April 2019).

Lebow, R. (2003) *The Tragic Vision of Politics: Ethics, Interests and Orders*, Cambridge: Cambridge University Press.

Longworth, J. (2016) 'The risks of remain – the economy', 6 June, available at http://www.voteleavetakecontrol.org/voting_to_stay_in_the_eu_is_the_risky_option.html (accessed 26 April 2019).

McQuail, D. (1987) *Mass Communication Theory: An Introduction*, London: Sage.

Miskimmon, A., O'Loughlin, B. and Roselle, L. (2017) *Forging the World. Strategic Narratives and International Relations*, Ann Arbor: University of Michigan Press.

Moore, M. and Ramsay, G. (2017) *UK Media Coverage of the 2016 EU Referendum Campaign*, London: King's College.

Mudde, C. (2004) 'The populist zeitgeist', *Government and Opposition* 39 (4): 541–63.

Oppermann, K. and Spencer, A. (2018) 'Narrating success and failure: congressional debates on the Iran nuclear deal', *European Journal of International Relations* 24 (2): 268–92.

Osborne, G. (2016a) 'HM treasury analysis on the EU referendum', 18 April, available at https://www.gov.uk/government/speeches/hm-treasury-analysis-on-the-eu-referendum-george-osbornes-speech (accessed 3 May 2019).

Osborne, G. (2016b) 'Leaving the EU would be a one way ticket to a poorer Britain', 16 May, available at https://www.gov.uk/government/speeches/chancellor-leaving-the-eu-would-be-a-one-way-ticket-to-a-poorer-britain (accessed 3 May 2019).

Osborne, G. (2016c) 'IMF Article IV Concluding Statement', 13 May, available at https://www.gov.uk/government/speeches/imf-article-iv-concluding-statement-chancellors-remarks (accessed 3 May 2019).

Patel, P. (2016a) 'Speech at the Spring conference of the association of licensed multiple retailers', 28 April, available at http://www.voteleavetakecontrol.org/priti_patel_speech_at_the_spring_conference_of_the_association_of_licensed_multiple_retailers.html (accessed 25 April 2019).

Patel, P. (2016b) 'Let's Take Back Control', *Sun*, 24 April, p.21.

Raab, D. (2016) 'The advantages of controlled immigration', 8 June, available at http://www.voteleavetakecontrol.org/gove_and_raab_eu_membership_makes_us_less_safe.html (accessed 25 April 2019).

Rimmon-Kenan, S. (2006) 'Concepts of narrative', in M. Hyvärinen, A. Korhonen and J. Mykkänen (eds), *The Travelling Concept of Narrative*, COLLeGIUM: Helsinki, pp. 10–19.

Ruback, T. (2010) '"Let me tell the story straight on": *middlemarch*, process-tracing methods and the politics of narrative', *The British Journal of Politics and International Relations* 12 (4): 477–97.

Spencer, A. (2016) *Romantic Narratives in International Politics: Pirates, Rebels and Mercenaries*, Manchester: Manchester University Press.

Stanley, B. (2008) 'The thin ideology of populism', *Journal of Political Ideologies* 13 (1): 95–110.

Stott, A. (2005) *Comedy*, Abingdon: Routledge.

Stuart, G. (2016a) 'Brexit is the left-wing choice', *Prospect Magazine*, 1 March, https://www.prospectmagazine.co.uk/politics/brexit-is-the-left-wing-choice (accessed 25 April 2019).

Stuart, G. (2016b) 'Gisela Stuart exposes the risks of staying in the EU', 13 April, available at http://www.voteleavetakecontrol.org/gisela_stuart_exposes_the_risks_of_staying_in_the_eu.html (accessed 25 April 2019).

Stuart, G. (2016c) 'The risks of remain – immigration', 6 June, available at http://www.voteleavetakecontrol.org/voting_to_stay_in_the_eu_is_the_risky_option.html (accessed 25 April 2019).

Taggart, P. (2019) 'Populism and "unpolitics"', in G. Fitzi, J. Mackert and B. Turner (eds), *Populism and the Crisis of Democracy. Concepts and Theory*, New York: Routledge, pp. 79–88.

Toolan, M. (2001) *Narrative: A Critical Linguistic Introduction*, London: Routledge.

Turner, M. (1996) *The Literary Mind*, Oxford: Oxford University Press.

Van Ham, P. (2002) 'Branding territory: inside the wonderful worlds of PR and IR theory', *Millennium: Journal of International Studies* 31 (2): 249–69.

Van Peer, W. and Chatman, S. (2001) 'Introduction', in W. van Peter and S. Chatman (eds), *New Perspectives on Narrative Perspective*, Albany: State University of New York Press, pp. 1–17.

Wales, K. (1989) *A Dictionary of Stylistics*, London: Longman.

White, H. (1973) *Metahistory: The Historical Imagination in Nineteenth-Century Europe*, Baltimore: Johns Hopkins.

Explanations for the Brexit policy fiasco: near-impossible challenge, leadership failure or Westminster pathology?

Allan McConnell and Simon Tormey

ABSTRACT
The inability of the Conservative Government led by Prime Minister Theresa May to deliver a Brexit deal by 29 March 2019 was a policy fiasco, condemned widely by Remainers and Leavers alike. The entire process was a unique combination of chaos, day-by-day unravelling of new proposals and gridlock. This article examines three main explanations for the fiasco that are prevalent in contemporary political discourse. Analysis is underpinned by conceptual literature straddling policy fiascos and policy studies. It examines three explanations (i) Brexit as an impossible policy challenge (ii) ineffectual leadership by Theresa May who took poor decisions and avoided plausible alternatives and (iii) Westminster as a partisan-fuelled institution incapable of reaching agreement on such a bi-partisan issue. The article concludes by considering whether any single explanation is sufficiently plausible, situating this analysis within long-standing debates on the nature of UK politics.

Introduction

After the 23 June 2016 referendum result in which 52% voted Leave and 48% voted Remain, Theresa May and the Conservative Government were left with the task of translating the 'will of the people' into a viable exit plan. Some such as International Trade Secretary Liam Fox stated that a Brexit agreement would be 'one of the easiest in human history' (BBC Today, Radio 4, 20 July 2017). In reality, extricating the UK from the European Union (EU) has presented the Westminster establishment and its political institutions with their greatest challenge of modern times. When article 50 of the Treaty of Lisbon was triggered in March 2017, the intent of the Conservative government was that it would lead and steward a process culminating in a withdrawl agreement, approved by the Westminster

Parliament and the EU, with the UK exiting by 29 March 2019. This deadline was not met, and the entire period until that date became characterized by a pathological combination of chaos, gridlock, constantly unravelling negotiations, serial failures to find a way forward, and intensely adversarial intra- and inter-party divisions.

Such divisions were highly evident across the political spectrum (from the Westminster elite to UK citizens). Dissatisfaction in both Leave and Remain camps produced a shared and dominant perception that the entire process had been a fiasco of unprecedented proportions (a point to which we will return). This special issue of the *Journal of European Public Policy* is timely because although Brexit-related matters will continue for many years and will undoubtedly by the subject of extended academic and journalistic critique, it provides an initial opportunity for critical analysis. While there are studies of multiple aspects of Brexit such as the socio-economic and national roots of the Leave majority (Henderson 2017), the fracturing politics of the British state (Jennings and Lodge 2019) and Cameron's decision to hold a referendum (Thompson 2017), there have been no direct attempts to tackle in a single analytical piece, the three common narratives (as per the title of this article) which seek to help explain the Brexit fiasco. Hence, the goal of this paper is to focus specifically on the period from the referendum result on 26th June 2016 until 29 March 2019, and consider competing explanations for the UK's 'fiasco' and failure to meet a vital legal and indeed political deadline. Given the nature of the special issue and the uncertainities of Brexit outcomes at the time of writing, we do not engage with the period after 29 March 2019 or seek to predict what might happen.

The paper begins by addressing foundational issues, including the nature of policy fiascos and the role of explanation. It then considers three main categories of explanation for the Brexit policy fiasco. Our intent in doing so is to help capture something of contemporary political discourse which seeks to explain why the UK government became incapable of delivering a Brexit-deal 'on time'. These are (i) Brexit as a near-impossible policy challenge, that any government would have been unable to address effectively (ii) Theresa May as an ineffective leader who took poor decisions and avoided plausible alternatives and (iii) Westminster as a partisan-fuelled institution incapable of reaching agreement on such a bi-partisan issue. Each of these explanations is underpinned by academic analyses of near intractable/wicked problems, ineffective decision makers, and pathological factors within institutions. We conclude by considering the 'sum up the parts' across the three explanations. In doing so we also argue that explanations for the Brexit fiasco have much in common with long-running debates on 'what is wrong' with politics and the political system in the UK.

Fiascos: thematic issues and explanations

The issue of what constitutes a policy fiasco, was first prompted by the seminal work of Bovens and 't Hart (1996) in their book *Understanding Policy Fiascos* and has been picked up and analysed further in studies of fiascos and failure (Hood et al. 2009, Brummer 2016, Gaskarth 2016, McConnell 2016, Oppermann and Spencer 2016) and in overlapping works on various form of policy failures (Bovens and 't Hart 2016, Kruck et al. 2018) and previously policy disasters (Dunleavy 1995, Gray and 't Hart 1998). Many debates therein revolve around whether a broadly undesirable state of affairs is an objective fact, a matter of interpretation, or both. Regardless of such debates, the definition by Bovens and 't Hart (1996: 15) is useful in the present context because it helps capture the real politick of such episodes (and in our case Brexit) through their definition of a fiasco as 'a negative event that is perceived by a socially and politically significant group of people in the community to be at least partially caused by avoidable and blameworthy failures of public policymakers'. It is clear that from across the political spectrum and straddling pro-Brexit and Remain camps, there is an overwhelming majority that the UK government's handling of the Brexit process until 29 March 2019 was a failure. For example, a series of surveys for NatCen Social Research (the UK's largest independent social research agency) over a two year period from February 2017 to February 2019 found a gradual slide in support for 'how well', the UK Government had handled the Brexit process. The final poll in February 2019 found that 80% of Leave voters and 85% of Remain voters indicated that Brexit had been handled 'badly' by the UK Government, with support for being 'well' handled, sitting at only 10% among Leave Voters and 5% among Remain voters (NatCen Social Research 2019: 8). Criticism of the UK from political elites across the political spectrum was the norm rather than the exception. An annual poll of MPs conducted by Ipsos Mori in November and December 2018 found that 70% of all MPs felt that the Prime Minister had done a poor job of negotiating Brexit, with more Conservative MPs feeling that the Prime Minister had done a bad job (47%) rather than a good one (34%) (The UK in a Changing Europe 2019).

In failing to achieve a critical goal for the future of the UK while attracting overwhelming criticism, the attribution of 'fiasco' is a reasonable one. In seeking to help explain this outcome, however, we come to the issue of what constitutes an adequate explanation. The issue of explanation in political science has come to the fore recently in a number of debates (Parsons 2007, Daigneault and Béland 2014, Dowding 2016, Compton and 't Hart 2019). The issues are complex, contested and indeed typical of a discipline noted for its plurality of approaches (Hay 2002). But given the high salience and controversy and criticism around Brexit, we seek to assess what can be called plausible descriptive explanations. As Hay (2017: 185) puts it: 'To explain an outcome, quite simply, has to be to tell a story which could credibly have produced that outcome'. Two issues, in particular, arise from this goal.

First, we seek to capture the core(s) of several different narratives (problem-based, agency-based and institutional-based) that permeate contemporary discourse, in terms of seeking to explain the Brexit fiasco. Second, we seek to minimize as much as possible, the potential for hindsight bias. We know the 'ending' of the story (fiasco) but then must construct a plausible explanation, beginning with pathologies (such as leadership misjudgements and institutional biases) and ending with fiasco/crisis. To minimize such explanatory risk as much as possible, we use insights from Mahoney and Goertz (2019) who point to the value of considering plausible courses of alternative action as a way of better understanding our objects or cases of interest. Plausibility does not mean that an alternative outcome under slightly different circumstances is inevitable. Rather it means there is at least one aspect of an issue that has *potential* to produce a different outcome overall, and there are no factors present that render a different outcome literally impossible (Mahoney and Goertz 2019). Here we can look to numerous experiences in British politics and member-state EU relations, to identify – in a non-deterministic way – potential alternatives to what actually occurred. Put another way, what follows is an examination of plausible alternatives, rather than predictions of what would have happened if different decisions had been taken.

In providing the foundations for explanation, we draw on and adapt generic insights to help explain political and policy phenomena. Parsons (2007) focuses on structural, institutional, ideational and psychological explanations. Brändström and Kuipers (2003) focus on political narratives to help explain policy failures and suggest a three-fold narrative of policy-maker failings, organizational mishaps and broader policy/system failures. We are mindful, however, of the point made by Bovens and 't Hart (2016) that grand explanations for all policy failures can be blunt and unhelpful, hence our focus here is only on Brexit, and on three levels explanations which capture something of contemporary attempts to make sense of the Brexit fiasco during the near two year period under study.

One is grounded in the idea of near-impossible policy challenges. Perhaps the most extensive treatment of such issues can be found is the literature on 'wicked' policy problems. While the initial 10 criteria for wicked problems as set out by Rittel and Weber (1973) have been much debated in subsequent decades (Koppenjan and Klijn 2004; Head and Alford 2015), the core assumptions are relatively straightforward. In essence, wicked problems are characterized by high levels of disagreement on the nature of the policy problem, high levels of disagreement on the desirability of any particular solution, and high levels of uncertainty around where any particular 'solution' will actually work. Related to wicked problems are 'intractable policy controversies' (Schön and Rein 1994) where issues cannot be resolved by appeals to 'the facts'. Broader still are issues of complexity and ambiguity (see Geyer and Cairney 2015, Peters 2019a), focusing on aspects of decision-making that render it extremely tough. For example, policy makers may be unable to take preferred decisions because structurally they are connected to, but effectively immobilized by, the power of significant veto players (Tsebelis 2002). Also relevant is the Condorcet Paradox (Gehrlein 2006). It is a form of political 'more is less', where the broader the range of options and possibilities, the less likely that a decision can be taken that satisfies a majority – even when second and third preferences are part of the decision-making process.

Another level of explanation lies with individual agents/decision makers (political leaders, senior officials) (McConnell 2016; Resodihardjo et al. 2016; Hinterleitner 2017). Fiascos as a product (in part) of political leadership has been approached by multiple disciplines and from different angles, particularly across political psychology and foreign policy decision-making (Brummer 2016). They include leadership traits and styles (Hermann 1999; Preston 2010), psychoanalytical traits (Goldman 2009), and the ability to perform under stress in crisis episodes (Post 2004). The pathologies inherent in different aspects of political leaderships are many but they include arrogance, fantasy thinking, clinging to unrealistic solutions, stereotyping of critics, and refusal to accept clear evidence.

A further explanation for fiasco, echoing much of the new institutionalism (Lowndes and Roberts 2013; Peters 2019b), resides in the pathologies of the institutional environment and processes within which individual agents operate. Such pathologies include blind spots to emerging threats (Bach and Wegrich 2019) and assuming that new threats are either insignificant and/or can be dealt with via existing ways of working. They also include strategic and lower levels of the institution, holding different instincts on the nature of the threat and the way forward (Boin and Renaud 2013).

We can now consider each of these three levels of explanation, setting out their core assumptions and interrogating each. We pay particular attention to plausible alternatives but do so in a non-prescriptive way. Our purpose is simply to examine and gain insight, rather than to make retrospective recommendations.

Brexit fiasco as a near-impossible policy challenge?

A persistent theme in the commentary has been the unenviably demanding nature of the task of delivering Brexit, to the point that it is has been explained as a near-impossible challenge that any government would have been unable to address effectively (Ericson 2018). Although not exhaustive, four factors continually appear in such a narrative.

First, there are the high levels of ambiguity (a classic wicked problems issue) in terms what 'Brexit' actually means. There are many possibilities, notably a clean break with every European institution ('Hard Brexit'), or dropping out of the single market while maintaining a customs union ('Soft Brexit'), as well as various permutations in-between (Emerson 2017). Oliver (2017: 3) writing in 2016, referred to 'fifty shades of Brexit' and the looming attempts to settle and reach agreement on one version as 'a diplomatic minefield of mega-proportions'.

Second, and following on, there was an issue of Northern Ireland and the impact that different variants of Brexit would have on the Good Friday Agreement and indeed Northern Ireland's place in the UK. As Gormley-Heenan and Aughey (2017: 506) comment: 'there was no reason to speculate about constitutional futures because the painstaking negotiations of the Agreement had established the only conceivable, mutually acceptable, template'. But with the UK voting to leave the EU, this delicate compromise came under threat. As a result, government seemed stuck between the EU's insistence that the Good Friday agreement be honoured (hence, indicating special provisions for free movement from Northern Ireland to the Republic of Ireland) and the insistence of the staunchly pro-hard Brexit European Reform Group (ERG) within the Conservative Party that there be no dilution of a Brexit settlement via a customs union of any other special measures. Such intense disagreement over the way forward is (again) a classic characteristic of wicked problems, but arguably it also fits with Schön and Rein (1994) and their analysis of intractable policy controversies, where political divisions overwhelm appeals to 'the facts'.

Third, there were high levels of uncertainty about how any proposal would play out once it was put before Parliament and voted upon. As Gamble (2019: 177) argues, 'Theresa May was trying to reconcile the irreconcilable, finding a formula which would satisfy simultaneously the contradictory demands of Leave Voters, the polarized factions in per party, the DUP, the business community, and the EU'. Amid such uncertainty, there were a large number of veto players, most with the capacity to stymie a version of Brexit they did not support, and especially in Parliament where there was the potential for any initiative to get mired – Condorcet style – in continual loops of transitive preferences, unable to produce a clear majority that would have satisfied all.

Fourth, and reinforcing uncertainties within Parliament, there was the role of the EU. As a supra-national set of institutions that emerged out of peacebuilding after the Second World War, it comprised of 28 member states, all interlocked politically and also economically in the world's largest second largest economy (behind the US). It was not in the EU's interests to make it easy for any state seeking to disrupt the 'common good' and secede from the EU (Bongardt and Torres 2017). The EU, therefore, was a significant veto player.

Do these four factors, individually or in combination, render any government as destined to become mired in issues similar to those encountered by Theresa May and the Conservative Government, with no realistic means of escape? While each element could be the subject of extended analysis on its own, we would suggest that the four aforementioned elements of near-impossibility, are immensely challenging for any government, but they are not insoluble.

In the face of multiple potential interpretations of Brexit, there were plausible alternatives to Theresa May's top-down and ambiguous 'Brexit means Brexit' as if there was not other interpretation (Allen 2018). The matter could have been handed to a non-partisan Commission or cross-party commission. Although not directly analogous, the Northern Ireland peace process, culminating in the 1998 Good Friday Agreement shares many similarities with Brexit, in seeking to craft and navigate a process leading to major 'constitutional' reform based on popular sovereignty, while overcoming diametrically-opposed views, forged in decades (at least) of bitter division and conflict. Alternatively, as Alexander (2019) suggests, a Brexiteer Prime Minister could have mandated Brexiteers to produce their own definition of Brexit. Whilst this may have produced a clearer, vision of a 'Hard Brexit' and been highly divisive, it may have been enough to concentrate the minds of MPs and break the deadlock. In some respects, such alternatives routes have echoes in the flip side of some of the wicked problems literature. While it emphasizes the near intractability of problems, it often overplays its fatalist hand (Peters 2019a) because in fact it also is imbued with a sense of optimism that wicked issues can be addressed for example through governance reforms, enhanced leadership and development of mutual understandings (Head and Alford 2015). In essence, attempting to address the ambiguities of 'Brexit' could have been addressed through greater leadership decentralizing of responsibility in various ways, seeking to build up capacity for ownership of a final recommendation.

On the related issue of the border between Northern Ireland and the Republic of Ireland, a plausible alternative approach would have been for the government to be much more forceful in challenging the EU's 'red line' that the border issue be resolved only by special provisions. We do not know what the outcomes of any such a move would have been, but the EU had proven itself highly adaptable and flexible throughout its almost seven decades of existence, for example via numerous opt-outs from the Schengen Agreement, Eurozone and various treaty provisions (Dinan 2014). Indeed Britain's reputation as an 'awkward partner' across multiple governments (George 1998), from holding a referendum in 1975 on whether to remain a member, or gaining concessions such as its contribution to the EU budget and opt-outs from the Euro and the Social Chapter, had demonstrated its independence and tenacity. In effect, there was a substantial precedent in the UK for testing and challenging the veto power of the EU itself, and the veto powers of its members under qualified majority voting procedures in the Council.

On the 'near impossibility' issue of uncertainty in terms how Parliament would react to any proposal brought before it. Such challenges are hardly new in the Westminster Parliament, but again, a different approach was possible. Attempting to mitigate could have been pursued at much earlier stage by (for example), discussions between the Government and Opposition parties (particularly the Labour Party whose Leader Jeremy Corbyn was not a Remainer) or by more extensive discussions between Theresa May, the Cabinet and backbenchers (Stern 2018; Alexander 2019). Such approaches based on a form of ground-up capacity-building or cross-party collaboration for change are not anathema in the Westminster system, and indeed have been used by governments of several political colours (such as the post 2010 Conservative-Liberal Democrat coalition). Also, there was potential for an impasse to be less likely if a second referendum required a ranking of preferences rather than a simple Yes/No. Doing so would not eliminate the risk of Condorect cycles (with no overall, and satisfied majority) but it would reduce the likelihood of impasse, and may also impact on MPs behaviours and voting as well (Kaye 2018)

The final component of near impossibility is that any government would need to contend with a veto player (the EU), whose interests did not lie in making it 'easy' for a member state to leave the EU (and especially if it sought to cherry-pick some of the advantages through a softer version of Brexit). A plausible alternative, drawing on the experiences of Denmark and Ireland where referendum votes rejected (respectively) the treaties of Maastricht and Lisbon, would be for the government to use the no vote to initiate a process of negotiation and then a further referendum (Alexander 2019). The issue here is not to suggest that such an approach would have been broadly popular or would have avoided the Brexit fiasco. It is simply a plausible alternative route, with elements of precedent in member state-EU relations.

In sum, the narrative that Brexit was a near impossible challenge, does not stand up to close scrutiny. It certainly has some credibility because the challenge of delivering 'on time' was exceptionally tough, but it is an over-stretch to portray it as a near-insoluble problem from which there is virtually no plausible escape route. Small contingency factors and variations in circumstances can make a significant difference (Shapiro and Bedi 2007), and therefore we should be cautious about conceding to a narrative that leaves little room for the potential impact of different leadership styles and tactics. We now, therefore, need to consider our second main explanation for the fiasco – ineffectual leadership by Theresa May.

Brexit fiasco as a product of ineffectual leadership by Theresa May?

The explanation here rests with the political agency, and the contention that Prime Minister Theresa May took risky decisions that – despite the availability of plausible alternatives – eventually locked-in the UK to a pathway with no obvious means of escape. May was accused routinely of 'magical thinking', 'fantasy thinking' and 'chasing unicorns' (see e.g., Ferrow 2018). While the previous section indicated the potential for a British Prime Minister to have plausibly tackled the Brexit challenge in a different way, here we focus on three critical decisions by Theresa May (a Remainer who was tasked with delivering a Brexit deal) that are at the core of this agency-based explanation for policy fiasco.

First, there was May's 2017 decision to call a General Election, less than two years after the previous one (Hobolt 2016). Initially, May's single-minded devotion to the task of delivering Brexit received plaudits from the right wing of May's own party as well as a strong showing in the polls. The PM won praise for her 2017 Lancaster House speech, which combined a tough Brexit stance with an acknowledgement of the importance of maintaining close relations with Europe. This position, blending 'frictionless trade' with control over national borders, became the motif of the Theresa May approach to delivering Brexit. Buoyed by opinion polls indicating the popularity of this position, May's decision was intended to facilitate the smooth passage of Brexit legislation (Heath and Goodwin 2017). Ultimately, however, instead of a hoped for 100 plus majority, the Conservative Party lost its majority in the House of Commons and became dependent on the support of Northern Ireland's Democratic Unionist party – a sectarian, anti-EU party opposed to any 'backstop' that would dilute the UK's withdrawal from the EU (Wincott 2017).

Second, in March 2017 May decided to trigger Article 50, thereby setting the clock running for a period of two years with a deadline of 29 March 2019 for obtaining a satisfactory withdrawal agreement from the EU. The intent was to put pressure on the EU to produce a formula that would reconcile frictionless trade with control over borders, but it led to a stand off in which the EU simply repeated its position that these two goals could not be reconciled.

Third, in terms of the strategic approach to the negotiations that followed, the prevailing wisdom of May and the negotiating team was a nostalgic view of Westminster sovereignty vs. the unaccountable leviathan of the EU (Weale 2016). The EU is a rules-based organization. It is also an intergovernmental body aware of the necessity for maintaining a tight line in its negotiations for fear of creating precedents that would be used by countries to promote their own national interest. Expert commentators repeated the dictum that the EU would not grant frictionless trade without recognition of the four fundamental freedoms that underpinned the single market. And yet, consistent with arguments about a clash between a more impositional UK 'policy style' and a more consensus-based EU one (Richardson 2019), May's own approach for the best part of two years was to insist on the possibility that this contradictory aim was possible via agreement with a 'veto player' that did not want the UK to leave the EU.

Taking all these points together, there is appeal in the contention that the strategic choices of Theresa May helped the UK proceed down a route which seemed to get more calamitous as time proceeded. This appeal seems even stronger when we consider that plausible alternatives existed for each.

May's decision to call another election in a climate of austerity and highly fractious debates over public services and the future of the UK was a high-risk gamble, especially because the traditional Conservative base of supporters could not be relied upon, given the divisive nature of Brexit and its prominence in the subsequent campaign (Heath and Goodwin 2017) The General Election in 2015 provided the Conservatives with a small but potentially workable Commons majority of 12. Quite plausibly, this majority may have been sufficient to weather the storms of Commons voting in the move towards a Brexit deal. Elite decisions almost inevitably involve aspects of formal and instinctive political risk-taking (Althaus 2008), with no guarantees that they will provide the desired outcome.

The decision to trigger Article 50 was also not essential at that time. The reason why May did so early in 2017 was clearly to create a sense of obligation amongst MPs. Yet in doing so it set the clock running before the UK's thinking had been tested with the EU. An alternative approach would have been to have a series of consultations with the EU *first*, and *then* when the outline of a withdrawal agreement was in sight, to trigger Article 50. A 'ticking clock' is one of the classic elements of crisis conditions and even although leaders may cultivate a sense of crisis in order to concentrate minds and galvanize support (Drennan, McConnell and Stark, 2015), there is a fine line between circumstances that can produce success or failure, especially because such outcomes are product of feedback loops, first – and second-order mechanisms, and reflexive agents who change and adapt their behaviour over time (Compton and 't Hart 2019). Put simply, triggering article 50 was a high risk gamble in the face of deep uncertainty and high potential veto power.

May's approach to negotiating with the EU also cast aside viable alternatives. The Lancaster House speech in January 2017 established a vision for how Brexit would be pursued. Given that there were a variety of ways in which Brexit could be interpreted, May could have turned to a process for establishing where consensus lies in the House of Commons, or could have simply laid out some choices, which might have been the subject for debate or discussion between the major parties (Stern 2018; Alexander 2019). Instead, the PM alighted on the one definition of Brexit that was always guaranteed to cause a hiatus with the EU: frictionless trade plus control over borders plus withdrawing from all European jurisdiction. In short, this was a bold but risky move designed to underpin May's own Brexit credentials.

The issue of why May's psychology resulted in a series of high risk choices will be an issue for future researchers, especially given a lack of charisma, enigmatic demeanour, weak campaigning style and proneness to inconsistencies (Prince 2017; Yolles and Di Fatta 2018). It is plausible that May best fits the 'compulsive leader' classification in the typology by Post (2004) of personality types responding to crisis and stress, rather than the 'narcissistic' or 'paranoid' leader. The former is characterized for a methodical eye for detail, and logical reasoning but often unsuited to crisis situations with high levels of ambiguity and uncertainty. The outcome can be pathological decision-making, including reframing issues to address them via familiar rules.

Yet this agency-based explanation for the Brexit fiasco, credible as it is, would we argue, does not properly situate May as an actor within the context of the Westminster system. Belying the myth of near-presidential powers, the Prime Minister is a strategic actor in a strategic context (Byrne and Theakston 2018). In many respects, May was simply doing what many of her predecessors had done in adopting a position and expecting that an institution that tends to produce majority one-party government, would get its way if one fights hard enough.

Brexit fiasco as a pathology of the Westminster system?

The Westminster model has been highly influential across much of the Anglosphere. Unlike other political systems operating on principles of federalism, presidentialism, consensus and written constitutions, the Westminster system is predicated on principles of a unitary (or at least Union state), the fusion of powers where the executive is derived in the majority party in the legislature, Parliamentary sovereignty, and civil service neutrality (Rhodes et al. 2011). The historic norm has been a 'fusion' of executive-legislature power powers, a strong and disciplined government vs. opposition divide, and the views of the government tending to prevail in terms of votes on the floor of the House of Commons (Russell and Glover 2017). The core of this third explanation, is that the Brexit fiasco was caused by the unsuitability of the Westminster model in being able to generate the consensus that Parliament needed to deliver a Brexit deal. Two issues are particularly important.

First, with May losing the Government's majority in the House of Commons, it became clear that the task of generating a majority for one particular iteration of Brexit would be demanding. In other political systems, this may have been the cue to search for areas of agreement between the major political parties which would then have delivered a policy based on a clear consensus or at least majority vote. But a pathway in the Westminster tradition had already been laid. As Richards and Smith (2017: 3) argue:

> The rationale for Theresa May calling an election is that it strengthens her Government's bargaining position over Brexit. Yet this majoritarian approach reveals the true nature of the British political tradition in its capacity to insulate against pressures for plurality and deliberation in the negotiations.

But once article 50 had been triggered, May's majoritarian instincts that the Party would fall into line behind the government (albeit with some persuasion), failed to account fully for an issue that had divided the Party for many years and provoked more backbench rebellions than any other issue, including under David Cameron in 2011 when 81 Conservative MPs defied the Whip in a vote on a referendum on EU membership (Cowley and Stuart 2012). If we think of Westminster as an institution with its own values and culture (see for example Judge 2019), then arguably what is laid bare here is a form of institutional blind spot (Bach and Wegrich 2019), where the unique value of the institution (in the case of Westminster, strong, majoritarian governments) also generates risks and frames of reference that are not sufficiently attentive to potential threats. As Hood (1998) argues, the 'achilles' heel' of the hierarchist organizations with its reliance on top-down authority and a 'more of the same' approach to addressing problems, is that it is vulnerable to the collapse of major initiatives.

Second, the absence of a codified constitution meant that much of the business of Westminster was based on convention and culture – indeed a British political tradition and a Westminster model that have been highly resilient in resisting pressures for reform (Richards et al. 2019). Problems began with the status of the referendum itself. Were MPs to regard the result as fixed in stone, a once in a generation vote which they were beholden to deliver? Would they be permitted to envisage a change in the 'will of the people'? Or was it that they should regard the result of the referendum as merely indicative, and allow the Westminster process itself to determine how and indeed whether Brexit was to be delivered at all? Prevarication on this point marked the early weeks and months after the result, with a heightening of political tensions as leading Brexiteers began to detect betrayal. The conventions and ambiguities of Westminster helped fuel traditional partisan divisions.

In sum, there is some credibility in these explanations, not least because they are compatible with numerous works on the capacity of Westminster to produce policy fiascos. Dunleavy (1995) in his examination of the propensity of Westminster to produce policy disasters (such as the poll tax, Child Support agency and exit from the European Exchange Rate Mechanism) argues that a key factor in inducing policy disasters is a form of political hyperactivism, borne out of a belief that party competition and a form of 'Westminster knows best' culture (or in reality – governments know best) is the way that issues should be addressed. Westminster remains an institution based heavily on the virtues of partisanship, but in the case of Brexit and a Remain/Leave divide that cut across across party lines (Hobolt 2016), there was a disjunction between its historical norms and its capacity to deliver. As Brändström et al. (2004) argue in their examination of historical analogies and crisis management, there is a danger for policy makers in assuming that past experiences (and successful resolutions) will play out the same way under new, complex unique circumstances.

The Brexit fiasco: reconciling multiple explanations

In the midst of and in the wake of 'crisis', and as a form of catharsis, societies gravitate towards simple explanations, and someone or something to blame as the 'villain' of the entire episode (Boin et al. 2016). The Brexit fiasco is no exception, and we have attempted here to capture something of the contemporary discourse via three main explanations. All are credible to some degree (even the near impossibility perspective, despite its over-stretching), and so how do we proceed from here?

In the first instance, each explanatory assumption is an eclectic mix of theories, frameworks and perspectives, stemming from different assumptions and interests, multiple methodological approaches and varying methods. It is not possible to bundle together and compare side by side, probing each in a quasi-scientific manner while projecting 'what if?' assumptions, as if we were tweaking variables under controlled laboratory conditions. We cannot recreate 'Brexit' in a laboratory, continually refining and modelling different causal factors (new definitions of Brexit, new prime ministers, different decisions, etc.) in order to prove with high levels of confidence that Brexit failures were the product of *X*.

Furthermore, explanations of policy success and failure that focus on linearity (X alone, unambiguously explaining Y), do not take into account complex interactions, dynamic feedback loops and the reflexivity of actors (Compton and 't Hart 2019). Indeed, when we add in the fact that political science as a discipline is pluralistic in the sense that it produces different explanations (with differing underlying ontological, epistemological and methodological assumptions) about any particular episode or phenomenon (Hay 2002), then arriving at a dominant, single and plausible explanation is problematic. For example, no matter how rigorously we might the case for example that it was 'May's fault' (an agency-based explanation)', or Brexit was a 'poisoned chalice' (a wicked problem explanation) we would always confront other plausible positions with different starting points in structural explanations (such as the pathologies of Westminster as an institution).

Our approach here is more in line with Cairney on (2007, 2013) who addresses the issue of multiple insights in the field of public policy. As Cairney (2013) suggests, different perspectives and different ontological and epistemological assumptions can pose problems in making like-for-like comparisons, but are less important if all we seek is new and plausible 'insights'. Our key insight here is that we should avoid defaulting to a single explanation alone. All three explanations are intertwined and compatible – each telling us something about the factors contributing to the Brexit fiasco. Furthermore, even if we felt Brexit was an 'impossible challenge' and the primary explanation of the entire episode, we cannot be certain that any alternative courses of action (and any movements in the flexibility of UK political institutions), would have been unable to alter a trajectory towards 'inevitable' failure'.

Ironically, the tendency towards single explanations aligns with classic political explanations for all manner of ills in the British political system. The history of post-war political commentary on the UK is replete with multifaceted analyses of 'what's wrong' and what should be done to fix it. Some suggest that contemporary policy problems are too complex and intermeshed with the global economy that the UK as a nation state cannot tackle them alone (O'Brien and Williams 2016; Kuttner 2019). Others focus on the quality of our political leaders and their ideas, arguing that we need 'new blood' and 'fresh thinking' (Weinberg 2012; Hardman 2018). Others focus on the Westminster system itself, arguing that we need voting reform, greater checks and balances and a written constitution (Dunleavy 1995; Hazell 1999).

Overall, our view is that in order to help explain a phenomenon as complex as the Brexit policy fiasco, we need to set aside such long-standing quests for theoretical parsimony of a kind that insists for example that agent-centred explanations are always to be favoured over structure-centred explanations (or vice versa). Agency is indeed important in understanding why Brexit turned out to be so frustratingly difficult to realize by 29 March 2019, but so are the institutions and processes within which actors are embedded – as well as the nature of the policy challenge itself. Without attention to each of these factors and the ways in which they interact within complex historical, social and economic contexts we will be unable to grasp the nature of this key episode in UK politics. Our task then is not to reduce the Brexit fiasco to a solitary explanation, but rather to help account for its complexity. Doing so means attending to the interplay of agents, institutions/processes and the unique policy challenge of exiting the EU within a specified timescale, and amid intense inter – and intra-party divisions.

Acknowledgements

The authors are grateful to the journal editors and anonymous reviewers for exceptionally helpful comments and suggestions.

Disclosure statement

No potential conflict of interest was reported by the authors.

References

Alexander, P. (2019) 'It could all have been so different: how Britain might have negotiated with Brussels', 20 March, available at https://blogs.lse.ac.uk/brexit/2019/03/20/it-could-all-have-been-so-different-how-britain-might-have-negotiated-with-brussels/.

Allen, N. (2018) ''Brexit means Brexit': Theresa May and post-referendum politics', *British Politics* 13 (1): 105–20.

Althaus, C. (2008) *Calculating Political Risk*, Sydney: UNSW Press.

Bach, T. and Wegrich, K. eds (2019). *The Blind Spots of Public Bureaucracy and the Politics of Non-Coordination*, Basingstoke: Palgrave.

Boin, A. and Renaud, C. (2013) 'Orchestrating joint sensemaking across government levels: challenges and requirements for crisis Leadership', *Journal of Leadership Studies* 7 (3): 41–6.

Boin, A., 't Hart, P., Stern, E.K. and Sundelius, B. (2016) *The Politics of Crisis Management: Public Leadership Under Pressure*. 2nd Edition. Cambridge: Cambridge University Press.

Bongardt, A. and Torres, F. (2017) 'A qualitative change in the process of European Integration', in N. da Costa Cabral, J.C. Gonçalves and N.C. Rodrigues (eds), *After Brexit: Consequences for the European Union*, London: *Palgrave Macmillan*, pp. 101–28.

Bovens, M. and `t Hart, P. (1996) *Understanding Policy Fiascoes*, New Brunswick: Transaction.

Bovens, M. and 't Hart, P. (2016) 'Revisiting the study of policy failures', *Journal of European Public Policy* 23 (5): 653–66.

Brändström, A. and Kuipers, S. (2003) 'From "normal incidents" to political crises: understanding the selective politicization of policy failures', *Government and Opposition* 38 (3): 279–305.

Brändström, A., Bynander, F. and `t Hart, P. (2004) 'Governing by looking back: historical analogies and crisis management', *Public Administration* 82 (1): 191–210.

Brummer, K. (2016) '"Fiasco prime ministers": leaders' beliefs and personality traits as possible causes for policy fiascos', *Journal of European Public Policy* 23 (5): 702–17.

Byrne, C. and Theakston, K. (2018) 'Understanding the power of the prime minister: structure and agency in models of prime ministerial power', *British Politics*, available at https://doi.org/10.1057/s41293-018-0087-7.

Cairney, P. (2007) 'A "multiple lenses" approach to policy change: the case of tobacco policy in the UK', *British Politics* 2 (1): 45–68.

Cairney, P. (2013) 'Standing on the shoulders of giants: how do we combine the insights of multiple theories in public policy studies?' *Policy Studies Journal* 41 (1): 1–21.

Compton, M. and 't Hart, P. (2019) 'Looping to success (and failure): second-order mechanism and policy Outcomes', in G. Capano, M. Howlett, M. Ramesh and A. Virani (eds), *Making Policies Work: First- and Second-Order Mechanisms in Policy Design*, Cheltengam: Edward Elgar, pp. 191–210.

Cowley, P. and Stuart, M. (2012) 'The Cambusters: the conservative European Union referendum rebellion of october 2011', *The Political Quarterly* 83 (2): 402–6.

Daigneault, P.-M. and Béland, D. (2015) 'Taking explanation seriously in political science', *Political Studies Review* 13 (3): 384–92.

Dinan, D. (2014) *Europe Recast: A History of European Union*, London: Red Glove Press.

Dowding, K. (2016) *The Philosophy and Methods of Political Science*, Basingstoke: Palgrave Macmillan.

Drennan, L., McConnell, A. and Stark, A. (2015) *Risk and Crisis Management in the Public Sector*. 2nd Edition, Abingdon: Routledge.

Dunleavy, P. (1995) 'Policy disasters: explaining the UK's record', *Public Policy and Administration* 10 (2): 52–70.

Emerson, M. (2017) 'Which model for Brexit?', in N. da Costa Cabral, J.C. Gonçalves and N.C. Rodrigues (eds), *After Brexit: Consequences for the European Union*, London: Palgrave Macmillan, pp. 167–88.

Ericson, A. (2018) 'Is Theresa May a bad negotiator, or is Brexit just an impossible proposition? Answer: yes', *Washington Post*, 14 December, https://wapo.st/2FxzVTB.

Ferrow, J. (2018) 'The land of unicorns: how magical thinking conquered British politics', available at politics.co.uk, https://www.politics.co.uk/comment-analysis/2018/08/15/the-land-of-unicorns-how-magical-thinking-conquered-british.

Gamble, A. (2019) 'The realignment of British politics in the wake of Brexit', *The Political Quarterly* 90 (2): 177–86.

Gaskarth, J. (2016) 'The fiasco of the 2013 Syria votes: decline and denial in British foreign Policy', *Journal of European Public Policy* 23 (5): 718–34.

Gehrlein, W.V. (2006) *Condorcet's Paradox*, Heidelberg: Springer.

George, S. (1998) *An Awkward Partner: Britain in the European Community*, 3rd Edition, Oxford: Oxford University Press.

Geyer, R. and Cairney, P. (eds) (2015). *Handbook on Complexity and Public Policy*, Cheltenham: Edward Elgar.

Goldman, A. (2009) *Destructive Leaders and Dysfunctional Organizations: A Therapeutic Approach*, Cambridge: Cambridge University Press.

Gormley-Heenan, C. and Aughey, A. (2017) 'Northern Ireland and Brexit: three effects on "the border in the mind"', *The British Journal of Politics and International Relations* 19 (3): 497–511.

Gray, P. and 't Hart, P. (eds) (1998). *Policy Disasters in Western Europe*, London: Routledge.

Hardman, I. (2018) *Why We Get the Wrong Politicians*, London: Atlantic.

Hay, C. (2002) *Political Analysis: A Critical Introduction*, Basingstoke: Palgrave Macmillan.

Hay, C. (2017) 'Explanation, prediction, causation – an unholy trinity? Appreciative comments on the philosophy and methods of science', *British Journal of Politics and International Relations* 15 (2): 180–6.

Hazell, R. (1999) *Constitutional Futures: A History of the Next Ten Years*, Oxford: Oxford University Press.

Head, B.W. and Alford, J. (2015) 'Wicked problems', *Administration & Society* 47 (6): 711–39.

Heath, O. and Goodwin, M. (2017) 'The 2017 general election, Brexit and the return to two-party politics: an aggregate-level analysis of the result', *The Political Quarterly* 88 (3): 345–58.

Henderson, A., Jeffrey, C., Wincott, D. and Wyn Jones, R. (2017) 'How Brexit was made in England', *The British Journal of Politics and International Relations* 19 (4): 631–46.

Hermann, M.G. (1999) *Assessing Leadership Style: A Trait Analysis*, Social Science Automation: Columbus.

Hinterleitner, M. (2017) 'Reconciling perspectives on blame avoidance behaviour', *Political Studies Review* 15 (2): 243–54.
Hobolt, S. (2016) 'The Brexit vote: a divided nation, a divided continent', *Journal of European Public Policy* 23 (9): 1259–77.
Hood, C. (1998) *The Art of The State: Culture, Rhetoric, and Public Management*, Oxford: Oxford University Press.
Hood, C., Jennings, W., Dixon, R,B, Hogwood, B. and Beeston, C. (2009) 'Testing times: exploring staged responses and the impact of blame management strategies in two examination fiasco cases', *Public Administration* 48 (6): 695–722.
Jennings, W. and Lodge, M. (2019) 'Brexit, the Tides and Canute: the fracturing politics of the British State', *Journal of European Public Policy* 26(5): 772–789.
Judge, D. (2019) *Political Institutions in the United Kingdom:* Oxford: Oxford University Press.
Kaye, S. (2018) 'Deal remain no-deal: Brexit and the Condorect Paradox', Blog, available at https://blogs.lse.ac.uk/politicsandpolicy/brexit-condorcet/.
Koppenjan, J.F.M. and Klijn, E.H. (2004) *Managing Uncertainties in Networks; A Network Approach to Problem Solving and Decision Making*, London: Routledge.
Kruck, A., Oppermann, K. and Spencer, A.2018). *Political Mistakes and Policy Failures in International Relations*, London: Palgrave.
Kuttner, R. (2019) *Can Democracy Survive Global Capitalism*, New York, NY: WW. Norton and Co.
Lowndes, V. and Roberts, M. (2013) *Why Institutions Matter: The New Institutionalism in Political Science*, Basingstoke: Palgrave Macmillan.
Mahoney, J. and Goertz, G. (2019) 'The possibility principle: choosing negative cases in comparative research', *American Political Science Review* 98 (4): 653–69.
McConnell, A. (2016) 'A public policy approach to understanding the nature and causes of foreign policy failure', *Journal of European Public Policy* 23 (5): 667–84.
NatCen Social Research (2019) 'Have the politicians delivered? Voters' judgement on the Brexit process', London: NatCen Social Research, available at https://whatukthinks.org/eu/analysis/have-the-politicians-delivered-voters-judgement-on-the-brexit-process/.
O'Brien, R. and Williams, M. (2016) *Global Political Economy: Evolution and Dynamics*, London: Palgrave.
Oliver, T. (2017) 'Fifty shades of Brexit: Britain's EU referendum and its implications for Europe and Britain', *The International Spectator: Italian Journal of International Affairs* 52 (1): 1–11.
Oppermann, K. and Spencer, A. (2016) 'Telling stories of failure: narrative constructions of foreign policy fiascos', *Journal of European Public Policy* 23 (5): 685–701.
Parsons, C. (2007) *How to Map Arguments in Political Science*, Oxford: Oxford University Press.
Peters, B.G. (2019a) *Policy Problems and Policy Design*, Cheltenham: Edward Elgar.
Peters, B.G. (2019b, forthcoming) *Institutional Theory in Political Science: The New Institutionalism*, 4th Edition, Cheltenham: Edward Elgar.
Post, J.M. (2004) *Leaders and Their Followers in a Dangerous World: The Psychology of Political Behaviour*, Ithaca: Cornell University Press.
Preston, J.T. (2010) 'Leadership and foreign policy Analysis', in R.A. Denmark (ed), *The International Studies Encyclopedia*, Vol. 8, Hoboken: Wiley-Blackwell, pp. 4856–74.
Prince, T. (2017) *Theresa May: The Enigmatic Prime Minister*, London: Biteback.

Resodihardjo, S.L., Carroll, S.J., Van Eljk, C.J.A. and Maris, S. (2016) 'Why traditional responses to blame games fail: the importance of context, rituals, and sub-blame games in the face of raves gone wrong' *Public Administration* 94 (2): 350–63.

Rhodes, R.A.W., Wanna, J. and Weller, P. (2011) *Comparing Westminster*, Oxford: Oxford University Press.

Richards, D., Diamond, P. and Wager, A. (2019) 'Westminster's Brexit Paradox: the contingency of the 'old' versus 'new' politics', *The British Journal of Politics and International Relations* 21 (2): 330–48.

Richards, D. and Smith, M. (2017) '"Things were better in the past": Brexit and the Westminster Fallacy of Democratic Nostalgia', British Politics and Policy at LSE, blog. 20 May, available at http://eprints.lse.ac.uk/81867/.

Richardson, J. (2019) *British Policy-Making and the Need for a Post-Brexit Policy Style*, London: Palgrave Macmillan.

Rittel, H.W.J. and Webber, M.M. (1973) 'Dilemmas in a general theory of planning', *Policy Sciences* 4 (2): 155–69.

Russell, M. and Glover, D. (2017) *Legislation at Westminster: Parliamentary Actors and Influence in the Making of British Law*, Oxford: Oxford University Press.

Schön, D.A. and Rein, M. (1994) *Frame Reflection: Towards the Resolution of Intractable Policy Controversies*, New York: Basic Books.

Shapiro, I. and Bedi, S. (2007) Introduction: contingency's challenge to political science', in I. Shapiro and S. Bedi (eds), *Political Contingency: Studying the Unexpected, the Accidental and the Unforeseen*, New York, NY: New York University Press, pp. 1–18.

Stern, S. (2018) 'Theresa May's handling of Brexit is a classic case of bad leadership', *The Conversation*, 12 December, available at https://theconversation.com/theresa-mays-handling-of-brexit-is-a-classic-case-of-bad-leadership-108646.

The UK in a Changing Europe (2019) 'New survey finds 70% of MPs think Theresa May has done a poor job of negotiating Brexit', available at https://ukandeu.ac.uk/new-survey-finds-70-of-mps-think-theresa-may-has-done-a-poor-job-of-negotiating-brexit/.

Thompson, H. (2017) 'Inevitability and contingency: the political economy of Brexit', *The British Journal of Politics and International Relations* 19 (3): 434–49.

Tsebelis, G. (2002) *Veto Players: How Political Institutions Work*, Princeton, NJ: Princeton University Press.

Weale, A. (2016) 'Nostalogic democracy triumphs over democratic internationalism', *The Political Quarterly* 87 (3): 352–4.

Weinberg, A. (2012). *The Psychology of Politicians*, Cambridge: Cambridge University Press.

Wincott, D. (2017) 'Brexit dilemmas: new opportunities and tough choices in unsettled times', *The British Journal of Politics and International Relations* 19 (4): 680–95.

Yolles, M. and Di Fatta, D. (2018) 'Agency, personality, and multiple identity types: understanding Theresa May', *Kybernetes* 47 (7): 1278–1306.

OPEN ACCESS

Can't get no learning: the Brexit fiasco through the lens of policy learning

Claire A. Dunlop, Scott James and Claudio M. Radaelli

ABSTRACT
It seems paradoxical to suggest that theories of learning might be used to explain policy failure. Yet the Brexit fiasco connects with recent approaches linking varieties of policy learning to policy pathologies. This article sets out to explain the UK government's (mis)management of the Brexit process from June 2016 to May 2019 from a policy learning perspective. Drawing on interviews with UK policy-makers and stakeholders, we ask how did the UK government seek to learn during the Brexit negotiations? We consider four modes of learning: reflexivity, epistemic, hierarchical, and bargaining. By empirically tracing the policy process and scope conditions for each of these, we argue that learning through the first three modes proved highly dysfunctional. This forced the government to rely on bargaining between competing factions, producing a highly political form of learning which stymied the development of a coherent Brexit strategy. We argue that the analysis of Brexit as a policy process – rather than a political event – reveals how policy dynamics play an important role in shaping the political context within which they are located. The article concludes that public policy analysis can, therefore, add significant value to our understanding of Brexit by endogenising accounts of macro political developments.

Introduction

There is something paradoxical in attempting to explain policy fiascos with theories of policy learning. We understand policy learning to mean the updating of beliefs about policy based on experiences, analysis or social interaction (Checkel 2001; Hall 1993; Heclo 1974). It evokes processes whereby policy actors gain a deeper or different understanding of the world around them, causing them to alter their causal beliefs and to change their behaviour. In a seminal article, Peter May (1992) connected policy learning and failure, but his argument was that evidence of failure should encourage reformulation of public policies. It is more counterintuitive to start with failure as outcome to be explained, as in the case of the Brexit process. Yet, the analysis of policy fiascos sits well with recent approaches linking varieties of policy learning to policy pathologies (Dunlop 2017; Dunlop and Radaelli 2013, 2018). This literature identifies four main modes of policy learning: reflexive, epistemic, hierarchical or bargaining (Dunlop and Radaelli 2013; for empirical applications see Di Giulio and Vecchi 2019; Polman 2018). The typology rests on two main claims: (1) the mode of policy learning in a particular context is determined by the nature of key policy setting variables; and (2) the effectiveness of learning through those modes is shaped by the presence or absence of scope conditions. This allows us to generate empirical expectations about the mode and effectiveness of policy learning in a particular context.

Applying the framework to Brexit, we set out to explain the UK government's (mis)management of the Brexit process since 2016 – this is our demarcation of the concept of policy fiasco. We ask how did the UK government seek to learn during the Brexit negotiations? Answering this question allows us to see how dysfunctional learning had an impact on the UK's handling of the issue. An important argument emerging from our analysis is that the politics of Brexit does not determine the policy. Rather, the policy process plays an important role in shaping the political context in which policy dynamics are located. Our argument does not deny that Brexit is a highly complex policy issue, the resolution of which will inevitably be long and arduous. Rather, our contribution is to show that the intractability of Brexit is in part due to dysfunctional forms of learning within government, which seriously hindered the development of a coherent policy response.

It is worth briefly reflecting on the analytical boundaries of the article. First, we examine the domestic Brexit negotiations: specifically, the policy actors that moved in and around the worlds of Whitehall and Westminster. While not denying the multi-level nature of Brexit, we must cede to the practical reality that analysis of the subnational (devolved governments) and supranational levels (the European Union) are simply beyond the scope of this article. Second, we use policy theory – learning in this case – to provide a more endogenous account of Brexit by illuminating the policy dynamics that shaped the political context in the UK. Our focus on the policy process avoids reducing the Brexit fiasco to the artefact of parliamentary arithmetic, but instead views the political impasse as contingent on – and in part a product of – dysfunctional modes of learning within government.

The analysis consists of two main steps. First, we assess the nature of policy learning around Brexit through each of the four modes. This involves mapping how these modes shifted over time in response to the sequencing of the Brexit process and changes in policy setting variables. Second, we explain the effectiveness of learning through each of the four modes by analysing the presence or absence of critical scope conditions. The analysis relies on process tracing of key decisions and developments related to the management of Brexit within the UK government between June 2016 and May 2019. This is informed by analysis of public documents, think tanks reports and media coverage over this period, together with seven anonymous interviews conducted with UK policy-makers and stakeholders in the summer of 2017 and 2018.

We argue that although the policy setting was well-suited to reflexive and epistemic learning immediately following the referendum, these were hindered because important scope conditions were not met (namely, open attitudes and negotiation settings, fluid group identities, a culture of trust, and the legitimacy of expertise). Learning shifted to the realm of hierarchy as the Article 50 negotiations got underway, but this was undermined by a breakdown of political authority and institutional instability following the June 2017 election. As a result, learning around Brexit was largely restricted to bargaining, the conditions for which (external conditionality and arena disaggregation) were partially met. However, as illustrated by the fate of the Withdrawal Agreement, this produced a highly dysfunctional form of learning that prioritised short-term political demands (namely, government survival and party management) over long-term strategic policy thinking (about Brexit).

The article proceeds as follows. The first section reviews the policy learning literature and the typology which we apply. The main analysis is structured around each of the four modes of policy learning: reflexivity, epistemic, hierarchical, and bargaining. The conclusion reflects on how the systematic analysis of learning, and policy theories more generally, can contribute to our understanding of policy fiascos.

Policy learning: literature and theory

The literature on learning is rich in typologies (for example, see Bennett and Howlett 1992; Dolowitz and Marsh 1996; Heikkila and Gerlak 2013, May 1992). The approach we consider here draws on explicit political science and adult education theories to identify different types or 'modes' of policy learning (Dunlop and Radaelli 2013). The framework posits that modes of policy learning are defined by two variables which relate to the policy setting. The first concerns the level of uncertainty or problem tractability, which is an important determinant of whether learning can be 'thick' or 'thin', and can be managed through technocratic or political processes (Checkel 2001). The second relates to the certification of actors; namely, whether actors exist that are viewed as holding legitimate expertise on a particular subject. On a nominal scale, these variables can be measured as low or high, thus producing a four-fold typology: reflexive, epistemic, hierarchical, and learning through bargaining (see Figure 1).

CERTIFICATION OF ACTORS	LOW	HIGH
LOW	2. Reflexive Learning	3. Learning through Bargaining
HIGH	1. Epistemic Learning	4. Learning through Hierarchy

Figure 1. Modes of policy learning. Source: Dunlop and Radaelli (2013: 603).

At its simplest, *reflexive* learning relies on a dialogue between actors who are open to new ideas and evidence about the world around them (Schön and Rein 1994). Learning is reflexive when this interaction leads actors to critically re-evaluate their core policy beliefs and to look at the policy world in novel ways. The policy setting variables that define reflexivity are equality of actors in the learning process (low certification) and radical uncertainty. In terms of scope conditions, reflexive learning is facilitated by: a relatively open attitude of the individual participants; the presence of policy instruments that allow collective problem-solving; and negotiation settings that permit overlapping identities and do not assign hierarchies; while an important negative scope condition (that is, hindrance) is at the level of attitudes, that is, suspicion and luck of trust about the intentions of the others.

Epistemic learning is typically found in policy settings characterised by radical issue uncertainty and the existence of a socially certified group of experts (Dunlop and Radaelli 2013). The absence of a recognised epistemic community (Haas 1992), or the presence of alternative, conflicting sources of epistemic knowledge, are therefore hindrances to learning. Other scope conditions include the availability of evidence-based policy instruments, such as impact assessments (IAs). These constitute an epistemic policy tool which provide *ex ante* policy appraisals, ensuring that the economic impact of different courses of policy action are documented, grounded in consultation and analysis, and available to the public. IAs are intended to guide policy objectives, but they can also serve other functions (Dunlop et al. 2012): political (to legitimate a pre-determined policy project); dialogic (to stimulate wider social debate about the conceptual terms of policy); or symbolic (i.e., a tick-the-box exercise).

In learning through *hierarchy*, knowledge is used by actors to exert control and is guided towards particular goals. Hierarchy is rooted in institutions – including formal structures, organisational roles, rules of the game, codes and norms – which shape the production, content and utilisation of knowledge (Dobbin et al. 2007). Some features of hierarchies have nothing to do with learning, e.g., authority supported by credible threats is not learning. But individual bureaucrats, government departments, and ministers within cabinets follow long-standing institutional rules. The hierarchical layers within the bureaucracy allow public managers to learn what to do, when and the role they are supposed to play. In this sense, the shadow of hierarchy is a learning mode. If the UK government (or the EU) could have imposed a deal on Parliament with authority supported by credible threats we would not have been in the territory of learning. But since this was not the case, there is a prima facie case for considering hierarchy as a mode of learning. To operate, this mode requires low uncertainty (no ambiguity about the behaviour that is expected when a policy problem appears) and high certification of actors (Dunlop and Radaelli 2013: 611). The scope conditions are stability within the organisation of the bureaucracies/government, and shared beliefs in the legitimacy of the different roles and echelons of the hierarchy.

Bargaining describes a mode of learning in which inter-dependent actors trade, bargain and exchange information to secure other objectives (Dunlop and Radaelli 2013: 610). Bargaining is common in policy settings with low actor certification and low uncertainty (high issue tractability): in this context, learning does not necessarily lead to the reconciliation of divergent preferences, but it can facilitate agreement on mutually beneficial outcomes. Learning through bargaining has two scope conditions. The first, external conditionality, can take the form of externally imposed time pressures. In a context of heightened uncertainty, deadlines facilitate bargaining by enabling actors to more accurately calculate the pay-offs of different bargaining strategies. The second condition is arena disaggregation. Bargaining may be easier where the boundaries of negotiating arenas are clearly defined and arena membership is fixed (Eberlein and Radaelli 2010). This enables complex issues to be compartmentalised, and facilitates the calculation of actor pay-offs through routinised interaction.

The following section applies the four modes of learning to Brexit. Importantly, we do not view Brexit as a static process. Rather, we recognise that the policy setting variables shifted over time as the negotiations progressed (from the pre-negotiation phase to the Article 50 negotiations, and then to parliamentary ratification of the Withdrawal Agreement). Importantly, from our perspective, these dynamic settings generated new opportunities for different types of learning (while often closing down others).[1] We explain the effectiveness of policy learning in each case by examining whether the scope conditions specified above were met (or not).

Learning reflexively

Of all the modes of learning we examine, Brexit is intuitively well-suited to the policy setting variables characteristic of reflexivity: low tractability (i.e., radical uncertainty) and low certification of actors. What Brexit means, how it can be achieved, and its real-world consequences have long been shrouded behind a heavy veil of ignorance. The scale of the policy challenge necessitated by legally untangling the UK from the EU across a vast swathe of policy areas was unprecedented. Not only was the potential number of alternative scenarios for Brexit unknown (and infinite), but the political and economic impacts of technical 'fixes' (e.g., for the Irish border) were almost impossible to quantify. It was also clear that few actors could claim to hold an exclusive monopoly of expertise on the subject.

In response to this policy impasse, the government might have been expected to encourage an extended period of reflection and consultation so as to facilitate mutual learning through reflexivity. However, the key scope conditions for doing so – an open attitude of individual participants to new ideas and information, non-hierarchical negotiation settings that allow overlapping identities and encourage dialogue, and participatory policy instruments for collective problem-solving – were largely absent both within and outside government. For the first twelve months of her premiership, Theresa May was almost impermeable to arguments aired in cabinet, her listening-and-learning ears sealed-off by the two powerful advisers, Nick Timothy and Fiona Hill (see Perrior 2017). Far from consulting widely with MPs from across her party, let alone seeking to forge a cross-party consensus, Theresa May instead relied on a small and narrow clique of eurosceptic MPs to formulate her early Brexit 'strategy' (James and Quaglia 2018). Yet in the absence of meaningful cabinet dialogue or agreement, this meant relying on the rhetorical tautology of 'Brexit means Brexit' to conceal the absence of rank-ordered preferences, and to silence dissenting voices.

The absence of reflexivity within government reflected the widespread culture of mistrust and suspicion generated by the referendum, and the cabinet splits this engendered (see Shipman 2017). In response, the May Government attempted (but largely failed – see below) to assert control over the process. The result of using different shades of formal power and parliamentary conventions was not a problem-solving trajectory, but further political confusion. Within cabinet, for example, mistrust gave rise to the development of institutional venues which were deliberately designed to minimise consultation and dialogue. Hence, in Autumn 2016, May established a smaller EU Exit and Trade (Negotiations) cabinet subcommittee (consisting only of the Prime

Minister, and five senior ministers) – not to increase organisational efficiency, but to reduce the risk of cabinet leaks. The use of informal procedures and conventions to assert power was also evident in the Impact Assessment process which we narrate below. Nor was Parliament immune. For example, the speaker of the House of Commons, John Bercow, broke with convention by allowing a vote on the amendment to a government business motion tabled by Conservative MP Dominic Grieve in January 2019. Similarly, in March 2018 Bercow cited a 1604 convention to deny the government the option of bringing the EU-UK Withdrawal Agreement back to Parliament for a third vote unless it contained significant changes. All these episodes show how the option of learning reflexively was stymied.

Turning to political parties, the Brexit negotiations exacerbated the clash between Remain-Leave identities. These identities fractured the existing parties, perhaps setting the path for historical re-composition of party cleavages (as signalled by the formation of Change UK by disaffected MPs). Negotiations with overlapping identities could conceivably have emerged via cross-party talks leading to a compromise between the Conservative and Labour Party. But, the commencement of these talks in spring 2019 came far too late in the process, by which point political strategising and mutual mistrust effectively ruled out any prospect of agreement between May and Corbyn on the UK's withdrawal.

Perhaps more surprising was the May Government's failure to encourage reflexive learning through engagement with external stakeholders, notably business. Distrust at the heart of government led No.10 to deliberately close down established channels of access to outsiders, rendering business consultation largely informal and ad hoc. At ministerial level, business leaders complained that Theresa May was 'elusive' compared to her predecessor, and that Brexit Secretary David Davis made it known that he was only willing to meet with those willing to speak positively about Brexit.[2] For example, Confederation of British Industry (CBI)[3] Director-General Carolyn Fairbairn was initially 'frozen out' of meetings with senior government officials after she publicly accused the Prime Minister of closing the door on the UK's open economy. Moreover, officials made it clear that lobbyists making any critical statements in the media about immigration, trade or the rights of EU citizens would be punished with an immediate cessation of access (Parker 2017). These political tensions were compounded by the centralisation of Brexit policy-making around No.10 and DExEU, and the downgrading of the Treasury. Business groups found DExEU to be a 'black hole' that was largely 'impenetrable' to industry, forcing them to increasingly 'sing the same tune' as ministers in order to be granted access.[4] Following the June 2017 election, the government took steps to repair relations with business by placing consultation on a more formal basis. To this end, a summit was convened by Brexit Secretary David Davis for UK business leaders in July 2017, and the Chancellor Philip Hammond established a new Brexit business advisory group to institutionalise relations (Gordon and Pickard 2017). Despite this, the ability of government and business to establish a meaningful dialogue on Brexit remained very limited; either because key decisions, such as ruling out single market membership, had already been taken (in secret), or deferred owing to a lack of political direction.

Finally, the prospect of encouraging reflexivity amongst the wider public was constrained by the gradual hardening of public attitudes on Remain and Leave into distinct group identities (Clarke et al. 2017). As Sorace and Hobolt (2019) detail, these constitute powerful normative lenses through which voters process information and interpret evidence, thereby reinforcing the polarisation of opinion. An alternative approach could have been to generate network-type settings from outside the formal venues of politics (Sabel and Zeitlin 2008) – i.e., beyond the cabinet, Westminster, and Whitehall – to facilitate a wider process of social learning (Hall 1993). For example, there were attempts to activate politically relevant knowledge from outside government and Parliament around Brexit with the creation of citizen's assemblies. Assemblies are particularly useful when Parliament is deadlocked and the government loses key votes on priorities, as in the case of Brexit. However, the idea gained little traction within government precisely because ministers had little incentive to (re)open the Brexit debate.

Somewhat paradoxically, despite the policy setting for Brexit being well-suited to this mode of learning (i.e., low tractability and low certification of actors) we find little evidence of reflexivity. On the contrary, the main scope conditions – namely, openness of attitudes, fluid negotiation settings, and a culture of trust – were largely absent. This encouraged a bunker-mentality in No.10, determined to keep control of the agenda, and using a discourse of obfuscation to deflect challenges. This position was untenable, however, once the UK triggered Article 50 in March 2017 and the Brexit negotiations got underway, as the government was now forced to stake out a position. In response, we see policy-makers attempting to move the process forwards through other modes of learning.

Learning epistemically

Although the intractability of Brexit satisfies the first policy setting variable, the prospects for any functional epistemic learning were stymied by the absence of any socially and politically legitimate experts. Indeed, the referendum was marked by an antipathy toward expertise, as infamously espoused by leave campaigner and cabinet minister Michael Gove. The presence of experts – most powerfully in the form of epistemic communities (Haas 1992) – is a critical variable in triggering epistemic learning as teaching. Haas argues that 'ideas would be sterile without carriers' (1992: 27), meaning that the values, norms and policy direction that give ideas purpose and form are derived from those who create them. The importance of this anthropomorphic conceptualisation of policy knowledge bears out in the empirical literature. Experts succeed in shaping decision-makers' preferences where they have both strong epistemic products – i.e., knowledge consensus – *and* when they deploy human skills effectively – persuasion, leadership, judgement.

No unified epistemic community existed to advise the government on Brexit. The most obvious candidate – the Bank of England (BoE) – had seen its analysis of UK withdrawal challenged as a matter of course. For example, when BoE economists published an evaluation of the possible impacts of various Brexit scenarios on the UK's monetary and financial stability in November 2018 (BoE 2018), the figures it quoted were roundly derided by leave supporting politicians (Treanor 2018). More damaging for the prospects of epistemic learning, they were curtly dismissed via social media as 'highly speculative' and 'too severe' by former BoE member Andrew Sentence and Nobel prize winning economist Paul Krugman (Partington 2018). Beyond these interventions, the wider production of contending claims (often through social media) on Brexit's impact made it impossible for the BoE to claim the authoritative high ground required by expert enclaves that aim to be principal teacher to policy-makers.

Despite the absence of any single, socially accepted knowledge carrier, epistemic lessons could have been generated. Another powerful channel for epistemic learning is the presence of evidence-based policy instruments, such as impact assessments (IAs). Key to the epistemic value of this instrument is how constellations of actors organise their interactions around IA as evidence-based trigger: instrumentally, symbolically, to exercise control, or dialogically. We argue that during the Brexit process, Whitehall's reliance on IAs vacillated between all four uses, ensuring that epistemic learning was dysfunctional. This instability, which fatally undermined the IAs' credibility, was generated by several factors: the early lack of transparency about the IAs; a range of competing goals held by different actors using the IAs; and the existence of competing IAs in the other nations of the UK, the European Commission and European Parliament. We briefly address each in turn.

Functional epistemic learning requires robust knowledge production processes open to scrutiny. Learning pathologies arise and policy capacity is damaged where the process of knowledge formation appears the preserve of 'invisible colleges' closed off from oversight (Regonini 2017). From the outset, the existence, scope and content of economic analyses of Brexit were the subject of contest. In December 2016, David Davis (then Secretary of State for Exiting the EU) confirmed the existence of 'about 57' sector assessments for individual parts of 85% of the economy. That same month, Parliament established a no disclosure policy to prevent public divulgence of any material that could be damaging to the Brexit negotiations. Throughout 2017, Freedom of Information requests were lodged by MPs and calls made by both Commons and Lords EU committees to have sight of the assessments. Despite assurances in June 2017 from DExEU that the list of sectors would be published 'shortly', Davis later asserted the need to balance 'our commitment to transparency with the need to protect information which could undermine the UK's ability to negotiate the best deal for the UK' (Davis 2017). But pressure continued to build and, in November 2017, Parliament dusted down and deployed an arcane procedure called a 'motion to return' (Defty 2017). From this point, the assessments (ultimately totalling 39) were released to EU committees in both Houses of Parliament and from then aspects were published or leaked before their final public disclosure in March 2018.

While it is not common practice for IAs to be released as they are being conducted, these are no ordinary sets of analyses. The lack of early disclosure to the relevant parliamentary committees, and uncertainty about just how many had been compiled ensured the IAs became a way to express dissent about the transparency and government dominance of the Brexit process. An analytical tool which was deployed with the promise of offering civil servants much needed forecasts and technical knowledge, became a tool that opened-up debate rendering either (or both) the analysis itself, or the government, suspect.

Further down the line, the government's use of IA changed. As the withdrawal deal was being agreed in late 2018, and with Davis having resigned from his position, Treasury assessments of the economic impact of the Chequers Plan were made public. The original aspirations outlined by Theresa May were predicted to result in a contraction in the UK economy of up to 3.9% over 15 years (HM Government 2018). The use of IA was highly political: not only was the actual agreed deal – which differed from the Prime Minister's favoured plan – not assessed, the 3.9% contraction was then compared to other less favourable scenarios of a free trade agreement (6.7% contraction) and no deal (9.1% contraction). This political approach by the government was then mirrored by politicians and commentators. Cherry-picking facts became the order of the day with the exclusion of economic growth used by Brexit supporters as the reason for the poor forecasts ('this is project fear') and the absence of regional breakdowns used by remainers to warn the forecasts were too optimistic ('we are looking into the abyss').

Yet, such criticisms are not entirely unjustified. The logic of IA is that policy-relevant knowledge about the socio-economic consequences of policy paths is knowable. The extent to which the impacts of Brexit can be reliably estimated is debateable. In such circumstances, IA as process and product has vehicular qualities – it can be used by political actors of all sides to carry radically different interpretations (see McLennan 2004 on vehicular ideas).

The final dimension to this dysfunctional epistemic learning is the presence of competing sites of knowledge production. While the struggle for access played out in Westminster, IAs were being prepared and published by other governments at sub and supranational levels, sector agencies (for example, Financial Conduct Authority [FCA] 2018) and think tanks (for example, the Institute for Government [IfG] – see Tetlow and Stojanovic 2018). The extent to which the presence of competing IAs substantively undermined the Whitehall analyses, or diluted the clarity of the message, is a story that remains to be told. What matters here is that their very existence was enough to undermine the credibility of the analysis as something which could contain debate regarding the fundamentals of policy. That said, though the detail of the IAs did not show up in policy outputs, as the original deadline to leave the EU (29 March 2019) loomed, they had some political purchase. The fact that IAs of all governments agreed that the issue was not one of the likelihood of economic damage, but rather of its magnitude, was important in destabilising Theresa May's Lancaster House assertion 'no deal is better than a bad deal'.

If anything, knowledge and access to knowledge became the territory of sharp political and institutional conflicts. The scope conditions for learning epistemically were violated. On the one hand, economic knowledge and the appraisal of the likely effects of policy options via experts in the BoE and specific policy tools like IAs did not make an impact on the strategy and choices of the main actors. On the other, the very presence of this knowledge became an issue of sharp confrontation between Parliament and the executive. In the end, who qualifies as an expert and the very meaning of what an impact assessment is and should do became fuzzy and controversial, casting doubts on the possibility of this type of knowledge utilisation in the Brexit process.

Learning through hierarchy

In a post-referendum context of high uncertainty and low certification, the operation of hierarchical learning through the British political system became highly dysfunctional. To be precise, while the symbols of formal hierarchy of the Westminster-Whitehall model (Richards et al. 2019) remained in place – namely, prime ministerial direction, cabinet responsibility and parliamentary procedures – the normal rules, norms, conventions and standard operating procedures underpinning them broke down. To explain why, we identify two scope conditions, the absence of which undermined the possibility of rule-based learning about Brexit.

The first scope condition is that roles and hierarchical lines are accepted, not contested. This condition was fatally undermined by the extent of ministerial divisions triggered by the 2016 referendum, compounded by the breakdown of cabinet collective responsibility following the 2017 general election. The impact of these political fault lines at official level was highly pernicious, eroding well-established norms of information sharing and coordination between Whitehall departments. Instead, it encouraged 'a culture of extraordinary secrecy' where key documents were 'over-classified' to prevent them from being shared between departments (Owen et al. 2018). Even 'rudimentary planning guidance' was made largely inaccessible, restricted to hard copies or secure computers only available to a limited number of officials in designated Whitehall reading rooms or a permanent secretary's office (Owen et al. 2018).

The relationship between (Brexit-supporting) ministers and senior civil servants was shaken, generating instability. Suspicion that Whitehall was 'institutionally anti-Brexit' spilled over into outright hostility, leading to the resignation of the UK's permanent representative to the EU (Sir Ivan Rogers) and undermining the position of the UK's lead official negotiator (Oliver Robbins). In the absence of clear policy goals, poor information flows and competing ministerial preferences, effective policy coordination proved 'impossible' and the alignment of departmental contingency plans was made 'very difficult' (Owen et al. 2018).

A key illustration of these problems was the planning guidance issued by the Cabinet Secretary to all departments to guide their Brexit preparations in March 2017. The difficulty of getting political agreement on key issues meant that there were large gaps, while the high level of security clearance needed to view the document, meant that critical information was not widely distributed to front line officials (Owen et al. 2018: 33). As a result, departments increasingly made their own assumptions about what preparations were necessary, guided by their minister's view of the consequences of different Brexit scenarios.

Institutional stability is a second scope condition for rule-based behaviour. Since the UK's accession in 1973, the model for EU policy coordination revolved around the 'quad' of the Cabinet Office, Foreign and Commonwealth Office (FCO), the UK Permanent Representation (UKRep) in Brussels and, on economic and budgetary issues, the Treasury (James 2011). Following the referendum, however, Prime Minister May subverted this structure by establishing a new Department for Exiting the European Union (DExEU) responsible for leading the Brexit negotiations, coordinating activity across government, and undertaking policy work related to the UK's future relationship with the EU. In addition, a new Department for International Trade was established to prepare and negotiate new trade agreements with non-EU countries after Brexit.

These institutional changes undermined learning by challenging the position of traditionally powerful departments, particularly the Treasury and FCO. Lines of responsibility were blurred by the fact that the UK's lead official negotiator, Oliver Robbins, had a dual reporting line to the Brexit Secretary and Prime Minister. As the IfG think tank documented, this created tensions with No.10, which ultimately had responsibility for the success or failure of the negotiations, and with departments who viewed DExEU as a departmental player, rather than as a more conventional broker (Rutter and McCrae 2016). Robbins' move to the Cabinet Office in September 2017 was an attempt to establish a clearer hierarchy by centralising responsibility as the Brexit negotiations entered a critical phase. But this had the effect of undermining the position of DExEU, contributing to its high turnover of ministers and senior officials (with only a single junior minister remaining in place since 2016), and eroding its capacity for institutional memory and accumulation of expertise over time. This limited DExEU's capacity to manage the Brexit preparations process, making it difficult to coordinate or assess the coherence of departmental plans.

More widely, the creation of DExEU depleted the internal resources and expertise of other departments through secondments, and sparked a bureaucratic turf war over ownership of key Brexit policy dossiers (Owen et al. 2018). Learning across all Whitehall departments was also seriously disrupted by heightened staff turnover triggered by the Brexit preparations. The IfG reports that officials took advantage of the promotional opportunities stemming from the creation of approximately 10,000 new posts created since the EU referendum. For example, turnover at DExEU was running at 9% a quarter at the end of 2017, compared to a civil service average of 9% a year (Sasse and Norris 2019).

Once the Brexit negotiations got underway, it was not surprising that the government defaulted to the standard operating procedures of the Westminster-Whitehall model (Richards et al. 2019), characterised by executive autonomy and centralised policy-making. That this proved wholly unsuited to the task in hand did not simply reflect the context of high uncertainty and low certification, however, but also strategic decisions (the 2017 election) and institutional reforms (the creation of DExEU) that fatally eroded political authority and institutional stability, which are essential for hierarchical learning.

Learning through bargaining

According to our theory, learning through bargaining was not appropriate under conditions of high uncertainty (Dunlop and Radaelli 2013). In this situation, the theory predicts that learning will be dysfunctional because actors cannot calculate the pay-offs of different bargaining strategies. This can be ameliorated, in part, if an important scope condition – external conditionality – is met. For example, externally imposed time pressures can incentivise bargaining by facilitating the calculation of pay-offs. In the case of Brexit, external pressures were imposed by the timing and sequencing of the EU's Article 50 process: namely, the two-year deadline for reaching a deal on withdrawal, and the sequencing (and separation) of this from the future relationship negotiations (see Armstrong 2017). Although these time pressures eased bargaining between rival factions to some extent, they also generated a limited form of learning that prioritised short-term political demands (e.g., government survival or party management) over long-term strategic policy thinking (over Brexit).

This dysfunctionality was compounded by the absence of a second scope condition – arena disaggregation – which enables bargaining to be compartmentalised and routinised (Eberlein and Radaelli 2010). The clearest illustration of arena overlap in the case of Brexit is the fact that the UK government was simultaneously bargaining with two sets of actors (Member of Parliament [MPs] and EU negotiators) in a two-level game. Yet even in the domestic context, if the principal venue for bargaining shifts over time as the negotiations progress, this expands the range of actors involved and makes the issue even more intractable. During the Brexit process, we observe a gradual process of expansion across three, overlapping arenas which undermined bargaining.

The first arena, in the immediate aftermath of the referendum, involved a small coterie of senior officials and MPs. In the political vacuum created by the Conservative leadership contest, an unofficial Brexit Cabinet, whose members were close to the Eurosceptic 'All Souls Group' within the party, became highly influential in shaping the learning process.[5] Given the Conservatives' slim parliamentary majority of 17, they concluded that the government had little choice but to adopt a hard Brexit position, which meant ending freedom of movement, to secure the support of pro-Brexit backbenchers.[6] Under Theresa May, this hardened into a broader electoral strategy, developed by No.10 Chief of Staff Nick Timothy and Director of Strategy Chris Wilkins, designed to address the wider social grievances that were perceived to have contributed to Brexit (Shipman 2017: 140–144).

The second arena of bargaining became particularly important following the Conservatives' loss of their parliamentary majority in June 2017 (see Wincott 2017), forcing May to increasingly bargain with her own cabinet and wider parliamentary party for survival. But this constrained the development of a coherent Brexit strategy, forcing key decisions on the future relationship to be deferred, and preventing government departments from undertaking effective preparations (Lloyd 2019). Time spent on intra-party bargaining also left the EU to set the agenda, monopolising the production of key negotiating texts and guidelines, thereby reducing its own scope for compromise and 'boxing in' the UK (Owen et al. 2018). As a result, UK negotiators were forced into a series of incremental and last-minute concessions to reach agreement with the EU. For example, May's Florence speech in September 2017 tentatively suggested that the UK might agree to a status quo transition period of 'around two years', agreement on which was only reached in March 2018. Similarly, to hammer out an agreement between competing factions within cabinet, the Prime Minister convened the Chequers summit in July 2018. The White Paper that followed – pledging to maintain a common rulebook for goods, but not for services, and to seek a 'facilitated' customs arrangement – represented a carefully crafted (but short-lived) cabinet compromise.

The Conservatives' precarious parliamentary position also necessitated careful bargaining between competing party factions; namely, the pro-Brexit Democratic Unionist Party (DUP) and the European Research Group (ERG), and two groups of former Remainers – those that favour a soft Brexit (the so-called Common Market 2.0), and those who support a second referendum. In an effort to secure passage of the Withdrawal Agreement, the government was often more willing to concede ground to the ERG, such as by accepting multiple amendments (Lloyd 2019: 32). It also made significant concessions to the DUP, offering them the *de facto* right to prevent UK-wide divergence from EU regulation, and a formal role in the future relationship negotiations.

The third arena, concerned with the passage of Brexit legislation, included the whole of Parliament. Despite the government's early attempts to limit its involvement, MPs gradually accrued important new powers over the Brexit process. For example, the EU Withdrawal Act took almost a year to get through Parliament and the government was forced to grant MPs a 'meaningful vote' on the final deal (Dixon and Williams 2018). Similarly, in a desperate attempt to secure parliamentary support for the Withdrawal Agreement, the government deliberately sought to portray this as a 'one shot' game, the reversion point of which would be a chaotic no deal Brexit.

Ultimately, however, this strategy was thwarted by MPs who used arcane parliamentary procedures to seize control of the legislative timetable. This culminated in March 2019 with a series of 'indicative votes', which can be interpreted as an attempt to facilitate learning through bargaining in three ways. First, the votes were used as a mechanism of generating information about MPs' preferences, and thus the scope of potential agreement in Parliament (Fox and Baston 2019). Second, the push by MPs to de-couple procedural issues from substantive ones sought to reduce the friction from bargaining, whereby agreement on the process may pave the way for agreement on the outcome. Third, the indicative votes attempted to circumvent the intractability of the Irish backstop issue in the Withdrawal Agreement by explicitly linking it to a range of *different* options on the future relationship – a process known an 'issue-aggregation' (Eberlein and Radaelli 2010).

The learning that resulted was dysfunctional in the sense that it still produced no agreement in Parliament, forcing the Prime Minister to request a further extension of the Article 50 process to 31 October 2019. But it did force May to change strategy and open cross-party talks with the Labour party in early April 2019 in an attempt to end the impasse. By shifting the Brexit process back to a small, closed negotiating arena, these talks represent the latest iteration of (dysfunctional) learning through bargaining. That these subsequently collapsed in May 2019, heralding Theresa May's own departure as Prime Minister, is perhaps a fitting epitaph to the limitations of bargaining under these conditions.

Conclusion

This article asked how did the UK government seek to learn during the Brexit negotiations? We found that although the policy setting was well-suited to reflexive and epistemic learning immediately following the referendum, these were hindered because important scope conditions were not met (namely, open attitudes and negotiation settings, fluid group identities, a culture of trust, and the legitimacy of expertise). Learning shifted to the realm of hierarchy as the Article 50 negotiations got underway, but this was undermined by a breakdown of political authority and institutional instability following the June 2017 election. As a result, learning around Brexit was largely restricted to bargaining, the conditions for which (external conditionality and arena disaggregation) were partially met. However, as illustrated by the fate of the Withdrawal Agreement, this produced a highly dysfunctional form of learning that prioritised short-term political demands (namely, government survival and party management) over long-term strategic policy thinking (about Brexit).

We conclude by reflecting on the broader theoretical and empirical contribution of the article. With respect to the wider theoretical literature on policy learning, we suggest that it makes a threefold contribution: (1) demonstrating the utility of analysing policy fiascos through time-sensitive policy learning theory, (2) examining temporal dynamics in granular policy processes to explain how learning shifts between different modes over time, and (3) assessing learning through the identification and empirical analysis of scope conditions. Taken together, these contributions point to the potential of learning as a theoretical lens on the policy process and macro-events like Brexit. Key policy dynamics – in this case, dysfunctional policy learning – did not simply reflect, but also served to shape the wider political context within which they are located. We assert that this ultimately contributed to the intractability of Brexit as a policy issue. The politics of Brexit do not simply determine the policy; but rather policy dynamics play an important role in shaping the political context within which they are located. Put differently, studies like ours serve to endogenise existing accounts of Brexit.

Finally, we recognise important limitations in our analysis. Notably, the fact that as a single country case study, the ability to generalise from our findings is necessarily limited. Some may also object that Brexit is sui generis, making comparison to other policy issues problematic. Nonetheless, we maintain that analysing a single case such as Brexit over time enables a depth of analysis that would otherwise not be possible. Furthermore, while the *politics* of Brexit has many unique characteristics, as a *policy* it arguably shares many of the same dynamics of process – including learning – as any other. Using policy theories to illuminate these therefore avoids reductionist political explanations, while potentially facilitating comparison with other prominent cases of policy fiascos. Doing so holds out the promise of being able to extract longer-term lessons from the Brexit experience.

Notes

1. We do not claim that learning during the Brexit process was perfectly sequential: while the possibility of learning through some modes (reflexive and epistemic) was apparent throughout the process, the policy settings conducive to other modes (hierarchy and bargaining) were more specific to particular time periods.
2. Interview with senior bank lobbyist in London, 14 June 2017.
3. The CBI is the largest association representing British business.
4. Interview with trade association representative in London, 18 July 2017.
5. Interview with bank lobbyist in London, 10 July 2017.
6. Interview with government minister in London, 20 February 2017.

Acknowledgements

Previous versions of this paper were presented at the Scuola Superiore dell'Università di Catania on 23 May 2019 and the University Association of Contemporary European Studies (UACES) 49th annual conference, Lisbon, 1–4 September 2019. We would like to thank all the participants of these events and in particular Fulvio Attinà, Francesca Longo, Stefania Panebianco, Monika Brusenbach Meislova and Nick Wright. We also thank our three anonymous reviewers, Jeremy Richardson and Berthold Rittberger. The conceptual work was informed by European Research Council (ERC) project – *Analysis of Learning in Regulatory Governance* (ALREG) (grant #230267). The usual disclaimer applies.

Disclosure statement

No potential conflict of interest was reported by the authors.

ORCID

Claire A. Dunlop http://orcid.org/0000-0003-2122-1075
Scott James http://orcid.org/0000-0002-4632-9288
Claudio M. Radaelli http://orcid.org/ 0000-0001-5056-5585

References

Armstrong, K.A. (2017) *Brexit Time: Leaving the EU – Why, How and When?* Cambridge: Cambridge University Press.

Bank of England (2018) *EU Withdrawal Scenarios and Monetary and Financial Stability: A Response to the House of Commons Treasury Committee*, London: Bank of England.

Bennett, C.J. and Howlett, M. (1992) 'The lesson of learning: reconciling theories of policy learning and policy change', *Policy Sciences* 25 (3): 275–94.

Checkel, J.T. (2001) 'Why comply? Social learning and European identity change', *International Organization* 55 (3): 553–88.

Clarke, H.D., Goodwin, M. and Whiteley, P. (2017) *Brexit: Why Britain Voted to Leave the European Union*. Cambridge: Cambridge University Press.

Davis, D. (2017) *Oral Evidence: The Progress of the UK's Negotiations on EU Withdrawal, HC 372*, Select Committee on Exiting the European Union 25 October.

Defty, A. (2017) Labour's 'motion for a return': what and why? 10 November UCL Constitution Unit, available at https://constitution-unit.com/2017/11/10/labours-motion-for-a-return-what-and-why/ (accessed 15 May 2019).

Di Giulio, M. and Vecchi, G. (2019) 'Multilevel policy implementation and the *where* of learning: the case of the information system for school buildings in Italy', *Policy Sciences* 52 (1): 119–35.

Dixon, R. and Williams, M. (2018) 'Amending legislation: a case study of the EU Withdrawal Act', in A. Lilly, H. White and J. Haigh (eds), *Parliamentary Monitor 2018*, Institute for Government, pp. 39–41.

Dobbin, F., Simmons, B.A. and Garrett, G. (2007) 'The global diffusion of public policies: social construction, coercion, competition, or learning?' *Annual Review of Sociology* 33: 449–72.

Dolowitz, D. and Marsh, D. (1996) 'Who learns what from whom: a review of the policy transfer literature', *Political Studies* 44 (2): 343–57.

Dunlop, C.A. (2017) 'Policy learning and policy failure: definitions, dimensions and intersections', *Policy and Politics* 45 (1): 3–18.

Dunlop, C.A., Maggetti, M., Radaelli, C.M. and Russel, D.J. (2012) 'The many uses of regulatory impact assessment: a meta-analysis of EU and UK cases', *Regulation and Governance* 6 (1): 23–45.

Dunlop, C.A. and Radaelli, C.M. (2013) 'Systematizing policy learning: from monolith to dimensions', *Political Studies* 61 (3): 599–619.

Dunlop, C.A. and Radaelli, C.M. (2018) 'The lessons of policy learning: types, triggers, hindrances and pathologies', *Policy and Politics* 46 (2): 255–72.

Eberlein, B. and Radaelli, C.M. (2010) 'Mechanisms of conflict management in EU regulatory policy', *Public Administration* 88 (3): 782–99.

Financial Conduct Authority (FCA) (2018) *EU Withdrawal Impact Assessment*, London, November 2018.

Fox, R. and Baston, L. (2019) 'Indicative votes: options, voting methods and voting systems', *Hansard Society Briefing Paper*, March.

Gordon, S. and Pickard, J. (2017) 'Ministers set up business advisory group with Brexit focus', *Financial Times*, 27 June.
Haas, P.M. (1992) 'Introduction: epistemic communities and international policy coordination', *International Organization* 46 (1): 1–36.
Hall, P.A. (1993) 'Policy paradigms, social learning and the state: the case of economic policymaking in Britain', *Comparative Politics* 25 (3): 275–96.
Heclo, H. (1974) *Modern Social Politics in Britain and Sweden*, New Haven, CT: Yale University Press.
Heikkila, T. and Gerlak, A.K. (2013) 'Building a conceptual approach to collective learning: lessons for public policy scholars', *Policy Studies Journal* 41 (3): 484–511.
HM Government. (2018) *EU Exit: Long-term Economic Analysis', Cm 9742, November 2018*, London: Stationery Office.
James, S. (2011) *Managing Europe from Home: The Changing Face of European Policy Making Under Blair and Ahern*, Manchester: Manchester University Press.
James, S. and Quaglia, L. (2018) 'Brexit, the city and the contingent power of finance', *New Political Economy* 24 (2): 258–71.
Lloyd, L. (2019) *The Brexit Effect: How Government has Changed Since the EU Referendum*, London: Institute for Government, 29 March, available at https://www.instituteforgovernment.org.uk/sites/default/files/publications/brexit-snapshot-final-web-vd.pdf.
May, P. (1992) 'Policy learning and failure', *Journal of Public Policy* 12 (4): 331–54.
McLennan, G. (2004) 'Travelling with vehicular ideas: the case of the third way', *Economy and Society* 33 (4): 484–99.
Owen, J., Lloyd, L. and Rutter, J. (2018) *Preparing Brexit: How Ready is Whitehall?* London: Institute for Government, 10 June, available at https://www.instituteforgovernment.org.uk/publications/preparing-brexit-how-ready-whitehall.
Parker, G. (2017) 'Theresa May ensures only Brexit key allows entry to No.10', *Financial Times*, 12 April.
Partington, R. (2018) 'Bank of England says no-deal Brexit would be worse than 2008 crisis', *The Guardian,* 28 November.
Perrior, K. (2017) 'Inside team Theresa', *Times Magazine*, 15 July.
Polman, D. (2018) 'Learning from practical experience: implementation epistemic communities in the European Union', in C.A. Dunlop, C.M. Radaelli and J.P. Trein (eds), *Learning in Public Policy: Analysis, Modes and Outcomes*, Basingstoke: Palgrave, pp. 123–144.
Regonini, G. (2017) 'Governmentabilities without policy capacity', *Policy Sciences* 50 (2): 163–78.
Richards, D., Diamond, P. and Wager, A. (2019) 'Westminster's Brexit paradox: the contingency of the 'old' versus 'new' politics', *British Journal of Politics and International Relations* 21 (2): 330–48.
Rutter, J. and McCrae, J. (2016) 'Brexit: Organising Whitehall to Deliver', Briefing Paper, London: Institute for Government, July.
Sabel, C.F. and Zeitlin, J. (2008) 'Learning from difference: the new architecture of experimentalist governance in the EU', *European Law Journal* 14 (3): 271–327.
Sasse, T. and Norris, E. (2019) *Moving On: The Cost of High Staff Turnover in the Civil Service*, London: Institute for Government, available at www.instituteforgovernment.org.uk/publications/moving-on-staff-turnover-civil-service.
Schon, D.A. and Rein, M. (1994) *Frame Reflection: Toward the Resolution of Intractable Policy Controversies*, New York, NY: Basic Books.
Shipman, T. (2017) *Fall Out: A Year of Political Mayhem*, London: William Collins.

Sorace, M. and Hobolt, S.B. (2019) 'A tale of two peoples: motivated reasoning in the aftermath of Brexit', *Working Paper*, London: London School of Economics and Political Science.

Tetlow, G. and Stojanovic, A. (2018) *Understanding the Economic Impact of Brexit*, London: Institute for Government, October, available at https://www.instituteforgovernment.org.uk/sites/default/files/publications/2018%20IfG%20%20Brexit%20impact%20%5Bfinal%20for%20web%5D.pdf (accessed 23 May 2019).

Treanor, J. (2018) 'Bank warns no-deal could see UK sink into recession', *BBC News*, 28 November, available at https://www.bbc.co.uk/news/business-46377309 (accessed 28 March 2019).

Wincott, D. (2017) 'Brexit dilemmas: new opportunities and tough choices in unsettled times', *The British Journal of Politics and International Relations* 19 (4): 680–95.

Divided they fail: the politics of wedge issues and Brexit

Tim Heinkelmann-Wild, Lisa Kriegmair, Berthold Rittberger and Bernhard Zangl

ABSTRACT
This paper develops a theory of wedge issue politics in modern democracies. It argues that wedge issues are associated with a politics of intransigence which differs from the politics of concessions that typically comes with non-wedge issues. This theory explains why Prime Minister Theresa May opted for a divisive approach to secure ratification of her Brexit agreement in the House of Commons. Due to the intra-partisan division within the Conservative Party, the government had an incentive to employ politics of intransigence. Playing a chicken game with recalcitrant party members, it relied on bargaining strategies to force party rebels to back down. This politics of intransigence further deepened intra-partisan divisions and thus prompted both sides to harden their stance. This vicious circle not only brought the Conservative Party to a breaking point but eventually led to government failure.

Introduction

It is a political science truism that individual actors' rational behaviors often generate collectively irrational results. The politics of Brexit within the governing Conservative party in the United Kingdom (UK) under Theresa May's premiership is a case in point. Brexit and the repeated failures to deliver it brought the Conservative party to a breaking point: It contributed to disastrous election results, it led to the fall of Theresa May's government, and it triggered the loss of a parliamentary majority for the succeeding government under Boris Johnson. We argue that these phenomena are the irrational results of rational strategies employed by factions within the divided Tory party, both opting for a *politics of intransigence* to force the other side to adopt their preferred Brexit policy: While Theresa May's government sought to compel intra-party rebels to support her policy of a comparatively soft Brexit on the one hand, Tory rebels' attempted to strong-arm Theresa May's government to pursue a hard Brexit.[1]

When governing parties in parliamentary democracies cannot avoid wedge issues, such as Brexit, different factions within the governing party generally tend to engage in a politics of intransigence. The main feature of what we label politics of intransigence is that actors engage in power bargaining strategies in order to force each other to back down (Schelling 1960), with each side signaling its firm commitment to refuse compromise and seeking to enhance the credibility of its commitment. Wedge issues are cross-cutting issues: Their presence causes intra-party divisions, which is why parties seek to avoid them when they can (de Vries and Hobolt 2012; Tzelgov 2014; van de Wardt et al. 2014; Hobolt and de Vries 2015). If governments are, however, confronted with a non-avoidable wedge issue that divides their party, we expect the different factions inside the governing party to adopt strategies of intransigence in the same way that Theresa May and recalcitrant members of parliament (MPs) from her own party confronted each other over the withdrawal agreement with the European Union (EU).

Our argument about wedge issues and their consequences for intra-party politics ties in with the literature on the rise of a new political cleavage between cosmopolitanism and communitarianism that cuts across the traditional left-right cleavage, which structured modern party systems (see, e.g., Kriesi *et al.* 2006; Hooghe and Marks 2009, 2018; Norris and Inglehart 2019). This literature posits that the new cleavage structure leads to a realignment of party-systems, which is a long-term rather than a short-term process. During this process of realignment, many political issues that map onto the cleavage between cosmopolitanism and communitarianism are likely to divide mainstream parties, which still mirror the left-right cleavage. While by no means a new phenomenon, wedge issues and political parties' responses to them are thus likely to become more and more important for an adequate understanding of today's party politics in modern democracies.

There is a fast-growing literature on the politics of wedge issues (see, for example, Kriesi 2007; Hooghe and Marks 2009; Bale *et al.* 2010; Parsons and Weber 2011; Hutter *et al.* 2016; Adam *et al.* 2017; Steenbergen and Scott 2004; Tzelgov 2014). One strand highlights that wedge issues provide political opportunities for challenger parties: politicizing these issues, they may exploit divisions within mainstream parties to gain voter support (Meguid 2005; de Vries and van de Wardt 2011; de Vries and Hobolt 2012; Adam *et al.* 2013; van de Wardt et al. 2014; Hobolt and de Vries 2015; van de Wardt 2015). Another strand argues that mainstream parties aim to avoid wedge issues in order to prevent the loss of voter support: They depoliticize the issue by, for instance, ignoring, distracting or blurring (Aylott 2002; Rovny 2012; van de Wardt 2014; Abou-Chadi and Krause 2018; Rauh 2019). Overall, this literature has contributed to our understanding of party politics in an age of realignment in today's democracies. We add to this literature by highlighting a particular aspect of wedge issues, which has not yet been theorized: How do mainstream governing parties react to a wedge issue, when strategies to avoid it are simply not available?

In the ensuing section, we theorize how unavoidable wedge issues prompt different factions inside mainstream governing parties to opt for a politics of intransigence. In the succeeding section, we apply our theory to the politics of Brexit inside the governing Conservative party under Theresa May's premiership. We show that intra-party divisions over the withdrawal agreement with the EU prompted Theresa May's government and Tory rebels to employ strategies of intransigence to force the other side to back down, ultimately leading to Theresa May's resignation. In the conclusion, we reflect on the scope of our theory.

The politics of wedge issues

The key feature of a wedge issue is that it cuts across party lines, and thus holds the potential of sparking intra-party divisions. Non-wedge issues, by contrast, give rise to conflicts along party lines, because they map onto the dominant political cleavages that gave rise to modern party systems (Lipset and Rokkan 1967; de Vries and Hobolt 2012; Tzelgov 2014; van de Wardt et al. 2014; Hobolt and de Vries 2015). In most advanced democracies, minimum wages are a non-wedge issue because the issue typically comes with political conflict between the main parties on the left and the right, reflecting the hitherto dominant left-right cleavage. By contrast, issues such as immigration or EU integration cut across the dominant left-right cleavage: They drive a wedge into mainstream parties in that they cause a heightened probability of intra-party conflict (Kriesi *et al.* 2006; Hooghe and Marks 2009, 2018; Hutter *et al.* 2016).

As indicated above, the literature on wedge issues underscores that mainstream parties typically try to avoid wedge issues. After all, taking a stance on wedge issues is likely to alienate parts of their constituencies and leads to the manifestation of latent intra-party divisions. Wedge issues also offer (potential) challenger parties the opportunity to draw core constituencies away from mainstream parties. Therefore, mainstream parties seek to depoliticize wedge issues through a *politics of avoidance* (see Figure 1). They will try to keep them off the political agenda, for instance by shifting a wedge issue to an arena outside of party competition (e.g., by holding a referendum). They may also try to manipulate the agenda by politicizing alternative issues (i.e., distracting), by denying the problem (i.e., neglecting) or by refraining from formulating unambiguous policy positions (i.e., blurring) (Sieberer 2006; Kam 2009; Parsons and Weber 2011; Green-Pedersen 2012; van de Wardt 2014; Hutter *et al.* 2016; Adam *et al.* 2017).

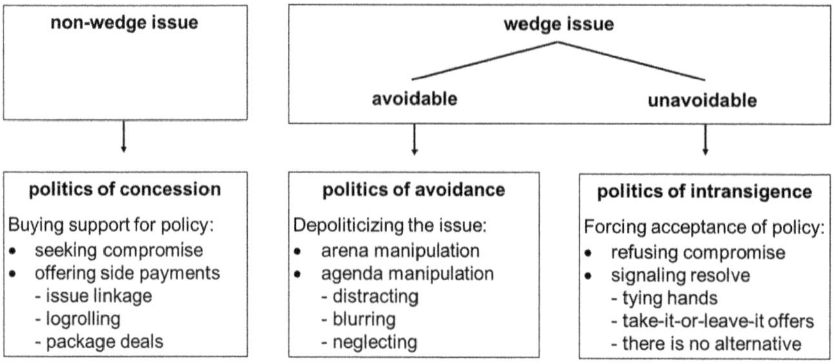

Figure 1. Politics within the governing party: wedge and non-wedge issues.

The literature on wedge issues, however, does not explore systematically how mainstream parties respond to a wedge issue, when avoidance is not an option. Mainstream parties are, for instance, often unable to avoid wedge issues when challenger parties politicize them successfully. Governing parties may also be unable to avoid these issues when parts of their constituencies require an unambiguous policy response against the backdrop of heightened problem pressure (see also, Lynch and Whitaker 2013: 328). The 2015 so-called 'migration crisis' in Europe is a case in point. The crisis caused divisions among and within mainstream conservative (center-right) and social-democratic (center-left) parties (as well as their constituencies), and governments were unable to avoid the issue, because it required an immediate policy response in frontline, transit and destination countries. For instance, Chancellor Angela Merkel had to enact a policy which brought the conservative governing sister parties to a breaking point while, at the same time, fueling the rise of a right-wing populist party in Germany.

If governments cannot avoid enacting wedge issue policies, they must cope – by definition – with resistance from a divided governing party. To ensure parliamentary support for their preferred policies in spite of intra-party resistance governments have in principle two options: They can embark on a politics of concessions or employ a politics of intransigence. We argue that the more a wedge issue divides the governing party, the stronger is the government's incentive to engage in a politics of intransigence vis-à-vis their MPs rather than offering concessions.

To begin with, governments usually draw on a *politics of concessions* when they deal with non-wedge issues that do not divide the governing party. In this case governments are in a strong position, because they can count on the overwhelming support of their party and thus on their MPs for parliamentary approval (see Figure 1). At most, a government's preferred policy might face resistance from individual MPs of their own party, which usually can be contained. Governments can 'buy' the required support from recalcitrant MPs through concessions, for instance by seeking a policy compromise or offering side payments through issue linkage, logrolling or package deals (Kam 2009: 29; Lynch and Whitaker 2013).[2] They can even make concessions to opposition parties in order to broaden domestic support for their policy.

When governments confront a wedge issue they cannot avoid, making concessions to secure the support within its own party is less likely to succeed. As wedge issues divide the governing party, governments have to overcome substantial intra-party resistance to enact their preferred policy. The government is in a weak position and cannot simply make concessions to buy the support from resisting MPs, since any attempt to secure the support from recalcitrant MPs is likely to provoke resistance by other MPs from within their own party.[3] Offering side payments also becomes more complicated as intra-party resistance to wedge issue policies stems always from a substantial constituency of the party represented by a sizable number of MPs. Finally, the government cannot buy support from opposition parties. While wedge issues typically divide not only the governing party, but also mainstream opposition parties, the opposition is likely to shy away from taking a clear stance on the wedge issue to avoid conflict amongst its own constituents. Being aware that the government lacks the governing party's undivided support for the policy in question, the opposition also has a strong incentive to seize this opportunity to increase the government's difficulties rather than help it gain parliamentary support.

Unable to secure support through concessions, governments will likely draw on a *politics of intransigence* to enact wedge issue policies (see Figure 1). Compared to non-wedge issues, wedge issues bring the government into a weaker position. The ensuing actor constellation resembles a chicken game, pitting the government against party rebels opposed to the governments preferred policy. In this intra-party chicken game (see Figure 2), it is rational for the government to commit to its preferred policy in order to force party rebels to back down. Governments will warn party rebels that they cannot and will not make any concessions. They will refuse

	Party rebels make concessions	**Party rebels are intransigent**
Government makes concessions	Compromise policy 3/3	Rebels determine policy 2/4
Government is intransigent	Government determines policy 4/2	Government failure 1/1

Figure 2. Chicken game within the governing party.

to compromise and try to enhance the credibility of their commitment to their preferred policy. For instance, governments can tie their hands to their policy position through costly signals such as increasing the audience costs of backing down (Fearon 1994; Slantchev 2006). To force recalcitrant MPs to yield, governments may also present their policy as a take-it-or-leave-it offer parliament may only accept or refuse. Instead of buying off recalcitrant MPs, governments will take off the table all alternative policy proposals and maneuver themselves into a position where yielding is not an option (Schelling 1960: 44; see also Dixit and Nalebuff 1991).

The more a government is able to signal resolve by committing itself credibly to its preferred policy, the more party rebels are facing an uncomfortable choice. They can accept a policy they dislike (payoff for party rebels: 2) or defeat their own government (payoff party for rebels: 1). To avoid this uncomfortable choice and force the government to yield, recalcitrant MPs are also likely to employ a politics of intransigence (payoff for party rebels: 4). They will commit themselves to insist on their preferred policy while trying to enhance the credibility of their insistence. The more party rebels can make this commitment credible, the more their government finds itself between a rock and a hard place. The government can stick to the proposed policy, thereby risking government failure (payoff for the government: 1), or it can make concessions, thereby alienating the party constituency in support of their original policy position (payoff for the government: 2). To avoid this uncomfortable choice, governments are likely to try to force party rebels to back down. They will seek to further enhance the credibility of their commitment so that their preferred policy prevails (payoff for the government: 4).

Through mutual intransigence both factions within the governing party enter an 'hypothetical test of nerve' (Hirshleifer 2001: 81). As it is individually rational for each side to counter intransigence with more intransigence, governments and party rebels not only make it increasingly difficult to reach a collectively rational compromise (payoffs: 3/3); they may even reinforce the divide within the governing party, spurring an escalation of intra-party conflict (Steenbergen and Scott 2004). Their respective pursuit of strategies of intransigence thus drives up the risk of the collectively most irrational outcome, whereby the inability to agree on a policy leads to a heightened probability that the government will fall, i.e., government failure (payoffs: 1/1).

In sum, when governing parties cannot avoid wedge issues, they give rise to a politics of intransigence that differs fundamentally from the politics of concession, associated with non-wedge issues. Once the self-reinforcing dynamic of the politics of intransigence sets in, the likelihood that the government and recalcitrant MPs can agree on a joint policy is contracting while the likelihood of government failure is increasing.

Intra-party politics and Brexit

In this section, we will apply our argument to the domestic politics of Brexit. As spelled out in the previous section, we focus on the interactions among the dominant factions in the governing Conservative party, and we delimit our analysis to the negotiation, adoption and approval process of the withdrawal agreement between the EU and the UK under Theresa May's premiership. In a first step, we demonstrate that Brexit is an unavoidable wedge issue for the Conservative party. Second, we show that intra-party conflict over Brexit as a wedge issue has fueled a politics of intransigence, increasing the probability of government failure. Third, we provide evidence for the self-reinforcing dynamics of the politics of intransigence, which further deepened the intra-party divisions within the Tory parliamentary party.

Brexit as a wedge issue

Brexit is widely seen as a picture book example of a wedge issue. For decades, the EU membership question divided the Conservative Party (Gamble 1996; McLean 2001; Clarke *et al.* 2017; Curtice 2017; Hayton 2018; Lynch and Whitaker 2018). Against the backdrop of the rise of the UK Independence Party (UKIP) and growing assertiveness of a group of Eurosceptic backbench MPs, prime minister David Cameron promised in 2013 to hold a referendum on the UK's EU membership in order to get the issue off the table (Hayton 2018: 231). This strategy of a politics of avoidance through arena manipulation has been described as a 'Mephistophelean pact' (Hooghe and Marks 2019: 1124) to cope with intra-party divisions on this issue (Jensen and Snaith 2016: 1308). While Cameron hoped a 'remain' referendum result would silence Eurosceptic fractions within his party, the decision to 'leave' led to an encompassing societal politicization of the membership issue in the UK. It also forced the governing party to take a stance and define its Brexit policy (Schimmelfennig 2018: 1166–67). After the 2016 referendum, a politics of avoidance was no longer feasible.

To show that the definition of the government's Brexit policy drove a wedge through the Conservative Party, we study debates in the House of Commons from the beginning of negotiations between the UK government and the EU on the withdrawal agreement through its various ratification attempts under Theresa May's premiership. We follow Lynch and Whitaker's (2013: 318) proposal to use 'speaking against the party' as an indicator for (unavoidable) wedge issues (see also, Heppell and Hill 2010; Sieberer 2015), which allows us to establish the nature of an issue even before a roll call vote takes places or in the absence thereof (Edwards 2007, Lynch and Whitaker 2013). Politicians generally engage in negative messaging to discredit opponents, induce defections, and ultimately change policy outcomes in line with their preferences (Weaver 2018; Heinkelmann-Wild and Zangl 2019). When negative communication is exchanged not solely between the government and the opposition, but within the governing party, we consider an issue to be a wedge issue. We focus on a specific type of negative communication that is especially conspicuous: the attribution of blame. Following Weaver (2018: 263), we conceive of blame attributions as deliberate communication of negative information about a target, at which responsibility for a negative policy outcome is directed. We utilize the blame attributions of MPs of the governing party to their own government as an indicator for unavoidable wedge issues. In operational terms, we conceive an issue as a wedge issue when the share of blame statements whereby MPs from the governing party target their own party exceeds a 25% threshold.

To demonstrate that Brexit is indeed a wedge issue, we analyzed the pattern of blame attributions in debates on the EU withdrawal agreement in the House of Commons in three distinct phases of the negotiations between the UK government and the EU.[4]

- The *pre-negotiation* phase beginning right after the referendum on 23 June 2016 up to the beginning of the so-called substantial negotiations[5] on 16 June 2017.
- The phase of *substantive negotiations* that lasted from 17 June 2017 until the adoption of the withdrawal agreement on 14 November 2018.
- The *ratification* phase lasting from the adoption of the withdrawal agreement by the UK government up to the initially envisaged Art. 50 deadline on 31 March 2019.

Within each phase, we searched for blame statements issued by MPs[6] from the governing Conservative Party.[7] For each blame statement, we coded whether the respective MP blamed actors from the governing or the opposition parties.[8] To assess whether Brexit was indeed a wedge issue we calculated the share of blame attributions that target the government rather than the opposition. Examples for blame attribution statements by Conservative MPs directed against the government include John Redwood, who criticized:

> When will the Government stand up to the EU, when will the Government say that they want a free trade agreement and they do not see the need to pay for it, and when will the Government rule out signing a withdrawal agreement that is a surrender document that we cannot afford?[9]

Similarly, Justine Greening contested the government's plan of a customs union 'in which we will have no say on the rules for a prolonged period' and wondered 'how this is in the UK's national interest?'[10] Moreover, Bob Stewart criticized that the government's EU withdrawal agreement 'is

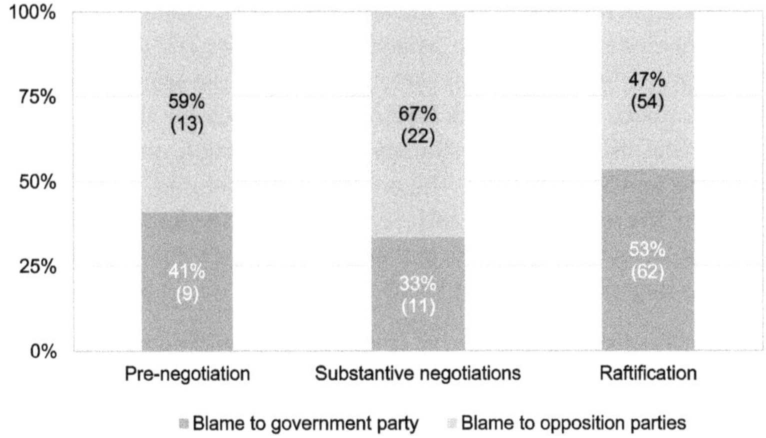

Figure 3. Conservative MPs' blame attribution patterns.

neither fish, nor fowl. It satisfies neither the remainers, nor those people who wish to leave the EU.'[11] And, Anna Soubry claimed that the government's 'slogan that no deal is better than a bad deal is nonsense.'[12]

Our analysis clearly demonstrates that Brexit constituted a wedge issue for the Conservative Party across all three phases. The 171 blame statements coded highlight that Brexit gave rise to intra-partisan blame attributions: The share of blame statements from Conservative MPs that targeted the government was constantly above our 25% threshold.[13] Moreover, in the ratification phase, even more than 50% of the blame statements from Conservative MPs targeted their own government rather than the opposition (see Figure 3).

In sum, the high share of intra-party blame attributions during the Brexit debates in the House of Commons demonstrates that Brexit constituted a wedge issue for the party in government throughout the whole process of negotiating and adopting the withdrawal agreement.

Brexit and the politics of intransigence

The divisive character of Brexit gave rise to a politics of intransigence. Theresa May's Conservative government did not try to 'buy' the support of recalcitrant MPs from its own party ranks through concessions. By committing itself to insist on its Brexit policy, the government attempted to compel party rebels – especially the members of the Eurosceptic 'European Research Group' (ERG) – to support the withdrawal agreement.

From the very beginning, the government employed strategies to signal its resolve to party rebels. First, the government's objective was to confront party rebels (and the Commons as a whole) with a take-it–or-leave-it offer, so that they would only be able to accept or reject the deal negotiated by Theresa

May. To underpin this strategy the government sought to keep parliamentary involvement to a minimum. For instance, the government sought to evade parliamentary scrutiny, as it kept secret potential Brexit scenarios and their estimated impact (Asthana and Mason 2016). Moreover, the government did not reveal its negotiation strategy and its position on Brexit (Brooks 2016; Mason and Stewart 2016). The prime minister refused 'a running commentary on the negotiations' and Secretary of State for Exiting the EU, David Davis, stated that it was 'not in the national interest' for the government to reveal its negotiation position (cited by Walker 2016). As a consequence

> a culture of extraordinary secrecy has developed. […] Key documents are over-classified, important information is not being shared between departments and those with a legitimate reason to be informed, such as Parliament, are kept in the dark. (Lloyd *et al.* 2018)

Theresa May's sidelining of the House of Commons even led to complaints by MPs that its role in approving the agreement would fall behind that of the European Parliament on the EU's side of the negotiations. Unsurprisingly, the role of the House of Commons in the approval process of the withdrawal agreement became a hotly contested issue. For instance, the government fought tooth and nail to prevent an amendment to the EU Withdrawal Act 2018, which was proposed by the Lords and supported by Conservative rebels. This amendment envisaged the Commons to provide binding instructions to the government in the case of a parliamentary rejection of the agreement, which would have torpedoed the prime minister's tactic to delimit the choice set.

Second, the government tried to make its preferred withdrawal agreement the only policy alternative worth pursuing. On the one hand, it tried to keep alternatives to its preferred withdrawal agreement off the negotiation table by running down the clock, therefore putting immense pressure on parliament to approve the deal. As early as April 2018, there were rumors that the government would delay the meaningful vote on the withdrawal agreement in the Commons until January 2019, thereby minimizing the time available for parliamentary debate (Crerar 2018). In December 2018, the meaningful vote on the withdrawal agreement was indeed called off (Elgot and Sabbagh 2018). It was only under the pressure of the threat of a no confidence vote that the prime minister announced that the vote would be held in January 2019. Labor leader Jeremy Corbyn criticized that the prime minister 'has cynically run down the clock trying to manoeuvre parliament into a choice between two unacceptable outcomes: her deal and no deal' (cited by Walker 2018). On the other hand, to focus the minds of its critics, the government sought to keep on the table the two alternative outcomes – a 'no-deal' Brexit and no Brexit at all – that, at the time, were most disliked among MPs. To put pressure on MPs to support the withdrawal agreement, the government rejected demands from Tory and Labor MPs to take these unwanted alternatives off the table, while at the same time warning that they can only be avoided if the government's agreement is accepted in the Commons. At first, the government warned that MPs had to accept the withdrawal agreement in order to avoid a 'no deal' Brexit (Mason and Stewart 2017). Theresa May cautioned: 'Avoiding no deal is only possible if we can reach an agreement or if we abandon Brexit entirely' (cited by Walker 2018). Later, the government also issued warnings that a rejection of the withdrawal agreement would run the risk of no Brexit. Foreign Secretary Jeremy Hunt argued: 'If we are going to deliver the clean Brexit that the British people want we have to get behind Theresa May' (Stewart and Walker 2018). While the warning of a 'no-deal' Brexit was geared towards 'soft' Brexiteers inside the governing party, the warning of 'no Brexit' was aimed at 'hard' Brexiteers – especially 'no-deal' Brexiteers from the ERG – to accept the prime minister's deal. This strategy of keeping the worst alternatives deliberately on the table evoked the intended reactions among Tory rebels, such as Simon Clarke, who complained that the government put 'a gun to my head' and that 'we have a very, very limited range of options left' (cited in Elgot *et al.* 2019). One MP opposing the agreement commented:

> I think the Government are playing the ultimate game of brinkmanship – it is deeply irresponsible – with Conservative Members, who are divided, as everybody knows. Unfortunately, the Government are flagging up to those who fear no deal as ultimately the worst thing that could happen, as they should do, that it is in some way acceptable, and they have never taken it off the table as we should have done two and a half years ago. (cited by Boffey 2018)

Finally, the government tied its hands by publicly portraying its own Brexit policy as the one eschewing alternatives. It publicly stated its unwavering resolve to stick to the withdrawal agreement. Government officials did not become tired of emphasizing that there is no viable alternative to their deal. Brexit Secretary Stephen Barclay claimed: 'It is a good deal, it is the only deal, and I believe that it is the right deal.'[14] The government also emphasized that it did not control the process, because of the EU's firm position: 'The EU Commission has been clear that this is the only deal. The idea that in the remaining days someone can go back to the Commission and negotiate a completely different deal is just not credible.'[15] Even after its rejection in the Commons in January 2019, the government refused to renegotiate the withdrawal agreement with the EU. Apparently, Theresa May went to Brussels without an intention to renegotiate. The EU's chief negotiator Michel Barnier complained in February 2019 that current exchanges with the British government were 'courtesy calls at best' with 'nothing on the table from the British side' (cited by Rankin 2019).

In reaction to the government's politics of intransigence, Conservative MPs opposed to the withdrawal agreement, ERG members in particular, engaged in similar strategies. Pledging rejection of the negotiated agreement, they sought to limit their own freedom of action to make the government budge from its uncompromising position. They declared that the content of any agreement would be judged 'by our red lines' (cited by Elgot 2018): 'Are we leaving the EU? Are we taking back control? Are we leaving the customs union and the single market? Will we get rid of free movement?' They thus committed themselves to reject any agreement that violated any of these red lines. Former Brexit Secretary Steven Baker warned:

> We are in a position as we move forward where colleagues will not tolerate a half-in, half-out Brexit [...] Of course the government are going to whip this vote extremely hard, but what I would say is the whips would be doing incredibly well if they were to halve the numbers, and my estimate is there are at least 40 colleagues who are not going to accept it [...] or indeed a backstop that leaves us in the internal market or customs union, come what may. (cited by Elgot 2018)

In the course of the parliamentary adoption proceedings of the withdrawal agreement, Conservative rebels even began to claim that a 'no-deal' Brexit was preferable to the government's agreement, thus committing themselves to an uncompromising position. Boris Johnson who stepped down as Foreign Secretary underlined that Britain should be 'actively preparing for no deal with ever more enthusiasm' (cited by Stewart and Boffey 2019). Steven Baker publicly proclaimed that the ERG would not budge from its rejection of the withdrawal agreement: 'I'll say to the government now, when meaningful vote three comes back I will see to it that we keep voting this down however many times it's brought back' (cited by Elgot *et al.* 2019).

Due to the wedge issue character of Brexit, the government as well as Tory rebels embarked on a politics of intransigence in which both sides stubbornly insisted on their preferred Brexit policies without a willingness to make substantive concessions. What is more, the intra-party divisions caused by Brexit became self-reinforcing over time. Brexit led to a politics of intransigence between Theresa May's government and the Tory rebels, and with no side willing to budge, each side responded to intransigence with intransigence, thereby intensifying intra-party conflict. We can empirically see this escalatory dynamic brought about by the politics of intransigence by looking at patterns of blame attributions in the House of Commons debates. To begin with, the *share* of blame attributions inside the Conservative party compared to blame attributions to members of the opposition has increased over time (see Figure 4). In the pre-negotiation and negotiation phases roughly one-third of blame attributions were directed at members from the own parliamentary party group. This share increased to over fifty

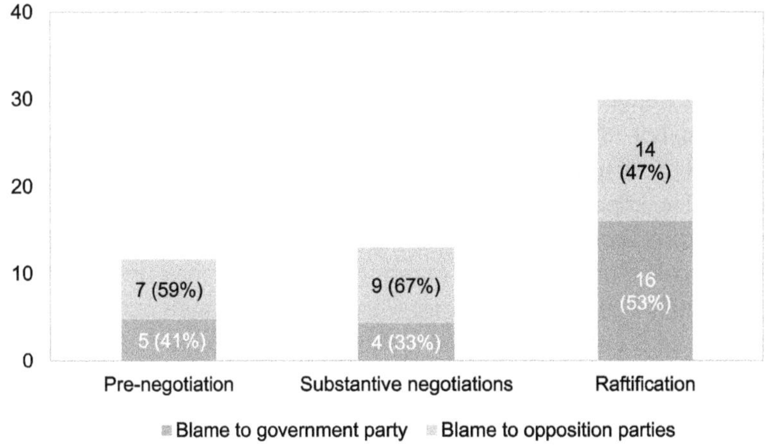

Figure 4. Frequency of Conservative MPs' blame attributions per 100 debate pages.

percent in the ratification phase. Moreover, the *frequency* of blame attributions inside the Conservative party increased considerably over time. The average number of blame attributions by non-Cabinet Tories to members of their own party, particularly to the government, increased by over 200 percent during the course of the negotiations of the withdrawal agreement. While the average number of blame attributions amounted to five per 100 debate pages in the pre-negotiation phase and four in the phase of substantive negotiations, the average number of blame attributions increased to sixteen during the ratification period, i.e., statements from Tory MPs that criticize their fellow MPs and the government. While the absolute number might seem low, on closer inspection it is in fact rather high. After all, the share of speaking time of Tory backbenchers in these debates amounts only to a comparatively small fraction.

In sum, the politics of intransigence has deepened the divide within the Conservative parliamentary party in the period under investigation. The hardening of positions from Theresa May's government and Tory rebels prompted a vicious circle, which not only prevented the approval of the withdrawal agreement, but also an agreement on a viable alternative to both 'no-deal Brexit' or 'no Brexit at all'. This intra-party divide has also contributed to disastrous results for the Tories in the 2019 elections for the European Parliament; it has brought the Conservative party to a breaking point, leading to the fall of Theresa May's government; and from the first day in office, it put a heavy burden on the new prime minister, Boris Johnson. While the protagonists acted rationally, the politics of intransigence produced irrational results: a government unable to agree on a policy and a prime minister who saw no other solution to this impasse than to step down.

Conclusion

In this paper, we aimed to contribute to scholarship on wedge issues. We argued that wedge issues give rise to a politics of intransigence with a potential for escalation, thus deepening the splits within the governing party and a heightened risk of government failure. We showed that our argument helps to understand an important aspect of the domestic politics of Brexit in the UK. It offers an explanation why rational actors, Theresa May's government and Tory rebels, embarked on a politics of intransigence despite their unwanted – and thus seemingly irrational – outcome. While we corroborated our expectations in the case of Brexit, we hold that it should hold explanatory leverage to a wider universe of cases.

With the rise of the new cleavage between communitarianism and cosmopolitanism (Kriesi *et al.* 2006; Hooghe and Marks 2009; Norris and Inglehart 2019), we are likely to observe a proliferation of wedge issues in modern democracies, especially where existing party systems have yet to adapt to the new cleavage. To the degree that governments are unable to avoid wedge issues, we expect to see more of what we labeled politics of intransigence: factions within governing parties engaging in political conflict over wedge issues, which brings about a heightened probability of policy and even government failure. Examples include US President Donald Trump's attempts to force Republican critics of his policies on controlling the border to Mexico to yield, or the near breakdown of the union between Germany's Christian Democrats and its Bavarian sister party, the CSU, over the admission of asylum seekers at Germany's borders. The heightened incidence of the politics of intransigence not only increases the risk of policy failure, it is also placing a strain on government survival. For instance, the Belgian government collapsed over the UN Compact for Migration, which drove a wedge through governing parties and coalitions in many modern democracies.

However, and this is putatively good news, once party systems have adapted to the new cleavage structure, the incentive for governments to engage in a politics of intransigence can be expected to decrease and the incentives for the traditional politics of concession to increase again. This might take longer in majoritarian democracies than in democracies with proportional electoral systems, since the latter would allow party systems to adjust more quickly. By then, the Brexit issue should be solved, one way or another.

Notes

1. In contrast to some observers, we thus see the irrationalities of Brexit not only as a result of the rational bargaining strategies employed by the UK and the EU (Caporaso 2018; Schimmelfennig 2018).
2. As resistance comes from a small number of MPs, the government can also rely on traditional measures of party discipline.

3. As a larger number of MPs rejects the government's policy, the traditional measures of party discipline are difficult to employ.
4. We examine a sample of 42 debates in the House of Commons from 23 June 2016 (the date of the Brexit referendum) until 31 March 2019. The debates were identified by keyword search in the Hansard database using the search terms: 'Brexit' or 'EU withdrawal' (for an overview, see Online Appendix).
5. We consider the second round of negotiations beginning on 17 July 2017 to signify the kick-off for the substantial negotiations as both negotiation teams presented their positions (whereas the first round was only concerned with procedural and organisational questions).
6. We only look at MPs from the Conservative parliamentary party that were not members of Theresa May's cabinet.
7. Blame attributions are characterized by three components: (i) the blame object, i.e., the issue for which blame is attributed; (ii) the blame sender, i.e., the actor that attributes blame for the blame object; (iii) the blame target, i.e., an actor to whom blame is attributed.
8. We considered all negative statements referring to Brexit and the withdrawal agreement between the UK and the EU, including the substance of the (draft) agreement and specific aspects thereof, proposals for its alteration and alternatives, or the negotiation process.
9. John Redwood, House of Commons 2018a: col 24.
10. Justine Greening, House of Commons 2018a: col. 25.
11. Bob Stewart, House of Commons 2018b: col. 709.
12. Anna Soubry, House of Commons 2017: col. 397.
13. A detailed overview of the coding and analysis is presented in the Online Appendix.
14. Stephen Barclay, Secretary of State for Exiting the EU, House of Commons 2019: col. 26.
15. Stephen Barclay, Secretary of State for Exiting the EU, House of Commons 2019: col. 40.

Acknowledgements

We wish to thank the three anonymous reviewers, the editor, as well as the participants of the research colloquium at LMU Munich, the biannual conference of EUSA in Denver 2019, as well as the ECPR General Conference 2019 in Wrocław for their constructive comments. We are specifically grateful to Catherine de Vries, Monika Brusenbauch Meislova, and Raphaela Hobbach. We also would like to thank Juliane Glovania, Louisa Klein-Bölting, Josef Lolacher, and Severin Süß for excellent research assistance.

Disclosure statement

No potential conflict of interest was reported by the authors.

Funding

This work was supported by the Deutsche Forschungsgemeinschaft [grant number 391007015].

ORCID

Tim Heinkelmann-Wild http://orcid.org/0000-0003-2699-6048

References

Abou-Chadi, T. and Krause, W. (2018) 'The Causal effect of radical right success on mainstream parties' policy positions: A regression discontinuity approach', *British Journal of Political Science*: 1–19. doi:10.1017/S0007123418000029.

Adam, S., Antl-Wittenberg, E.-M., Eugster, B., Leidecker-Sandmann, M., Maier, M. and Schmidt, F. (2017) 'Strategies of pro-European parties in the face of a Eurosceptic challenge', *European Union Politics* 18(2): 260–282. doi:10.1177/1465116516661248.

Adam, S., Maier, M., de Vreese, C. H., Schuck, A. R. T., Stetka, V., Jalali, C., Seeber, G. U. H., Negrine, R., Raycheva, L. and Berganza, R. (2013) 'Campaigning against Europe? The role of euroskeptic fringe and mainstream parties in the 2009 European parliament election', *Journal of Political Marketing* 12(1): 77–99. doi:10.1080/15377857.2013.752245.

Asthana, A. and Mason, R. (2016) 'Brexit divisions emerge as Whitehall draws up leave scenarios', *The Guardian*, 31 August.

Aylott, N. (2002) 'Let's discuss this later', *Party Politics* 8(4): 441–461. doi:10.1177/1354068802008004005.

Bale, T., Green-Pedersen, C., Krouwel, A., Luther, K. R. and Sitter, N. (2010) 'If you can't beat them, join them? Explaining social democratic responses to the challenge from the populist radical right in Western Europe', *Political Studies* 58(3): 410–426. doi:10.1111/j.1467-9248.2009.00783.x.

Boffey, D. (2018) 'Belgium's government loses majority over UN migration pact', *The Guardian*, 9 December.

Brooks, L. (2016) 'Nicola Sturgeon calls on Theresa May to be more open over Brexit', *The Guardian*, 7 September.

Caporaso, J.A. (2018) 'Europe's triple crisis and the uneven role of institutions: the Euro, refugees and Brexit', *JCMS: Journal of Common Market Studies* 56(6): 1345–61.

Clarke, H., Goodwin, M. J. and Whitelely, P. (2017) *Why Britain voted for Brexit: An individual-level analysis of the 2016 referendum vote*, Cambridge: Cambridge University Press.

Crerar, P. (2018) MPs and peers flex muscles as countdown to meaningful vote begins, *The Guardian*, 29 March.

Curtice, J. (2017) 'Why leave won the UK's EU referendum', *Jornal of Common Market Studies* 55(S1): 19–37.

de Vries, C.E. and Hobolt, S.B. (2012) 'When dimensions collide: the electoral success of issue entrepreneurs', *European Union Politics* 13(2): 246–68. doi:10.1177/1465116511434788.

de Vries, C. E. and van de Wardt, M. (2011) 'EU issue salience and domestic party competition', in K. Oppermann and H. Viehrig (eds), *Issue salience in international politics*, Oxon: Routledge, pp. 173–188.

Dixit, A. and Nalebuff, B. (1991) 'Making strategies credible', in R. Zeckhauser (ed.), *Strategy and Choice*, Cambridge: MIT Press, pp. 161–84.

Edwards, E. (2007) United we stand? Examining dissent within political parties on issues of European integration, Paper prepared for the EUSA Tenth Biennial International Conference, Montreal, Canada, 17-19 May, 2007.

Elgot, J. (2018) 'At least 40 Tory MPs would reject Chequers-style plan, says ex-minister', *The Guardian*, 9 October.

Elgot, J., Mason, R. and Stewart, H. (2019) May's final warning to Tory rebels: back me or lose Brexit, *The Guardian*, 13 March.

Elgot, J. and Sabbagh, D. (2018) 'Theresa May postpones Brexit deal vote: Prime minister to make statement to MPs as pound falls to lowest level in 18 months', *The Guardian*, 10 December.

Fearon, J. d. (1994) 'Domestic political audiences and the escalation of international disputes', *The American Political Science Review* 88(3): 577–92.

Gamble, A. (1996) 'An ideological party', in S. Ludlam and M. J. Smith (eds), *Contemporary British conservatism*, London: Macmillan Education UK, pp. 19–36.

Green-Pedersen, C. (2012) 'A giant fast asleep? Party incentives and the politicisation of European integration', *Political Studies* 60(1): 115–130. doi:10.1111/j.1467-9248.2011.00895.x.

Hayton, R. (2018) 'British conservatism after the vote for Brexit: The ideological legacy of David Cameron', *The British Journal of Politics and International Relations* 20(1): 223–238. doi:10.1177/1369148117737278.

Heinkelmann-Wild, T. and Zangl, B. (2019) 'Multi-level blame games: blame-shifting in the EU', *Governance*. doi:10.1111/gove.12459.

Heppell, T. and Hill, M. (2010) 'The voting motivations of conservative parliamentarians in the Conservative party leadership election of 2001', *Politics* 30(1): 36–51. doi:10.1111/j.1467-9256.2009.01366.x.

Hobolt, S.B. and de Vries, C.E. (2015) 'Issue entrepreneurship and multiparty competition', *Comparative Political Studies* 48(9): 1159–85. doi:10.1177/0010414015575030.

Hooghe, L. and Marks, G. (2009) 'A postfunctionalist theory of European integration: From permissive consensus to constraining dissensus', *British Journal of Political Science* 39(1): 1–23. doi:10.1017/S0007123408000409.

Hooghe, L. and Marks, G. (2018) 'Cleavage theory meets Europe's crises: Lipset, Rokkan, and the transnational cleavage', *Journal of European Public Policy* 25(1): 109–135. doi:10.1080/13501763.2017.1310279.

Hooghe, L. and Marks, G. (2019) 'Grand theories of European integration in the twenty-first century', *Journal of European Public Policy* 26(8): 1113–33. doi:10.1080/13501763.2019.1569711.

House of Commons (2018a) 'EU customs union and draft withdrawal agreement', 22 October.

House of Commons (2018b) 'EU withdrawal agreement', 18 December.

House of Commons (2019) 'EU withdrawal agreement: legal changes', 7 January.

Hutter, S., Grande, E. and Kriesi, H. (2016) *Politicising Europe: Integration and mass politics*, Cambridge: Cambridge University Press.

Jensen, M.D. and Snaith, H. (2016) 'When politics prevails: the political economy of a Brexit', *Journal of European Public Policy* 23(9): 1302–10. doi:10.1080/13501763.2016.1174531.

Kam, C.J. (2009) *Party Discipline and Parliamentary Politics*, Cambridge: Cambridge University Press.

Kriesi, H. (2007) 'The role of European integration in national election campaigns', *European Union Politics* 8(1): 83–108. doi:10.1177/1465116507073288.

Kriesi, H., Grande, E., Lachat, R., Dolezal, M., Borschier, S. and Frey, T. (2006) 'Globalization and the transformation of the national political space: Six European countries compared', *European Journal of Political Research* 45(6): 921–956. doi:10.1111/ejpr.2006.45.issue-6.

Lipset, S.M. and Rokkan, S. (1967) *Party systems and voter alignments: Cross-national perspectives*, New York: Free Press.

Loyd, L., Owen, J. and Rutter, J. (2018) How ready is Whitehall?, Institute for Government, London.

Lynch, P. and Whitaker, R. (2013) 'Where there is discord, can they bring harmony? Managing intra-party dissent on European integration in the conservative party', *The British Journal of Politics and International Relations* 15(3): 317–39. doi:10.1111/j.1467-856X.2012.00526.x.

Lynch, P. and Whitaker, R. (2018) 'All Brexiteers now? Brexit, the Conservatives and party change', *British Politics* 3(1): 31–47.

Mason, R. and Stewart, H. (2016) 'Theresa May in 'U-turn' over pre-article 50 Brexit debate in parliament', *The Guardian*, 12 October.

Mason, R. and Stewart, H. (2017) 'Tory Brexiters to protest to No 10 about deal on £60bn divorce bill', *The Guardian*, 29 November.

McLean, I. (2001) *Rational choice and British politics*, Oxford: Oxford University Press.

Meguid, B. M. (2005) 'Competition between unequals: The role of mainstream party strategy in niche party success', *The American Political Science Review* 99(3): 347–359.

Norris, P. and Inglehart, R. (2019) *Cultural backlash: Trump, Brexit, and the rise of authoritarianism populism*, Cambridge: Cambridge University Press.

Parsons, C. and Weber, T. (2011) 'Cross-cutting issues and party strategy in the European Union', *Comparative Political Studies* 44(4): 383–411. doi:10.1177/0010414010393474.

Rankin, J. (2019) 'EU officials: UK only 'pretending to negotiate' over Brexit impasse', *The Guardian*, 13 February.

Rauh, C., Bes, B. J., & Schoonvelde, M. (2019). Undermining, defusing or defending European integration? Assessing public communication of European executives in times of EU politicisation. *European Journal of Political Research*, 18(2): 260. doi:10.1111/1475-6765.12350.

Rovny, J. (2012) 'Who emphasizes and who blurs? Party strategies in multidimensional competition', *European Union Politics* 13(2): 269–292. doi:10.1177/1465116511435822.

Schelling, T.C. (1960) *The Strategy of Conflict*, Cambridge, Mass. Harvard Univ.

Schimmelfennig, F. (2018) 'Brexit: differentiated disintegration in the European Union', *Journal of European Public Policy* 25(8): 1154–73.

Sieberer, U. (2006) 'Party unity in parliamentary democracies: A comparative analysis', *The Journal of Legislative Studies* 12(2): 150–178. doi:10.1080/13572330600739413.

Sieberer, U. (2015) 'Using MP statements to explain voting behaviour in the German Bundestag: An individual level test of the Competing Principals Theory', *Party Politics* 21(2): 284–294. doi:10.1177/1354068812472584.

Slantchev, B.L. (2006) 'Politicians, the media, and domestic audience costs', University of California. eScholarship, available at http://www.escholarship.org/uc/item/58c3h5zg.
Steenbergen, M.R. and Scott, D.J. (2004) 'Contesting Europe? The salience of European integration as a party issue', in G. Marks and M.R. Steenbergen (eds), *European Integration and Political Conflict*, Cambridge: Cambridge University Press, pp. 165–92.
Stewart, H. and Boffey, D. (2019) 'Theresa May suffers historic defeat in vote as Tories turn against her', *The Guardian*, 16 January.
Stewart, H. and Walker, P. (2018) 'I can't support Brexit plan but I do support May, says David Davis', *The Guardian*, 9 July.
Tzelgov, E. (2014) 'Cross-cutting issues, intraparty dissent and party strategy: the issue of European integration in the House of Commons', *European Union Politics* 15(1): 3–23. doi:10.1177/1465116513509307.
van de Wardt, M. (2014) 'Putting the damper on: Do parties de-emphasize issues in response to internal divisions among their supporters?', *Party Politics* 20(3): 330–340. doi:10.1177/1354068811436047.
van de Wardt, M. (2015) 'Desperate needs, desperate deeds: Why mainstream parties respond to the issues of niche parties', *West European Politics* 38(1): 93–122. doi:10.1080/01402382.2014.945247.
van de Wardt, M., de Vries, C.E. and Hobolt, S.B. (2014) 'Exploiting the cracks: wedge issues in multiparty competition', *The Journal of Politics* 76(4): 986–99.
Walker, P. (2016) 'David Davis: revealing Brexit plans is against national interest: EU exit secretary faces tough questions from MPs as Hilary Benn says he will not try to obstruct the withdrawal process', *The Guardian*, 20 October.
Walker, P. (2018) 'Commons to vote on May's Brexit plan in week of 14 January', *The Guardian*, 17 December.
Weaver, R.K. (2018) 'The nays have it: how rampant blame generating distorts American policy and politics', *Political Science Quarterly* 133(2): 259–89. doi:10.1002/polq.12771.

Political, process and programme failures in the Brexit fiasco: exploring the role of policy deception

Darrin Baines, Sharron Brewer and Adrian Kay

ABSTRACT

We propose a conceptual framework of policy deception to help identify, analyse and explain Brexit as a policy fiasco. The framework casts light on the political use of the device of an in/out European Union (EU) referendum by David Cameron. The paper develops the argument that the referendum did not offer a binary choice between two policy options for the United Kingdom's (UK) relationship with the EU representing different, but commensurable preferences, because one option was 'baseless' in that it was unfounded in any policy analysis. The label of policy deception usefully reveals that many of the political, process and programme failures at the heart of the Brexit fiasco have their roots in the referendum. We conclude that the concept of policy deception contributes usefully to emerging work on why the Brexit policy fiasco occurred, and is likely to be a fruitful topic for future work.

Introduction

Brexit may well be remembered as a monumental policy fiasco (Dunlop, James, & Radaelli, 2019; Jennings & Lodge, 2019; Kovac, 2019; McConnell & Tormey, 2019). However, the analysis of such failures is never a neutral or objective endeavour (Bovens & 't Hart, 1996; Brändström & Kuipers, 2003; McConnell, 2016). Failures are never neatly classified but are constructed, declared and argued over in labelling processes that are not necessarily evidence-based (Bovens & 't Hart, 2016). This presents a challenge to those wishing to identify, analyse and explain Brexit as a policy fiasco.

In this special issue, McConnell and Tormey (2019) argue that the inability of the Conservative government led by Prime Minister Theresa May to deliver a Brexit deal by 29 March 2019 was a policy fiasco. They examine three main explanations for this: (1) Brexit as an impossible policy challenge; (2) ineffectual leadership by Theresa May, who took poor decisions and avoided plausible alternatives; (3) Westminster as a partisan-fuelled institution incapable of reaching an agreement on such a bi-partisan issue. The authors conclude that the Brexit fiasco cannot be reduced to a solitary explanation. Instead, analysts should focus on accounting for its complexity by attending to the interplay of agents, institutions/processes and the unique policy challenge of exiting the European Union (EU) within a specified timescale and amid intense inter- and intra- party divisions.

Dunlop et al. (2019) use a policy learning perspective to locate the Brexit fiasco in the period from June 2016 to May 2019, in contrast we concentrate our analysis in the run up to the 2016 referendum. Replacing David Cameron, Theresa May reported in the House of Commons that 'when I first became Prime Minister in 2016 there was no ready-made blueprint for Brexit' (May, 2018). Well over three years later, and after two general elections called on the issue of Brexit, there is still no blueprint. In October 2019, the journalist Martin Kettle wrote, 'Brexit won the vote. But it's an ideology not a policy. When its supporters tried to turn it into policies, as they are still trying to do, it fell apart' (Kettle, 2019). In this paper, we argue that that the referendum did not offer a binary choice between two policy options for the United Kingdom's (UK) relationship with the EU representing different, but commensurable preferences, because one option was 'baseless' in that it was unfounded in any policy analysis.

Following McConnell's (2016) criteria, we argue that the Brexit policy fiasco is a perfect storm of the following combined failures: political (failure of Cameron's political performance in terms of winning the referendum and achieving his primary goal of a renegotiated agreement between the UK and the EU), process (failure to initiate and complete the necessary policy-making processes for exiting the EU) and programme (failure to design a policy framework for UK's future relationship with the EU). We ask the question: Was the Brexit policy fiasco a case of policy deception? The paper develops the claim that the Leave option may be classed as such because it was a baseless voting option that deceived some voters into believing that leaving the EU was an established and available policy pathway.

Policy fiascos

Our analytic position is based upon the etymology of the word 'fiasco', which is theatre slang for 'failure in performance' and deriving from the Italian 'far fiasco', meaning to 'suffer a complete breakdown in performance' (Ayto, 2011). Used in the current context, fiascos are failures of political performance. However, the etymology of the word suggests that such failures may also involve deception. Before 'fiasco' was used in theatre, it derived from the Italian phrase to 'make a bottle'. Why performance failures were linked to the bottles is unclear and disputed but, a 'fiasco' is a type of round-bottomed Italian bottle with its own tight-fitting straw basket. In 1574, a government decree fixed the capacity of the mezzo quarto bottle, with a vessel's capacity certified by a lead seal applied to its outer straw casing that stop purchasers seeing the contents inside. However, producers soon started re-using certified baskets on substandard vessels containing less liquid. As this fraud became commonplace, the Italian government subsequently decreed that the seal should be moved to the bottle's mouth to stop deceit.

The Brexit referendum was electoral process designed to enable voters to choose between the options an 'Remain' and 'Leave', supposedly two equivalent 'vessels' containing different policy contents. If these binary ballot options were the same 'size', as measured by the official standards set for referendums, then the electoral process would be democratic and the choices equal. Thus, the UK's Electoral Commission was tasked with choosing two official campaign groups that could be trusted to fill the two 'standard-sized' Brexit options fairly. By choosing 'Britain Stronger In' ('Remain') and 'Vote Leave' ('Leave'), the Electoral Commission put its seal of approval on their approaches, which may have misled voters into believing they were both trustworthy and viable policy pathways. At the time of the referendum, many voters were unable to see through the 'straw casing' created by the Electoral Commission's approval of Vote Leave as the official exit campaign, which stopped them seeing that the Leave option was an empty vessel, a policy deception.

Paper overview

Our purpose is to analyse whether Brexit should be labelled a 'policy fiasco' and to develop the concept of policy deception in the terms of how David Cameron, the Electoral Commission and Vote Leave helped create the Brexit policy fiasco. We first outline our conceptual framework of policy deception. Next, we analyse how Cameron's handling of the 2016 referendum led to his political failure by creating the Leave option for dramatic effect. Third, we discuss how the Leave option was included on the ballot paper even though it was not an equivalent thing in policy terms to the Remain option, which lead to a policy process failure. Fourth, we examine the multiple rationalities in the Leave option and how different situated contexts and logics of Brexit and the policy tasks set by the referendum result leading to programme failure when the UK government tried, post-referendum, to deliver the Leave option. Finally, we discuss how these political, process and programme failures combined to create the Brexit policy fiasco. We draw the conclusion that Brexit was a policy fiasco and that policy deception may deserve further exploration as a concept in policy studies.

Conceptual framework

In 2019, the former Conservative prime minister, John Major, commented that, 'When the nation voted on Brexit, they did so out of fiction and undeliverable promises' (Kennedy, 2019). In our conceptual framework, we recast this Brexit fiction as policy deception. President Emmanuel Macron stated, 'Brexit is the choice of the British people … pushed by those who predicted easy solutions … those people are liars' (Merrick, 2018). We agree that the British people were misinformed, but we disagree with Macron's classification of this misinformation as lies. We believe there is an important difference between lies and deceit and that, to fully understand the Brexit policy fiasco, understanding the difference between them as different types of untruth is vital.

While policy studies has long identified a gap between constructions of policy success or failure and the actual value of a policy estimated by applied policy analysis (Bovens & 't Hart, 1996), the possibility of deception implied by the gap has not been explored. Policy deception refers to the case where there are politically constructed public beliefs that a policy exists but these beliefs have no basis in any actual analysis that develops and compares systematically policy options, through some process and by some criteria. In our framework, we borrow heavily from Searle (2017), who uses money as an example of deception. He reports that modern currencies are 'baseless' because they are not backed by anything. If customers enter a bank with $20 notes and ask to receive their value, they will not receive gold but instead similar paper notes. Searle (2017) argues that governments or banks do not use 'lies' because systematic deception does not require a 'conscious intentional liar'. Instead, he views deceptions as widespread illusions or systematic falsehoods that are related to, or built into, social systems. For example, monetary value is not real but 'observer-relative'. The worth of your money depends upon your own valuation of its power, and your personal valuation does not have a linear, fixed relationship with the ascribed face value of the notes (Searle, 2017). Therefore, the orchestrated belief that money has an intrinsic worth is a systematic deception.

We argue that a similar logic applies to the face value of a vote for the Leave option during the Brexit referendum. This option was baseless with no intrinsic value as policy. Whatever worth people ascribed to the value of their vote was observer-relative and could not be cashed-in for any agreed set of policies or political outcomes. Moreover, Cameron's failure to secure agreed terms for leaving before the referendum results were known contributed to the difficulty of cashing-in the UK's decision to exit at a value acceptable to the government, parliament and many of the electorate. Therefore, although formal negotiations about the UK's future relationship with the EU have not yet been completed, Brexit may only be deliverable at a substantial economic loss to the UK rather than producing the substantial benefits promised by the Leave campaign. As a result, there is likely to be a significant difference between the expected and realised benefits of Britain's withdrawal. Using Searle's reasoning, this cost will be incurred because the Leave option was not based upon an agreed set of policies, with a known underlying policy analytical value.

To establish the validity of our approach to policy deception, we provide an account of the idea that the Leave option was real, organised and deliverable as a system-wide deceit enabled by the decision to list the Leave option alongside Remain on the Brexit ballot paper. To fully understand why the Brexit fiasco occurred, we must focus on how voters were systematically deceived into believing the Brexit referendum was no different from normal election campaigns in the sense that each of the voting options were real.

The Electoral Commission's remit was to ensure that the referendum was run with integrity and transparency of campaign funding and spending (Electoral Commission, 2015). At the time, there was no mechanism in place to ensure that Leave was real in the sense that the option was deliverable within a reasonable timeframe. As Cameron vowed to automatically implement the referendum outcome, the latter was now presented as an achievable policy alternative. If the referendum had not been declared by Cameron as a binding in/out choice, choosing to leave could have acted as a protest vote that stimulated wide-scale political debate and reform but with no real expectation that the UK would exit the EU. As political events forced Cameron to implement his in/out proposals, voters were faced with the Leave policy option, which was baseless in terms of contents, planning and delivery.

Applied in the current context, we could also say that there was a common misconception that, because it appeared on the ballot paper, the Leave option was backed by the 'something' of a UK successfully functioning outside the institutions of the EU. According to the ontological analysis by Searle (2017), the common misconception that baseless objects, such as money, are real is due to widespread systematic deception, which is possible because some objects and people have 'status functions' imposed upon them (Searle, 2017).

Political failure

Policy deception occurs when there is widespread belief amongst voters that a baseless policy option has substance, even though the option is not backed by something deliverable in the ways promised. In this section, we argue that the Leave option policy deception was first stimulated by Cameron's misjudged political decision-making, which forced him to hold an EU referendum that with a baseless Leave option. The former Conservative prime minister, John Major, described Brexit as 'the worst foreign policy decision in my lifetime' (Price, 2019). Here, we outline how Cameron's political failure occurred, and suggest that his poor decision-making resulted in a widespread policy deception during the Brexit referendum.

According to McConnell (2010), political failures occur when detrimental policy outcomes affect the ability of parties and individuals to obtain or to retain their positions in government and in the political system. In this section, we argue that Cameron's personal decision to hold the Brexit referendum resulted in his personal political failure of having to resign his premiership. This occurred for three main reasons. First, this failure may be classed as Cameron's own fault because he personally chose the referendum policy option when other options were available. Next, he decided to make the result of the referendum politically binding when this political commitment was unnecessary. Third, he risked his premiership on achieving a Remain victory, when he could have distanced himself completely from the referendum outcome by choosing not to lead the Remain campaign. Given the combination of such factors, Brexit has been called Cameron's 'great miscalculation' (Glencross, 2016).

According to Brummer (2016), inflexible leaders who exhibit deficiencies in information gathering and processing seem more likely to end up causing foreign policy fiascos. Cameron's decision to stick steadfastly to his plans to hold an EU referendum to resolve 'party management issues' despite concerns from coalition partners, advisers and even Eurosceptic conservatives, suggests inflexibility (Oliver, 2016; Shipman, 2016; Smith, 2016). Alternatively, Cameron's victories in both the Alternative Vote referendum in 2011 and the Scottish referendum in 2014, along with his unexpected majority in the 2015 general election, gave him a reassuring run of political success. As such, Cameron may have become increasingly confident in his role as premier and believed that he could continuously win voter backing at the ballot box. This may have shaped his willingness to pursue his plans for an EU referendum regardless of the risks. This hypothesis fits with the common criticism that Cameron was a political risk-taker (Daddow, 2015; Smith, 2018).

Cameron thought an EU referendum would be a turning point in his battle against Euroscepticism (Hobolt, 2016; Vasilopoulou, 2016). By offering an in/out ballot, he believed that he could simultaneously appease the Eurosceptics in his party, offer a less extreme political alternative to the UK Independence Party and end the growing political agitation by getting a better membership deal from an EU leadership fearful of a British exit.

Telegraph article

Cameron became prime minister of a coalition government in May 2010 because his Conservative party was not popular enough to govern alone. By 2012, he was accused of losing control as leader because of, among other matters, the rebellious call by 81 Tory members of parliament for an EU exit referendum (Kirkup, 2012). Cameron responded by writing an article for *The Daily Telegraph*, stating that he was 'not against referendums on Europe' but 'we need to be absolutely clear about what we really want, what we now have and the best way of getting what is best for Britain. We need to answer those questions before jumping to questions about referendums' (Cameron, 2012, para.2).

In his article, Cameron also addressed the political issue of which democratic process would give voters the most influence, writing that the 'problem with an in/out referendum is that it offers a single choice, whereas what I want – and what I believe the vast majority of the British people want – is to make changes to our relationship' (Cameron, 2012, para.9). Within a year, he changed his public position from political caution to openly accepting a simple in/out referendum. This unobligated change of course eventually led to his political failure.

Bloomberg speech

Cameron's initial attempts to resolve the Europe issue were ineffective. In January 2013, he tried to create a turning point in his political fortunes by announcing at the London headquarters of the private media company, Bloomberg, his intention to negotiate a new settlement with the EU and to hold an in/out referendum on the UK's membership (Cameron, 2013). As leader of a coalition government, he knew that his pro-Europe partners, the Liberal Democrats, would not readily support a membership ballot. As it was generally expected that another coalition government would be formed after the upcoming 2015 general election, this position was unlikely to change. Therefore, the decision to announce an in/out referendum alongside the intention to radically renegotiate the institutional arrangements governing the UK's membership was a strategic move rather than a plan that would necessarily materialise instantly. At home, his performance was regarded as a success with its intended political audience (Daddow, 2015). Delighted at the promise of an in/out referendum, Conservative MPs in Parliament 'greeted Cameron with massive cheering and waving of order papers' (Hoggart, 2013).

During the Bloomberg speech, David Cameron announced that 'democratic consent for the EU in Britain is now wafer thin' and 'those who refuse to contemplate consulting the British people, would in my view make more likely our eventual exit' (Cameron, 2013). In contrast to the shackles applied by existing EU institutions, he would give the UK people the freedom to either support his new deal or leave the existing arrangements. As the situation required urgent reform, the enabling legislation would be passed as soon as the Conservative government won the next election, and a referendum would be held within the first half of the next parliament.

Process failure

In 2016, UK Parliament's foreign affairs select committee reported that Cameron's government committed an act of gross negligence and deepened the uncertainty surrounding the impact of Brexit by instructing Whitehall not to make any contingency plans for a vote to leave the EU (Select Committee on the Constitution, 2016). The Government had initially suggested it was the responsibility of Vote Leave to explain what Leave would mean to the voters (Smith, 2016). The Treasury report released in April 2016 only outlined the economic impact from three possible models, but did not analyse the viability of the Leave option in full (HM Treasury, 2016). The former Cabinet Office Minister, Oliver Letwin, told the committee that no Brexit plans were ordered because it was possible they would leak and seen as unwarranted interference in the referendum campaign.

Cameron's failure to initiate and to complete the steps necessary to make Leave a policy option to be implemented before the 2016 referendum is a form of process failure on three counts. First, no process existed for transitioning any member state out of the EU, so this ballot option was technically 'baseless' in the sense used by Searle (2017). Second, Cameron personally negotiated and agreed terms with the EU for remaining but not for leaving. Third, the Leave option that appeared on the ballot paper was not equal in political feasibility to the renegotiated Remain choice. The metaphorical Leave bottle was empty, but Cameron never expected it to be opened, so the lack of content did not matter.

Article 50

To withdraw from the EU, member states must follow the legal and political processes outlined in Article 50 of the Treaty on European Union, which states that 'Any Member State may decide to withdraw from the Union in accordance with its own constitutional requirements' (European Parliament, 2016). European Council guidelines state that the EU shall negotiate and conclude an agreement with any country that notifies its intention to leave, setting out the arrangements for withdrawal and specifying the institutional framework for future relations. Following the Brexit referendum, the UK government triggered Article 50 in March 2017, with the legal withdrawal scheduled to occur on 29 March 2019.

Given the complexities involved in securing an exit process with 27 EU partners with no pre-written blueprint, negotiating an exit deal within two years of triggering Article 50 was probably unrealistic. In 2016, the House of Lords reported that the government's failure to set out its exit plans 'caused uncertainty and confusion in the aftermath of the referendum' (Select Committee on the Constitution, 2016, p. 7) and recommended that,

> Parliament may wish, in future, to ensure that detailed consideration is given to how the result of any referendum will be implemented in advance of the vote itself occurring, and to whether explicit provision should be made in the enabling legislation either to implement the outcome automatically or to instruct the Government to act on the result.

The policy process for leaving the EU failed because the government did not negotiate implementable (EU-approved) plans for the UK's withdrawal. This process failure contributed to the Brexit policy fiasco.

Just as monetary denominations printed on paper notes are not backed by government gold reserves, the Leave option on the ballot papers was not backed by EU-approved, physically deliverable plans. Therefore, voters were systematically deceived by the official ballot if they believed their votes were exchangeable, upon demand, for new institutional arrangements for a UK outside the EU.

Programme failure

To leave the EU, parliament had to invoke Article 50 then negotiate an exit deal (within strict EU rules) agreeable to the other 27 member countries and to design and prepare for the implementation of a whole new suite of domestic policy to substitute for previous EU competences. To date, Brexit may be classed a programme failure because the policy outcomes suggested by the official Leave campaign have not been initiated within two years of triggering Article 50 (Vote Leave, 2016). It may be judged as being unsuccessful because the necessary and proposed programmes have not been designed and implemented within the expected timeframe. Trying to make the Leave option real has involved prolonged, but fruitless negotiations and imposed unexpected costs on the UK by creating economic uncertainty and the exit of investment, workers and firms.

Vote Leave framework

On 15 June 2016, during the last week of the campaign, Vote Leave published 'A framework for taking back control and establishing a new UK–EU deal after

23 June' (Vote Leave, 2016). The document states that, following a Leave victory, the UK government will need to create a roadmap outlining to parliament the legislative steps needed to give effect to the public's vote. According to Vote Leave (2016), there is no need to rush this important process because the 'principles of the new settlement are clear and will be based on free trade and friendly intergovernmental cooperation'. Reflecting upon past experiences, the document also claims that it will be possible to negotiate a new settlement with the EU by the 2020 general election. According to the Leave framework, the following circumstances would enable quick progress:

(1) Tariff-free trade between the UK and the EU already exists, so the parties will not need to negotiate the tariff lines on which duties will be abolished, only to continue the status quo.
(2) Regulatory equivalence already exists, so detailed negotiations about the mutual recognition of product standards will be unnecessary because regulations are currently identical. Since non-tariff barriers are few, there will be no need to negotiate their abolition.

As the actual progress of trade negotiations since the referendum suggests, Vote Leave's claims were misleading (Edgington, 2019). Exiting the EU has not proven to be easy. To date, securing a deal agreeable to all member states and getting parliamentary agreement to change domestic law has not yet been possible. There is a real chance of the UK crashing out without a deal in 2020 following Boris Johnson's win at the 2019 election (Woodcock, 2019). As no-one can predict the future, Vote Leave's misleading claims in their framework cannot be called lies, but they can be labelled deceptive and very unlikely to occur in practice.

The purpose of publishing the framework for taking back control just before the referendum vote was not to portray the truth but to support the systematic deception that Leave was a deliverable policy option. Ironically, the document also clearly acknowledges that Leave was an empty policy bottle that would not be filled until after a referendum success. In a political sleight of hand, Vote Leave tried to convince voters that EU leaders and the British parliament would be happy to fill the empty vessel once the Leave option had been chosen, even though they had no proof that an exit would lead to the ready flow of enabling policies and laws. Using Searle's example, this is similar to saying that the paper money in your pocket today is baseless, but in the future (if you vote for it) there will be gold.

Discussion

That Brexit is a complex phenomenon comprising a set of highly contingent combinations of factors over an extended temporal sequence is widely accepted in the academic literature (McConnell & Tormey, 2019; Thompson, 2017). Its evaluation as a policy fiasco, however, is much less settled, either within the live arenas of ongoing Brexit politics or from the viewpoints of academic spectators. In their review of the study of policy failures over the last twenty years, Bovens and 't Hart (2016) revisit their long-standing argument that the fiasco label is not a neutral classification that may be applied externally according to objectively verifiable standards but rather something constructed in the 'framing contests' of politics.

In the practical politics of a referendum campaign, it is hard for voters to observe and to disentangle what is real. For instance, the Leave battle bus was emblazoned with the words 'We send the EU £350 million a week. Let's fund our NHS instead'. According to Cameron (Cameron, 2019, p. 688): 'It wasn't true. As Boris rode the bus around the country, he left the truth at home. We didn't send £350 million a week to the EU'. Regardless of the truth, the battle bus had a greater impact than Remain's conventional, staged political events. This is probably because the Vote Leave did not feel constrained by standard policy rationality or evidence provided by experts. Instead, their campaign was aimed at giving voters the opportunity to develop new, post -EU identities with claims about post-EU programmes that were not grounded in policy analysis. For instance, Vote Leave stated that voting to exit could generate benefits by stopping the UK bearing substantial costs when Turkey joins the EU (Ker-Lindsay, 2018). In reality, as a member state, the UK will not have to bear any costs of the country becoming an EU member any time soon because Turkey has no reasonable chance of meeting the entry requirements (the EU's 35 Accession chapters) in coming decades. In response, Cameron's advisers suggested that he announced that the country would not become an EU member while he was prime minister. He (Cameron, 2019, p. 669) writes:

> But I felt that would be irresponsible – the country was in the EU's waiting room for a reason. And by saying a veto was necessary now was tantamount to accepting that it could join shortly. So, paralysis had me in its grip. I was caught between being a campaigner and being a prime minister, and I chose the latter, it truly was asymmetric warfare, I made the wrong choice.

As this example suggests, Cameron experienced role conflict as the lead of the Remain campaign. While he was floundering, Vote Leave were able to make a whole range of deceptive policy promises and claims that, ultimately, helped them win the referendum. Therefore, we may conclude that Cameron caused the Brexit programme failure because he could not successfully perform his conflicting roles of EU negotiator, prime minister and political campaigner. In consequence, his failings helped create the Brexit policy fiasco.

Political failure

Given that the Brexit fiasco ended Cameron's career as prime minister, when did his political failure begin? According to Wright and Cooper (2016), the Bloomberg address was the 'start of the end of David Cameron'. This is because his change of direction created the possibility of an undesirable political outcome. Given this error in choosing an EU ballot, the writers ask whether Cameron was in favour of a referendum himself? They reply, 'We don't know for sure but the answer is probably not. That being said, Cameron certainly felt he had little choice over the issue' (Wright & Cooper, 2016: para. 12). However, Cameron knew the political risks because two of his predecessors, Margaret Thatcher and John Major, had been forced to resign over Europe divisions in the Conservative party.

Despite being advised otherwise, Cameron thought the referendum announcement was a gamble worth taking because, according to Wright and Cooper (2016), he believed the referendum would never happen. At the time, the prime minister calculated that Labour under Ed Miliband would not back the ballot plan, whereas his coalition partners were passionately opposed. Most importantly, in 2013, senior Tories – including Cameron – realistically thought they had no chance of winning an overall majority in the 2015 general election and that another coalition was likely. As a result, most people believed that the referendum pledge would be the first thing to go in coalition talks. If this was the case, there are grounds to claim that Cameron's referendum pledge was designed to deceive both Eurosceptics at home and political leaders in Europe.

Process failure

The Brexit referendum resulted in a process failure because the Conservative government was unable to deliver the baseless Leave option. The prolonged political negotiations held after Article 50 was triggered demonstrate that, at the time of the referendum, the Leave option was baseless. In Searlean terms, voters were systematically deceived by the promise of post-EU institutional arrangements backed by the necessary political, legal and economic arrangements. We suggest that Leave was not an implementable policy option but a baseless political positioning that the prime minister did not initially expect to enact in practice or predict would ever need implementing. Even as the UK formally leaves the EU on 31 January 2020, we still do not know much about the UK's future relationship with the EU and any terms decided will not be those suggested at the time of the referendum.

As the Leave option was introduced for political effect only, Cameron did not put the policy procedures in place to create a viable exit plan, secure agreement for that plan from other EU member countries or have a clear and deliverable way to deliver the Leave option. As events forced Cameron to implement his political promise, the Leave option became a systematic deception that misled voters into believing that the official alternative to Remain was backed by something. Because EU leaders refused to accept the status function assigned to the Leave option, the post-referendum policy process failed to deliver the promised EU exit, thus contributing to the Brexit policy fiasco.

Programme failure

Given the lack of details about the type, nature and outcomes of policy programmes after an exit, Vote Leave deceived voters by suggesting imaginary political changes with imaginary socio-economic consequences. The key question is: why were so many voters deceived? Although there is a complexity of possible answers, Searle's (2017) ontology of deception provides important insights. First, the Electoral Commission gave Vote Leave the status function of being an official campaign group, which implied to many voters that their claims were legitimate. Next, the hypothetical value of the policy programmes suggested by the Leave campaign did not have to be based upon anything real. To work as a political currency, Vote Leave's claims only had to secure collective acceptance and did not have to be 'cashed in' at the time votes were cast.

The Brexit programme failure has its foundations in the political promises made by Vote Leave. The lack of pre-agreed terms for Britain's exit meant that Vote Leave could invent their own policy programmes and designate their face value without fear of contradiction. They could print their own 'baseless' political currency. In a conventional general election, parties produce manifestos outlining their proposed policies. In the EU referendum campaign, neither Remain nor Leave produced a traditional manifesto. However, the remain option had the clearly defined policy position of staying in the EU under the terms negotiated by Cameron and with forty years of accumulated policy development, whilst Vote Leave had no equivalent set of policies. In this void, Vote Leave made numerous policy claims and promises during the ten-week referendum campaign that did not later materialise and were able to claim that voters could 'take back control'. Such promises may be viewed as 'illusions' that, in themselves, they were baseless.

Vote Leave was established to run one campaign only and did not have to consider the consequences of deceiving the public in any further elections. They were in a unique political position. Under contemporary institutional rules, the government, Parliament and the Electoral Commission had no jurisdiction over the truth content of Vote Leave's political campaigns. Whilst Cameron led a traditional political campaign, his opponents had free reign to implement their version of populism, with official approval from the UK's electoral institutions. The bottle was empty, voters were being systematically deceived, but Vote Leave had the official seal of parliament, the prime minister and the Electoral Commission.

Cameron's political gamble

Whether Cameron should be held accountable for the Brexit policy failure depends not on what he did but on the available counterfactuals that he did not follow. Thompson (2017) argues that Cameron's referendum decision was a gamble premised on the following assumptions. First, there was no prospect of the Conservative party winning the 2015 general election. Second, the other EU member states, particularly Germany, would not risk Britain leaving. Third, there was no realistic chance of a Leave vote winning.

David Cameron's memoirs were published in September 2019. He reports pursuing a 'renegotiation and referendum' strategy from 2015 because he was convinced that a poll would happen in the near future anyway and, under a more Eurosceptic Tory government, would probably not offer the possibility of EU reform. Reflecting upon this decision, Cameron (2019, p. 623) states:

> Writing all this now, I completely accept that my strategy failed to achieve the outcome I desired. But at the time – and subsequently – I believed that the risks of doing nothing were greater. As I have said many times, that doesn't mean I have no regrets, or do not believe that things could have been done differently or better in terms of the negotiation, or the campaign, or indeed the timing. But it is why I don't regret the central decision to adopt a strategy of a renegotiation and referendum.

According to Thompson (2017), the Brexit fiasco was not the accidental product of Cameron's personal failings or the idiosyncrasies of his judgement in relation to his party. At some point before the planned 2020 election, it was probable (but not inevitable) that the issue of EU membership would need to be addressed within the Conservative party. Although Cameron used a risky strategy to solve this problem, Thompson (2017) suggests that the problem was not with his judgement but with the fundamental political weakness of Britain's position inside the EU. In other words, the counterfactual situation would probably have resulted in a fiasco of some description or other, albeit at a slower pace.

Before the 2016 referendum, Cameron used political means to create the false impression that Britain was powerful in Europe and that he had the power to renegotiate the EU–UK relationship. In truth, his ploy did not work because the EU's leaders – particularly in Germany – realised that Britain was not well placed to renegotiate its position. Rejected in Europe, Cameron wished to create a good impression at home (Smith, 2016). With no real basis for claiming that he could secure a new deal, the prime minister resorted to the political device of announcing an in/out EU referendum as a means of diminishing Euroscepticism and improving his chances of winning the 2015 general election. By doing so, he made the Leave campaign's case by signalling to the British people that they had little control within the EU and should be given the opportunity to leave. Unfortunately, Cameron did not predict that Vote Leave would be fronted by the team of Boris Johnson and Dominic Cummings. During the ten-week referendum campaign, the popular politician and the astute political strategist fought the Remain campaign and won the majority of voter support (Shipman, 2016).

Is Leave deliverable?

Given our claim that the Leave option was a policy deception, the question remains of whether the referendum result can ever be delivered? During the General Election in 2019, Boris Johnson (who replaced Theresa May as prime minister in July 2019) used the slogan 'Get Brexit Done'. The use of this message implies that: (i) Leave is a real, deliverable policy option, (ii) Parliament, the EU and Remainers are stopping the Conservative government following this possible political pathway, and (iii) the failure to deliver the referendum result was a policy fiasco caused by key political stakeholders since the 2016 poll. In response, the former Conservative deputy prime minister, Michael Heseltine, said the slogan was a 'great delusion' because it heralded years of further negotiations not an instant end because 'The most you can do, if there were to be a massive Tory majority, is to get through the legislation to enable you to begin the talk about what the future relationship will be' (Buchan, 2019). In contrast to Johnson's optimism that all the details of our future relationship will be in place by December 2020, experience to date suggests that Brexit may not be done quickly, and will involve even more years of political and economic uncertainty (Rankin, 2019).

Given that UK voters were systematically deceived, how can the Conservative government negotiate an exit option that convinces voters that the baseless Leave option is deliverable? Again, working with Dominic Cummings as a chief special adviser to the prime minister, Johnson introduced the Withdrawal Agreement Bill, which passed (at second reading) on 20 December 2019 by 358 votes to 234, with a majority of 124. The legislation was required to ratify the withdrawal agreement made with the EU and ensures that the UK will leave Europe by 31 January 2020 (Hope & Sheridan, 2019). In an accompanying speech in the House of Commons, Johnson told parliament, 'This is the time when we move on and discard the old labels of Leave and Remain' (Hope & Sheridan, 2019). He added, 'In fact, the very words seem tired to me – as defunct as Big-enders and Little-enders, or Montagues and Capulets at the end of the play'.

Given our argument that the Leave option is a baseless, systematic deception, Johnson's speech is an interesting development. Trying to deliver the undefined Leave alternative has been consistently problematic for the Conservative government and led to a political failure for Theresa May. Speaking in December 2019, the ex-Conservative government minister, Kenneth Clarke, said that the situation remained the same, 'I could never get out of Boris – and nobody so far could get out of Boris – what he has in mind for the eventual deal. To say they're generalities is an understatement' (Walker, 2019). In this policy void, by claiming that the Leave label is no longer relevant, the prime minister has been able to swerve the issue of whether this referendum option is deliverable or not. As far as UK legislation is concerned, the requirements of the Brexit poll will be delivered by 31 January 2020, but with detailed negotiations and policy development to follow.

Conclusion

In this paper, we argue that the greatest trick pulled during the 2016 referendum was way in which David Cameron, the Electoral Commission and Vote Leave convinced voters that the Leave option did exist. Even if Vote Leave had been honest in their campaigning and had lost the referendum, many people would have been convinced that Brexit was possible and could be delivered at some future point. In contrast, our analysis suggests that the referendum option (with its official seal of approval from the Electoral Commission), together with Vote Leave's political campaigning, deceived many voters and stimulated their emotions in ways that encouraged them to choose an empty policy bottle. If conventional, instrumental politics led by experts and analysts had played a bigger part in designing and describing the complexities of leaving the EU, then the straw casing of deceit may have been removed, exposing an empty political vessel. However, this raises the interesting question for further debate of whether, in post-truth politics, voters wish to be deceived because they desire particular policy outcomes regardless of the underlying truths.

Declaring Brexit a policy fiasco is not a neutral endeavour. Labelling political failures as fiascos is not an exercise based upon indubitable, objective facts, but relies upon the construction of narratives that embody debatable, subjective points of view. For many, the perspective that Leave was a baseless, systematic deception may conflict with their version of the truth. As an addition to the current policy studies literature, we argue the Brexit fiasco story should begin with Cameron and his construction of Leave as a (baseless) referendum option. Based upon this perspective, we conclude that Brexit should labelled a policy fiasco based upon political, process and programme failures that were intertwined with Cameron's policy deception, given the seal of approval by the Electoral Commission.

Acknowledgments

The authors would like to thank the editors of the special issue, Berthold and Jeremy, as well as three anonymous referees for their constructive and useful contributions to the development of the paper.

Disclosure statement

No potential conflict of interest was reported by the author(s).

References

Ayto, J. (2011). *Dictionary of word origins*. New York: Arcade Publishing.

Bovens, M., & 't Hart, P. (1996). *Understanding policy fiascoes*. New Brunswick: Transaction Publishers.

Bovens, M., & 't Hart, P. (2016). Revisiting the study of policy failures. *Journal of European Public Policy*, *23*(5), 653–666.

Brändström, A., & Kuipers, S. (2003). From 'normal incidents' to political crises: Understanding the selective politicization of policy failures. *Government and Opposition*, *38*(3), 279–305.

Brummer, K. (2016). 'Fiasco prime ministers': Leaders' beliefs and personality traits as possible causes for policy fiascos. *Journal of European Public Policy*, *23*(5), 702–717.

Buchan, L. (2019, November 25). General election: Tory peer urges voters to reject Johnson's 'grand delusion' and back Lib Dems. *Independent*.

Cameron, D. (2012, June 30). We need to be clear about the best way of getting what is best for Britain. *The Telegraph*, 30 June.

Cameron, D. (2013, January 23). *EU speech at Bloomberg*. Retrieved from https://www.gov.uk/government/speeches/eu-speech-at-bloomberg

Cameron, D. (2019). *For the record*. London: William Collins.

Daddow, O. (2015). Performing Euroscepticism: The UK Press and Cameron's Bloomberg speech. In K. Tournier-Sol & C. Gifford (Eds.), *The UK challenge to Europeanization* (pp. 151–171). London: Palgrave.

Dunlop, C. A., James, S., & Radaelli, C. M. (2019). Can't get no learning: The Brexit fiasco through the lens of policy learning. *Journal of European Public Policy*. doi:10.1080/13501763.2019.1667415

Edgington, T. (2019). Brexit: What trade deals has the UK done so far? *BBC News*. Retrieved from https://www.bbc.co.uk/news/uk-47213842

Electoral Commission. (2015). *Referendum on membership of the European Union*. London: UK Parliament.

European Parliament. (2016). *Article 50 TEU: Withdrawal of a member state from the EU*. Briefing PE 577.971. Brussels: European Parliamentary Research Service.

Glencross, A. (2016). *Why the UK voted for Brexit: David Cameron's great miscalculation*. London: Palgrave.

HM Treasury. (2016). *HM Treasury analysis: The long-term economic impact of EU membership and the alternatives*. London: UK Government Cm 9250.

Hobolt, S. B. (2016). The Brexit vote: A divided nation, a divided continent. *Journal of European Public Policy, 23*(9), 1259–1277.

Hoggart, S. (2013, January 24). In, out, in, out? That's not really what it's all about. *The Guardian*.

Hope, C., & Sheridan, D. (2019, December 20). Stop calling each other Leavers or Remainers, Boris Johnson says, as Brexit Bill overwhelmingly passed. *The Telegraph*.

Jennings, W., & Lodge, M. (2019). Brexit, the tides and Canute: The fracturing politics of the British state. *Journal of European Public Policy, 26*(5), 772–789.

Kennedy, R. (2019, December 6). John Major: UK's former conservative PM breaks party ranks to urge voters to reject Brexit. *Euronews*.

Ker-Lindsay, J. (2018). Turkey's EU accession as a factor in the 2016 Brexit referendum. *Turkish Studies, 19*(1), 1–22.

Kettle, M. (2019, October 16). At first, I accepted Brexit. Now it's become clear that we must not leave the EU. *The Guardian*.

Kirkup, J. (2012, June 28). Cameron's backbenchers demand EU referendum. *The Telegraph*.

Kovac, M. (2019). The Brexit fiasco and the failure of Article 50 of the Treaty on the Functioning of the European Union. *Baltic Journal of Law & Politics, 12*(1), 172–192.

May, T. (2018, November 15). PM statement on Brexit negotiations. Retrieved from https://www.gov.uk/government/speeches/pm-statement-on-brexit-negotiations-15-november-2018

McConnell, A. (2010). Policy success, policy failure and grey areas in-between. *Journal of Public Policy, 30*(3), 345–362.

McConnell, A. (2016). A public policy approach to understanding the nature and causes of foreign policy failure. *Journal of European Public Policy, 23*(5), 667–684.

McConnell, A., & Tormey, S. (2019). Explanations for the Brexit policy fiasco: Near-impossible challenge, leadership failure or Westminster pathology? *Journal of European Public Policy*. doi:10.1080/13501763.2019.1657485

Merrick, R. (2018, September 28). Emmanuel Macron calls Brexit campaign leaders 'liars', in extraordinary attack. *Independent*.

Oliver, C. (2016). *Unleashing demons: The inside story of Brexit*. London: Hodder & Stoughton.

Price, C. (2019, December 6). Sir John Major gives PM election headache. *The Telegraph*.

Rankin, J. (2019, November 25). 'Get Brexit done'? The reality will be far more difficult and tortuous. *The Guardian*.

Searle, J. R. (2017). Money: Ontology and deception. *Cambridge Journal of Economics, 41* (5), 1453–1470.

Select Committee on the Constitution. (2016). *The invoking of Article 50*, HL Paper 44. London: House of Lords.

Shipman, T. (2016). *All out war: The full story of how Brexit Sank Britain's political class*. London: Harper Collins.

Smith, J. (2016). David Cameron's EU renegotiation and referendum pledge: A case of déjà vu? *British Politics, 11*(3), 324–346.

Smith, J. (2018). Gambling on Europe: David Cameron and the 2016 referendum. *British Politics, 13*(1), 1–16.

Thompson, H. (2017). Inevitability and contingency: The political economy of Brexit. *The British Journal of Politics and International Relations, 19*(3), 434–449.

Vasilopoulou, S. (2016). UK Euroscepticism and the Brexit referendum. *Political Quarterly, 87*(2), 219–227.

Vote Leave. (2016). *A framework for taking back control and establishing a new UK-EU deal after 23 June*. Retrieved from www.voteleavetakecontrol.org

Walker, P. (2019, December 23). Boris Johnson should 'stop campaigning and start governing', says Ken Clarke. *The Guardian*.

Woodcock, A. (2019, November 28). Boris Johnson's Brexit policy risks no-deal crash-out next year that will trigger a recession and return to austerity, expert IFS analysis indicates. *Independent*.

Wright, O., & Cooper, C. (2016, June 24). The speech that was the start of the end of David Cameron. *Independent*.

The Brexit car crash: using E.H. Carr to explain Britain's choice to leave the European Union in 2016

Justin O. Frosini and Mark F. Gilbert

ABSTRACT

This article uses E.H. Carr's discussion of causation in *What is History?* as a methodological frame for studying the causes of Brexit. It contends that, in final analysis, the underlying reason why millions of British citizens rejected European Union membership was the conviction that British freedom and independence was at risk. The power of the EU to make British law was never entirely accepted by a significant part of the British political class from the very beginning of Britain's engagement with Europe. This residual opposition to European integration strengthened as a result of the Treaties of Maastricht and Lisbon, and gained an additional boost from the growing social and economic divides of British society, and the impact of migration from the EU. The Brexit car crash was an accident waiting to happen.

Introduction

This article treats Brexit as an event whose causes are rooted in the political development of Britain since the 1970s. Brexit is as British as Wimbledon. This is not to dispute that 'the sentiments that led to this outcome (Brexit) are by no means a distinctively British phenomenon' (Hobolt 2016: 1260). There is anti-elitist populism in other European Union (EU) countries, notably Italy and France; immigration is an issue everywhere; some of the critiques of European unity aired for decades in British political discourse are now finding an audience elsewhere.

But anti-EU feeling is more pronounced in Britain. Explaining Brexit means providing a plausible answer to the central question that the June 2016 vote has posed, which is why membership of the EU was regarded by so many ordinary people as a condition almost of subjugation. On Brexit morning, thousands of citizen activists celebrated by proclaiming 'Freedom' and 'Independence'. On 25 June 2016, the *Daily Mail*'s headline was 'Take a Bow Britain!' The rest of the front page read: 'it was the day that the quiet people of Britain rose up against an arrogant, out-of-touch political class and a contemptuous Brussels elite'.

To explain Brexit is in other words about understanding why so many 'quiet people' greeted the victory of the 'Leave' campaign as a *liberation*. Such an inquiry does not come easily to academics who are professionally engaged in the study of the EU and its history. But unless one grasps that the 2016 Brexit campaign was premised upon a narrative of restoring democracy and freedom, one can end up typecasting the 17.4 million British citizens who voted Leave as merely irrational, ill-informed or even xenophobic/racist. Many Leave voters were one or more of those things; some advocates of Brexit in the press were all four. But we should not neglect the positive political ideology of the Brexiteers. The people who voted 'Leave' were voting *for* something, not just *against* the EU, or elites, or social injustice. This article attempts to show what that something was.

Smoking can be dangerous

Our starting point is E.H. Carr's famous example of a car crash to explain how historians approach causality. In *What is History?* Carr examines the case of Robinson, a smoker in need of his fix from the tobacconist on the other side of a road, who is knocked down and killed while crossing at a blind corner where 'visibility is notoriously poor' by Jones, who is returning from a party where he has 'consumed more than his usual ration of alcohol', and is driving a car whose brakes are defective (Carr 1973: 104–5). What is the cause of Robinson's death? Jones' drunkenness? The blind corner? The faulty brakes? The answer, of course, is that these causes fatefully combined. As Carr says, 'the historian deals in a multiplicity of causes' – though one should not simply list causes without attempting to weigh them. 'The relative significance of one cause or one set of causes or of another, is the essence of (a historian's) interpretation' Carr avers (Carr 1973: 103), and most historians do ultimately identify one cause or set of causes that 'in the final analysis' they regard as overriding in any particular case (Carr 1973: 90).

Note that pure chance and human agency played a part in the accident, too. Robinson's death was paradoxically both over-determined and extremely casual, as students always point out when one uses his demise as a teaching tool. Jones might have knocked down Atkinson five minutes earlier, as he walked his dog down a dark stretch of road. Robinson's craving for nicotine might have been delayed by a phone call. Robinson ought certainly to have looked right and left before he crossed the road, or have used the level crossing further down the street. Such contingencies manifestly do matter for the outcome of events: Had Franz Ferdinand cancelled the rest of his visit to Sarajevo after the first attempt to assassinate him failed, the most important opponent of the war party in Vienna would have survived (Lebow 2000–2001).

Carr's settled view, however, was that we should not waste too much time on happenstance. Scholars should construct their explanations around what he somewhat vaguely calls 'real' generalizable causes. We take this to mean that the historian should isolate the crucial socio-economic, intellectual, institutional, and political variables of any given case – the ones that would plausibly have produced similar outcomes had they been present in other times and places – and explain how they combined over time to produce a particular result.

What follows is a necessarily compressed police superintendent's accident report of the process that led a substantial part of the British people not just to reject the United Kingdom's membership of the EU, but to reject it in a spirit of euphoria. Compressed, because for reasons of space we focus upon just three of the 'generalizable causes' that were fundamental for creating the climate whereby a referendum against EU membership could be won by the EU's opponents.

The first of these causes is intellectual: it is the deep-rooted conviction that membership of the EU is incompatible with the doctrine of parliamentary sovereignty. This concern drove right-wing intellectuals like Enoch Powell and socialist thinkers like Douglas Jay and Tony Benn to reject even joining the European Economic Community (EEC). Jay – in a forensic 1968 critique of the European project – contended that the EEC had a 'constitution which is illiberal and undemocratic not merely in legal form but in basic philosophy ... it is rooted in an essential distrust of the people' (Jay 1968: 33). Tony Benn's first visit to the Berlaymont prompted him to confide to his diary that the 'huge building', 'in the shape of a cross' was 'absolutely un-British'. Benn felt like 'a slave going to Rome'; despite the fact that he was 'an elected man', the Commissioners had 'more power' and 'no accountability to anybody' (Benn 1990: 180). Such convictions showed remarkable tenacity after 1973 and flared into new flame during the parliamentary guerrilla war over the ratification of the Maastricht Treaty. They have never been doused since.

The second 'generalizable cause' is the role of the press. Britain's mass circulation newspapers, most of which supported membership of the EEC, from the early 1990s onwards made the EU a symbol of elitism, privilege and bureaucracy. Had any other country had a press remotely like the British one, it might be leaving the EU too. We have no space to explain why this shift of position occurred (a prosopographical study of the chief columnists of those newspapers and their proprietors would be a useful exercise), but the newspapers' unscrupulousness popularized the notion that the EU was an external enemy robbing Britain of sovereignty, and made it impossible for any British prime minister after John Major to defend membership on other than narrow economic grounds.

The third generalizable cause that we isolate is the elephant in the room of the Brexit vote, migration. Since the 1980s, millions of Britons, especially in London, have benefited from the services-based economy that was the legacy of Margaret Thatcher and John Major – and of the EU single market in goods and services. Large swathes of the country, however, were not so blessed: resentments against economic disparities within Britain welled over into fury against the EU when largescale migration within the EU became an issue after 2004. The single market, the British discovered, also meant freedom of movement for people. And they couldn't do anything about flows of people without 'taking back control'.

The constitutional debate on Britain and Europe

Take Back Control', the slogan adopted by the Brexiteers in the 2016 referendum campaign, rendered into plain English an intricate constitutional debate spanning at least five decades. The core argument of this debate is that the United Kingdom's entry into the EEC/EU demolished parliamentary sovereignty, a pillar of Britain's uncodified constitution. The most passionate advocate of this position was Enoch Powell, who bears the same intellectual relationship to Brexiteers as Jean Monnet possesses to the European movement. Powell argued that the question of joining the Common Market was the 'most fundamental of all', namely, 'what nation are we to be' (Powell 1971: 36). If the political unity of Europe meant that Britain would become a province or county in a larger whole then, Powell contended, no potential economic benefit was worth the price of membership.

In the early 1970s, Powell stated that if the British people understood that such a renunciation of national sovereignty was the goal of the EEC, then they would never agree to give their allegiance to a European entity. But if so, then it would be 'dishonourable and foolish' for British people to allow its leaders to sign the Treaty of Rome on their behalf. It was not right to join the EEC unless one could do it 'ex animo', with a 'genuine and hearty intention that in the fulness of time political as well as economic union shall come out of it' (Powell 1971: 70).

Powell's opposition to EEC membership was the other side of the coin to his opposition to immigration to Britain from the former Commonwealth. In both cases, he believed that elites were imposing a radical transformation in whom the British were. For Powell, parliament was *literally* the soul of the nation. In no continental country did the legislative assembly occupy the same centrality for the nation's sense of self. Speaking in Lyon, Powell said:

> Take parliament out of the history of England and that history itself becomes meaningless. Whole lifetimes of study cannot exhaust the reasons why this

> fact has come to be, but fact it is, so that the British nation could not imagine itself except with and through its parliament. Consequently the sovereignty of our parliament is something other for us than what your assemblies are for you (Powell 1971: 67).

Powell's evocation of parliamentary sovereignty was not the effusion of a romantic reactionary. Similar arguments were also voiced by eminent jurists such as Lord Denning who famously referred to the incoming tide of European law, observing that 'it flows into the estuaries and up the rivers. It cannot be held back, Parliament has decreed that the Treaty is henceforward to be part of our law. It is equal in force to any statute' (Bulmer vs Bollinger 1974).

Opponents of EEC membership were appalled by the consequences on parliamentary sovereignty that the tide of European law, and its claim to supremacy, implied. In their opinion, when Edward Heath led Britain into Europe through the European Communities Act 1972, a first step was taken towards weakening the 'classic' concept of supremacy of Parliament. Indeed, when the United Kingdom joined the EEC, an established case law of the then European Court of Justice (ECJ) already existed. More precisely, the doctrine of supremacy which emerged in prominent cases such as *Van Gend en Loos* (1963) and *Costa v Enel* (1964) was incorporated into the legal system of the United Kingdom by means of the European Communities Act. As the Lords underlined:

> If the supremacy [...] of Community law over national law of Member States was not always inherent in the EEC Treaty it was certainly well-established in the jurisprudence of the European Court of Justice long before the United Kingdom joined the Community. Thus, whatever limitation of sovereignty Parliament accepted when it enacted the European Communities Act 1972 was entirely voluntary. Under the terms of the Act of 1972 it has always been clear that it was the duty of a United Kingdom court [...] to override any rule of national law found to be in conflict with any directly enforceable rule of Community law (*Factortame II* 1991).

The key question is whether that decision was 'entirely voluntary'. Were Members of Parliament really aware of the consequences for Parliamentary supremacy when they approved the 1972 act? Were the British people truly aware of all of the direct effect of EEC law when they voted in the referendum of 1975? If we assume that the decision taken by the House of Commons was 'entirely voluntary', then from a constitutional perspective one could argue that Powell and other anti-marketeers were wrong and that parliamentary supremacy had not been demolished at all. The argument generally adduced to proclaim that the conditions of Parliament's legislative supremacy necessarily remain in the United Kingdom's hands, is the fact that the EEC Act 1972 contains a rule of interpretation according to which 'future Acts of Parliament are not to be interpreted in a way that conflicts with the supremacy of directly effective Community law' (Hartley 2004: 162; Patrono and Frosini 2015: 997–998). Put another way there is an 'implied supremacy clause' inserted in any Act of Parliament enacted since 1972 to the effect that any inconsistency between the Act and European law should be resolved in favour of the latter unless Parliament expressly indicates that it intends to derogate from EU law. In brief, the prevalence of EU law over British law finds its source in an Act of the British Parliament and therefore its supremacy remains intact.

There are, however, two counter arguments to this.

The first is that once Britain entered the EEC there was no way of leaving – at any rate until the Lisbon Treaty made Brexit possible. The EEC was, as one scholar has argued, 'a house without exit doors' (Musolff 2000). Indeed, the famous Costa v. Enel case of 1964 underlined that alongside the principle of supremacy there was also a principle of uniformity: no changes could be made to the treaties (including the decision of a member state to leave) without the unanimous consensus of all the other member states. This was important because, as people like Douglas Jay argued from the outset, the Treaty of Rome wasn't a traditional international treaty with a get-out clause.

> In a normal Treaty, the British Government's and Parliament's power of independent decision is renounced to an extent clearly known and set out in the Treaty. Parliament also retains the power at any time to denounce the Treaty, usually with a stated period of notice, and regain its full sovereignty. Under the Rome Treaty, however, the British Parliament would hand over to the Council of Ministers and the Commission the power of legislating in the future, in ways not known at the time of signing the Treaty, on the internal affairs of this country (Jay 1968: 31)

Second, the idea of imposing a uniform legal system across the Community has been criticized by some so-called legal pluralists. Writing a few years after the ratification of the Maastricht Treaty, Carol Harlow pointed out that '[t]here is a serious mismatch between the priorities of the EC and national legal orders and that the impact of the superior order on national legal systems may be both unexpected and detrimental' (Harlow 1996: 199). In a nutshell, many scholars regard excessive harmonization of the legal systems of the member states as a form of centralization and a way of stifling pluralism.

Such arguments illustrate that the relationship between the European Union and British parliamentary sovereignty really is problematic. In the last few years, doubts have if anything grown on this score even among leading scholars of EU and Constitutional Law. For instance, Paul Craig has criticized the 'locks and limits' of the EU on the sovereignty of the member states (Craig 2011: 48), while Michael Gordon and Michael Dougan provocatively ask 'Who Won the Bloody War Anyway?' (Gordon and Dougan 2012: 37).

No, no, no!

Convinced that EEC membership would bring economic gains, many ardent Eurosceptics, such as Bill Cash, Margaret Thatcher, or the journalist Christopher Booker, campaigned in favour of Britain's membership (Mrs Thatcher's 1975 flags jumper remains mythical to this day). The positive attitude of most Tories towards the EEC persisted even after the toppling of Edward Heath. Once the battle to reduce the amount of Britain's net contribution to the Community budget was won, Thatcher became a driving force in pushing through the Single European Act (SEA) of 1986. SEA embraced many Conservative ideas on simplifying trade and reducing non-tariff barriers, but from the point of view of national sovereignty, in Thatcher's own words, 'the price which we would have to pay to achieve a single market with all its benefits ... was more majority voting in the Community' (Thatcher 1993: 553).

So long as she was premier, Thatcher took a pragmatic approach to the perils to British national sovereignty represented by further European integration. In the 1980s, at any rate until Neil Kinnock dragged the Labour Party to more centrist ground, the principal 'Eurosceptics', a word that was first used in 1986, were on the left. Even Thatcher's 1988 Bruges Speech – so often dismissed as the first manifesto of Euroscepticism – epitomizes her essentially commercial and competitive view of the European project: an extract from it is even included in a book entitled the *Pro-European Reader* (Leonard and Leonard 2002: 92–94). But then things went sour. Skirmishes with the Socialist President of the Commission, Jacques Delors, became ever more frequent. Events came to a head in 1990 as the EEC launched two new intergovernmental conferences on monetary and political unity. The clash became frontal. The Finchley MP raced towards a head-on collision with the Europhile side of her party. On 30 October 1990 Thatcher gave her famous 'No! No! No!' speech in the House of Commons in which she explicitly warned that the supremacy of parliament was in danger; subsequently, Thatcher was ousted as leader of the Conservative Party and replaced as Prime Minister by John Major.

Thatcher fell primarily because of Europe and many within the Conservative Party would never forget it. Indeed, hard core Thatcherites considered her overthrow to be little less than a coup d'état. On 7 February 1992 Britain signed the Maastricht Treaty. But despite the astuteness with which John Major negotiated opt-outs on the social chapter and the European Monetary Union (EMU), the concessions to Britain's position were regarded as insufficient by a small group of approximately 20 Tory MPs whom an exasperated Major dubbed 'the bastards'. Egged on by the Lady herself, a tug of war immediately began over the treaty's ratification. Indeed, two political scientists have even misguidedly suggested that British Euroscepticism resulted from 'one woman's prejudice' (Fontana and Parsons 2015: 89). The problem was not the individual prejudice of any politician, however eminent, but the issue of sovereignty. It was a Labour member, Peter Shore, speaking in a debate on the Social Protocol on 22 July 1993, who expressed the rebels' core argument against Maastricht most eloquently:

> The British courts or Whitehall is not the primary threat to Parliament. That threat is massively present in the treaties of the European Community that proclaim the supremacy of Community law over British law, and in its courts of justice that can and do strike down and render nugatory any Act of this Parliament that conflicts with European law. Through the Maastricht treaty, it will massively extend its powers to large new areas of policies, including the ultimate power of imposing fines on this country if its rulers dared to pursue policies contrary to those imposed by the European Community … All this and more is at the heart of the Maastricht treaty (Shore 1993).

Over the ratification of the Maastricht Treaty John Major was subjected to the most strenuous parliamentary test of any contemporary British leader – Theresa May now perhaps excepted. As a baffled Major wrote:

> How had so much bad blood welled up so fast? How had members of what had so recently been a winning team turned against each other, plotted against each other, betrayed each other, careless of the opportunity this was building for their common enemy? … Was there something I could have said, some policy I could have adopted … which might have begun my party's journey back to sanity? (Major 1999: 384–5)

The answer to these questions was no. After Maastricht, 'Europe' became a stark question of right or wrong. By the 2001 general elections, such Conservatives were a majority in the parliamentary party and the then party leader, William Hague, shared their views: indeed, he was elected *because* he shared their views. The 2001 manifesto, *Time for Common Sense*, promised to fight for a 'network Union', a 'flexible Europe of nations' in which Britain would keep the pound, re-negotiate the EU's basic law to keep a veto over all new legislation, and give Westminster 'reserved powers' against EU encroachment on British parliamentary sovereignty. Any new transfers of sovereign parliamentary power to the EU would require a referendum (Conservative Party 2001). Had Hague won the 2001 election, Britain would have undergone a traumatic clash with the EU somewhat earlier. Instead, the Conservatives were defeated by a humiliating margin, in part because of their position on Europe, which was then widely regarded as too extreme. The Eurosceptic wing of the party did not care, however. They had put the issue of lost sovereignty and lost freedom centre stage.

'Get Britain out of the EU'

The British press kept it there for the next fifteen years. After Maastricht was ratified, resistance to the European project was carried on largely by the principal daily newspapers and their chief columnists. The British press constructed a climate of hysteria around the whole issue of Europe that set the intellectual agenda. Since the fall of Thatcher in 1990 hardly a day has gone by without at least one of Britain's newspapers attacking Europe on some issue or another (Levy et al. 2016). Even non-EU institutions were targeted – indeed, they were tarred with the EU brush. British newspapers, for example, ran a relentless campaign against the Court of Human Rights' judgment on prisoners' voting rights handed down in 2005. For many years much of the British press has been dominated by Eurosceptic media tycoons and commentators such as Christopher Booker, Simon Heffer, Richard Littlejohn, or Charles Moore. The dominating role of Rupert Murdoch, in particular, has led some observers to pose the question of whether one can consider freedom of the press to be fully guaranteed in the British system (Daddow 2012).

Fake news was not invented in 2016. Ever since 1992 the EU Commission has collected headlines from British newspapers and meticulously exposed falsehoods. The Commission has faced an impossible task, however. Its average rebuttal is read about 1,000 times. The website of the *Daily Mail*, which according to the Commission is the worst offender, by contrast garners 225 m visitors each month despite the fact that many of its headlines appear to have been written by journalists as inebriated as Jones when he knocked down Robinson (European Commission). Some of the news stories disproved by the EU defy belief: the 1998 headline 'Bananas must not be excessively curved says EU' (*Sun*, March 1998) is notorious, but what about: 'EU to force British rhubarb to be straight' (*Sun*, June 1996) or 'EU says strawberries must be oval' (*Sun*, March 1998). Then there are stories on 'untouchable' subjects such as 'EU threatens poppy appeal with tax' (*Evening Standard*, November 2003), or 'Her Majesty to be removed from British passports says EU' (*Daily Telegraph*, September 2007). A few headlines can only be described as surreal: 'EU is forcing cows to wear nappies' (*Daily Mail*, October 2014).

What such articles had in common was the message that Britain's right to live freely by its own laws was being infringed. Foreigners were not just ruling us, they were interfering with our everyday life. For 20 years, the British press, especially the *Daily Mail*, has taken every opportunity to point the moral that Britain needed to 'take back control', be it control over rhubarb – or its borders and economic policy.

The more ludicrous tabloid headlines were, of course, only a diversion in a prolonged attack on all extensions of EU competency, the highlights of which were the campaigns against giving up the pound in the first Blair government, against the so-called EU Constitution, and against the Lisbon Treaty, which provoked the *Daily Express* to publish a headline on 4 November 2009 that proclaimed 'Britain: The End'. The failure of the government headed by Gordon Brown to heed the massive opinion poll majorities supporting a referendum on the Lisbon Treaty was the 'final straw' that led many Eurosceptics in parliament and the press to advocate leaving outright – a course of action that Lisbon made possible (Francois 2016). The principal pro-Brexit newspapers downplayed the economic risks consequent upon this choice – journalists in the *Daily Mail* and *Daily Telegraph* competed from 2009 onwards to denigrate the EU's economic performance and to dwell upon the opportunities open to Britain if it became a sort of Singapore writ large off the coast of the EU. But ultimately, parliamentary sovereignty was the crux of the matter: even hesitant Eurosceptics aware of the potential costs of leaving the EU thought it trumped economic concerns. On the eve of the referendum, Ambrose Evans-Pritchard, one of the most reflective Eurosceptic commentators, consciously or unconsciously evoked Enoch Powell to justify his vote in favour of leaving:

> With sadness and tortured by doubts, I will cast my vote as an ordinary citizen for withdrawal from the European Union. Let there be no illusion about the trauma of Brexit. Anybody who claims that Britain can lightly disengage after 43 years enmeshed in EU affairs is a charlatan or a dreamer, or has little contact with the realities of global finance and geopolitics. Stripped of distractions, it comes down to an elemental choice: whether to restore the full self-government of this nation, or to continue living under a higher supranational regime, ruled by a European Council that we do not elect in any meaningful sense, and that the British people can never remove [...] (Evans-Pritchard 2016)

Paradise lost

There was a curious disjuncture in British public life in the 2000s. Its principal newspapers, which still sold millions of copies a day and which were swift to move on line with attractive, innovative websites, pumped out anti-EU propaganda with vigour. Tony Blair, Gordon Brown and David Cameron all conducted EU policy with an eye to the next day's headlines: they had to. Yet the people were less obsessed. Although opinion polls consistently showed that a substantial minority of people – it oscillated between 10–20 percent – wanted to leave the EU and that a plurality wanted to reduce its powers, and although this plurality increased after the Treaty of Lisbon's ratification in 2009, until 2016 there was never a groundswell of public opinion for leaving outright (Ormston 2015: 19–20; Swales 2017: 4).

Indeed, Britain became a more 'European' place in the 2000s. Older British people took advantage of freedom of movement to renovate cottages in rural France and Spain and to boost flagging wine consumption in those countries. Britain's flourishing economy created jobs for highly qualified Europeans who found opportunities that their domestic job markets had denied them. There was widespread awareness that membership of the EU single market was a crucial variable in attracting inward flows of capital, especially from non-European states like Japan and the United States. To quote Tony Blair:

> As any inward investor will tell you, increased investment depends on two things above all others. Britain's modern, flexible economy. And its membership of the world's largest market. There are 380 million consumers in the European Union. In the next ten years, with enlargement, there will be 100 million more. They are the big prize that attracts the likes of Ford, Toyota, Nissan, Microsoft (Blair 1999).

In this mood of openness, Blair's policy of 'constructive engagement' with Europe seemed more sensible than the anti-Europeanism of William Hague and his immediate successors as leader of the Conservative Party, including David Cameron, whose modernizer's credentials stopped short of embracing the EU: in 2009, the Tory Party even withdrew from the European People's Party (EPP).

But paradise would soon be lost. The Euro crisis, which gave credibility to Eurosceptic propaganda against the single currency, and the arrival after 2004 of working class Europeans to do jobs that native British workers believed should belong to them, upset this optimistic mood. Britain was one of only three countries (Ireland and Sweden were the others) that allowed full freedom of movement from the new member states after accession (citizens of Bulgaria and Romania were not given the same rights after their accession in 2007). The result was an entirely predictable (though unpredicted) influx of EU citizens, which, coming on top of already high non-European immigration, caused public opinion to perceive that Britain no longer controlled its own borders. As one influential commentator has noted: 'if there is a paramount reason for Britain's shock decision to leave the EU it is the seething discontent of a large part of public opinion created by twenty years of historically unprecedented immigration and the insouciant response of the ... political class to this change' (Goodhart 2017: 118).

The numbers are striking: in 2004 just over one million EU citizens were resident in the UK; by 2014 this figure had increased to almost exactly three million, with the overwhelming majority of the new residents coming from the EU-8 countries, notably Poland (Vargas-Silva and Fernández-Reina 2018: 4). When one notes that the number of non-EU residents also increased from three million to over five million between 2000 and 2014, public disquiet was unsurprising: migration on this scale imposed a major burden on public services and the transformation of whole areas of towns. Peterborough, a medium-sized cathedral city in eastern England, became the fastest-growing urban area in the United Kingdom as a result of migration from EU-8 countries (Grinnell 2014). Add to the mix the fact that EU-8 workers were often found jobs at rock-bottom wages by agencies that undercut local workers in economically deprived areas, and the fact that this immigration was anyway taking place during a time of salary stagnation, the conditions were ripe for a backlash against both migrants and the EU. The surge in migration from the EU-8 was greeted with hysteria by the press, which surpassed itself with the virulence of its headlines and the tendentiousness of its facts on the issue of 'Britain's Wide Open Borders' (Allen 2016: 12). It was also exploited by the United Kingdom Independence Party (UKIP) and its leader Nigel Farage, an able demagogue.

Yet as Christopher Bickerton and Richard Tuck have pointed out, beneath this opposition to migration lay the conviction that national sovereignty had been lost, not only prejudice against foreigners, or economic distress. When the British grasped that 'whomever they voted into Parliament, nothing significant could be done about EU immigration unless Britain left the EU', they 'suddenly realized that the basic political structures in which they lived had been transformed, and that there was literally nothing they could do about it', at any rate by normal parliamentary means (Bickerton and Tuck 2017).

David Cameron was responding to this hardening of public opinion against the EU when, on 23 January 2013, he made his Bloomberg speech pledging that there would be a referendum on the question of EU membership during the next parliament. The prime minister warned frankly that 'democratic consent for the EU in Britain is now wafer thin' (Cameron 2013). When UKIP got 27.5 percent of the vote in the 2014 European elections, it was an unmissable sign that the many voters who thought the EU needed its wings clipping were shifting out of the 'reform' camp and into the 'leave' camp. Euroscepticism was going mainstream (Startin 2015).

Not looking right and left

To reprise Carr, by May 2015, when Cameron scored a surprise election victory that enabled him to govern without the Liberal Democrats, Robinson needed to look right and left very carefully indeed before he crossed the road. The chances of an accident occurring at the junction where British politics and the EU met had risen sharply. British public opinion was no longer willing to accept an integration process that proceeded by 'a form of ratchet' (Hill 2019: 39) and which led to more and more decisions being centralized in Brussels.

This is why David Cameron's February 2016 negotiation with the rest of the EU to get Britain an exemption to stay out of any further moves towards political integration, and to restrict the rights of EU migrants to 'non-contributory in-work benefits' for four years, met with derision by the Eurosceptic press and its readers (Gov. UK 2016). By then, nothing short of Gaullist press conference diplomacy to cap the number of migrants could have won Cameron a reprieve. Cameron's misstep prompted Boris Johnson to announce, in a formidable article in the *Daily Telegraph*, that he would campaign for 'Leave'. In his piece, Johnson acknowledged that the 'federalist vision' of Europe was not 'an ignoble idea', though it was one 'we do not share', worried that a vote to leave the EU would cause 'fresh tensions' between Scotland and the rest of the UK, but obsessively returned to the question of sovereignty lost. Every argument first used by Powell and Jay in the 1960s was rehashed, especially the fact that EU law is 'irreversible – since it can only be repealed by the EU itself'. He concluded:

> We have given so much to the world, in ideas and culture, but the most valuable British export and the one for which we are most famous is the one that is now increasingly in question: parliamentary democracy – the way people express their power ... This is the only opportunity we will ever have to show that we care about self-rule. A vote to Remain will be taken in Brussels as a green light for more federalism, and for the erosion of democracy. (Johnson 2016).

As the referendum campaign began, the Jones of public opinion was drunk at the wheel with such arguments, which was all the more reason why the British government needed step carefully. Instead, it tried to scare Jones into swerving. During the referendum campaign, Downing Street relied on 'Project Fear', bombarding the electorate with economic data suggesting that leaving the EU would be a disaster. On 18 April 2016, Chancellor George Osborne unveiled a treasury analysis that predicted a fall in household incomes of £4,300 by 2030 if Brexit took place; the same document estimated income tax rises of 8–10p in the pound. Most voters were unmoved by obviously spurious predictions for a decade and a half hence (Shipman 2017: 247–48). Will Straw, who fronted 'Stronger In', the official campaign for a Remain vote, has suggested that the key Remainers complacently believed that 'the two golden laws of politics were going to win it for us in the end – that risk kicks in towards the end and people vote for the status quo, and secondly that prosperity trumps all other issues'. He added wryly: 'both of these laws proved false in this election' (Shipman 2017: 598).

This giant misjudgement was based upon a London-centric vision of British prosperity. Britain's economy was geographically skewed, productivity and wages were stagnant and too many people were obliged to work long hours (Tilford 2016: 1). South East England and some other privileged parts of the country were thriving, most of the country was not. The great unanticipated fact of 23 June 2016 was turnout: several million lower income people who did not usually vote, and who were hence off the radar of the Remain campaign's inept polling operation, cast a ballot. The keenest Leavers were the poorest working class people, who thought by startling margins that leaving the EU wouldn't make the economy worse, and that immigration had caused British life to deteriorate (Swales 2017: 25–26). More accurately, perhaps, they couldn't imagine it being worse. These voters lapped up the nativist narrative propagated by Nigel Farage. Arron Banks, the South African millionaire who bankrolled Leave.EU, Farage's campaign vehicle, said:

> we went to the north, we went to Bolton, we went to Halifax. Nigel was wildly popular there. They say he was toxic. He was toxic inside the M25, in the rarefied air there. But outside of there he was anything but toxic. (Shipman 2017: 589)

Cameron compounded his insouciance over the power of prosperity to decide the referendum with a blasé attitude – in public at least – towards the 'special status' deal he had negotiated with the EU. In effect, he treated it as the policy of the government, but not necessarily of the Conservative Party. Over 100 Tory MPs followed the lead of Boris Johnson and Michael Gove and campaigned to leave. This mattered, because while Nigel Farage could sway the former mill towns of Yorkshire and the coastal towns of Lincolnshire or Kent, he was not so effective with respectable middle class opinion. Tim Shipman, in his account of the referendum campaign, quotes Tony Blair's spin doctor Alistair Campbell saying:

> If it had just been Nigel Farage and the right-wing papers, and a few Tory oddballs, it would have been fine. It wouldn't have happened without Boris Johnson and Michael Gove ... They took it to a different level (Shipman 2017: 600).

'In the actions of all men, and especially of princes, where there is no court of appeal, one judges by the result' (Machiavelli 1961: 101). Cameron failed abysmally: he is one case where it is hard to see a school of historical revisionism coming to the rescue. In hindsight, Cameron ought to have driven a harder bargain with the EU; should have been more in touch with the public mood, not loftily aloof; should have made Michael Gove realize that he was expected to toe the party line, or else. He did none of those things.

Johnson and Gove, by contrast, displayed the unscrupulousness in pursuit of victory that a Prince needs. Machiavelli's reminder that the 'princes who have achieved great things have been those who have given their word lightly, who have known how to trick men with their cunning, and who have, in the end, overcome those abiding by more honest principles' might have been written with Johnson and Gove in mind (Machiavelli 1961: 99). They acquiesced in every one of the exaggerations and outright lies fabricated by the Vote Leave campaign, above all the slogan that leaving the EU would save £350 million every week, which they knew was fake news, but which unquestionably was effective with the electorate. In the end, they tipped the balance. As Dominic Cummings, the guru of the official Vote Leave team, acknowledged:

> If about 600,000 people – just over 1% of registered voters – had decided differently, IN would have won. This is a small enough margin that it could easily have happened if quite a few specific events and decisions had turned out differently (Cummings 2017).

Like the death of Robinson, the car crash on 23 June 2016 was extremely contingent on the personal behaviour of a handful of key individuals. Had Gove put loyalty to his friend the prime minister ahead of his longstanding opposition to EU membership; had Cameron and Osbourne had the common sense to implement an expansionary spring budget targeted at deprived areas instead of middle class tax cuts; had the Labour Party – its virtual absence from this article is significant – campaigned for Remain in its northern heartland with greater vigour, then Britain might have voted narrowly to remain.

Such counterfactuals, which, in so far as they require only a minimal rewrite of actual events, meet a crucial criterion of plausibility, do not alter the fact that Brexit was an accident waiting to happen. Since the Maastricht Treaty became law, but especially in the last decade, the EU project has become increasingly identified in Britain with a democratic recession; with a transfer in perpetuity of powers that should rightly belong to the sovereign parliament elected by the British people. The 'British are a parliamentary nation', said the intellectual progenitor of the Leave movement, 'if our values are in danger, and if our freedom and independence is in danger, it is because Parliament is endangered, and endangered in the only way an institution can be – by inner loss of conviction' (Powell 1978: 134). Yet one of the great ironies of the 'Brexit Fiasco' is that events have shown that Britain's most ardent Leavers are less convinced by the centrality of Parliament than they claim. Indeed, they have been willing to sidestep it to get the Brexit they want. In other words, there has been a huge twist in the tale which the psychologist Wilhelm Wundt would have defined as a 'heterogony of ends' (Wundt 1886: 250). Brexit itself, rather than parliamentary sovereignty, has become the object to be defended at all costs (Frosini 2019: 3–4), but that is another story that could lead to another Jones-Robinson style accident.

Chronicle of a car crash

In the final analysis, the referendum outcome was testimony to the power of ideas, albeit ideas brutally simplified and sometimes cynically propagated. Jay's and Powell's stringent critiques of the dangers presented to Britain's democracy by European integration had been coarsened by two decades of tabloid journalism and boiled down to a potent campaign slogan – 'Let's take back control' – that touched atavistic emotions and mobilized genuine grievances. It also touched upon an uncomfortable truth, namely that the seemingly inexorable growth in the functions and power of the EU does not sit easily with traditional British constitutional precepts.

It is the nature of the historical methodology proposed by E.H. Carr that the weight of causation could be placed elsewhere. Other historians might well argue that we have underestimated the extent to which English ethnic and cultural bigotry (Spiering 2014) played a part in driving anti-EU sentiment, or have neglected entirely imperial nostalgia, or have said little about the strange death of British social democracy, or the existence of a cleavage between 'Somewheres' and 'Anywheres' (Goodhart 2017). All of these are legitimate 'generalizable causes' which other scholars might easily weigh heavily in the balance. In *What is History?* Carr argued that historical interpretation is like looking at a mountain: it looks different from every angle of vision (Carr 1973: 26–27). In this article, we plead guilty to having sketched the mountain from one angle in particular. But this angle is an important one, since the euphoria and sense of liberation that many voters genuinely felt on 24 June 2016, and the tenacity with which Brexiteers have since resisted compromise, is inexplicable unless you can compel yourself to look at Brexit from this point of view.

Acknowledgements

This article is one of the outcomes of co-teaching a course at SAIS Europe entitled 'Uncertainty and Political Change in Consolidated Democracies' and we would like to thank our students for their contributions. Furthermore, this article benefited from the forthright comments of three external reviewers, who did their job very capably. Part of this research was conducted at the Center for Constitutional Studies and Democratic Development and funded by the George Lawrence Abernethy Endowment.

Disclosure statement

No potential conflict of interest was reported by the authors.

References

Allen, W.L. (2016) *A Decade of Immigration in the British Press*, Oxford: Migration Observatory.

Benn, T. (1990) *Against the Tide: Diaries 1973-76*, London: Arrow.

Bickerton, C. and Tuck, R. (2017) *A Brexit Proposal*, available at https://briefingsforbrexit.com/a-brexit-proposal-by-christopher-bickerton-and-richard-tuck/ (accessed 13 September 2019).

Blair, T. (1999) 'Speech at the London Business School: Making the case for Britain in Europe', London, 27 July, available at https://www.theguardian.com/business/1999/jul/27/emu.theeuro2 (accessed 13 September 2019).

Cameron, D. (2013) 'Speech at Bloomberg', London, 23 January, available at https://www.gov.uk/government/speeches/eu-speech-at-bloomberg (accessed 13 September 2019).

Carr, E.H. (1973) *What is History?* London: Pelican.
Conservative Party (2001) 'Time for common sense (Manifesto)', available at http://www.conservativemanifesto.com/2001/2001-conservative-manifesto.shtml (accessed 13 September 2019).
Craig, P. (2011) 'The European Union act 2011: locks, limits and legality', *Common Market Law Review* 48: 1915–1944.
Cummings, D. (2017) 'On the referendum #21: Branching histories of the 2016 referendum and 'the frogs before the storm', available at https://dominiccummings.com/2017/01/09/on-the-referendum-21-branching-histories-of-the-2016-referendum-and-the-frogs-before-the-storm-2/ (accessed 13 September 2019).
Daddow, O. (2012) 'The UK media and Europe: from Permissive consensus to Destructive Dissent', *International Affairs* 88 (6): 1219–1236.
European Commission (1992–2017) 'Index of Euromyths', available at https://blogs.ec.europa.eu/ECintheUK/euromyths-a-z-index/ (accessed 13 September 2019).
Evans-Pritchard, A. (2016) 'Brexit vote is about the supremacy of Parliament and nothing else: Why I am voting to leave the EU', *Daily Telegraph on-line*, 13 June.
Fontana, C. and Parsons, C. (2015) 'One woman's prejudices: Did Margaret thatcher cause Britain's anti-Europeanism?', *JCMS: Journal of Common Market Studies* 53 (1): 89–105.
Francois, M. (2016) 'The appalling handling of the Lisbon treaty sowed the seeds of Brexit', https://brexitcentral.com.
Frosini, J.O. (2019) 'Is Brexit ripping up the unwritten constitution of the United Kingdom', *The Italian Journal of Public Law* 11 (1): 1–7.
Goodhart, D. (2017) *The Road to Somewhere*, London: Penguin.
Gordon, M. and Dougan, M. (2012) 'The United Kingdom's European Union Act 2011: Who won the bloody war anyway?', *European Law Review* 37 (1): 3–30.
Gov. UK (2016) *The Best of Both Worlds: The United Kingdom's Special Status in a Reformed European Union*, London: HM Government.
Grinnell, P. (2014) 'Population growth rate is fastest in UK but Peterborough people are not that happy' *Peterborough Telegraph*, 29 January.
Harlow, C. (1996) 'Francovich and the problem of the disobedient state', *European Law Journal* 2 (2): 199–225.
Hartley, T.C. (2004) *European Union Law in a Global Context*, Cambridge: Cambridge University Press.
Hill, C. (2019) *The Future of British Foreign Policy: Security and Diplomacy in a World After Brexit*, Cambridge: Polity.
Hobolt, S.B. (2016) 'The Brexit vote: a divided nation, a divided continent', *Journal of European Public Policy* 23 (9): 1259–1277.
Jay, D. (1968) *After the Common Market: A Better Alternative for Britain*, London: Penguin.
Johnson, B. (2016) 'There is only one way to get the change we want – Vote Go', *Daily Telegraph*, 22 February.
Lebow, R.N. (2000–2001) 'Contingency, catalysts and international system change', *Political Science Quarterly* 115 (4): 591–616.
Leonard, D. and Leonard, M. (eds) (2002). *The Pro-European Reader*, Basingstoke: Palgrave.
Levy, D.A.L., et al. (2016) *UK Press Coverage of the EU Referendum*, Oxford: Reuters Institute.
Machiavelli, N. (1961) *The Prince*, London: Penguin.
Major, J. (1999) *John Major - The Autobiography*, London: HarperCollins.

Musolff, A. (2000) 'Political imagery of Europe: A house without exit doors?', *Journal of Multilingual and Multicultural Development* 21 (3): 216–229.

Ormston, R. (2015) *Disunited Kingdom? Attitudes to the EU Across the UK*, London: NatCen Social Research.

Patrono, M. and Frosini, J.O. (2015) 'Two Grand Old Ladies Face to Face: The United Kingdom and the United States of America Constitutions Compared', *Victoria University Wellington Law Review* 46: 989–1009.

Powell, J.E. (1971) *The Common Market: The Case Against*, London: Elliot Right Way Books.

Powell, J.E. (1978) *A Nation or No Nation?: Six Years in British Politics*, Ritchie, R. (ed.), London: Batsford.

Shipman, T. (2017) *All Out War: The Full Story of Brexit*, London: William Collins.

Shore, P. (1993) 'Hansard volume (House of commons debates)', *22 July, 229:550–51*.

Spiering, M. (2014) *A Cultural History of British Euroscepticism*, London: Palgrave.

Startin, N. (2015) 'Have we reached the tipping point? The mainstreaming of Euroscepticism in the UK', *International Political Science Review* 36 (3): 311–323.

Swales, K. (2017) *Understanding the Leave Vote*, London: NatCen Social Research.

Thatcher, M. (1993) *Downing Street Years*, London: Harper Collins.

Tilford, S. (2016) *Brexit Britain: The Poor Man of Western Europe*, London: Centre for European Reform.

Vargas-Silva, C. and Fernández-Reina, M. (2018) *EU Migration to and from the UK*, Oxford: Migration Observatory.

Wundt, W. (1886) *Ethik. Einer Untersuchung der Thatsachen und Gesetze des sittlichen Lebens*, Stuttgart: Verlag Von Ferdinand Enke.

No match made in heaven. Parliamentary sovereignty, EU over-constitutionalization and Brexit

Susanne K. Schmidt

ABSTRACT

The abundant literature on the UK's Brexit-decision has focused on explaining the politicization and preference formation leading up to the referendum. But the institutional background has received much less attention. I argue that as a common-law country with a tradition of parliamentary sovereignty, the UK exhibits institutional features that pose a significant mismatch to the prevailing policymaking mode in the European Union. The latter relies heavily on the constitutionalization of the EU-Treaties with the four freedoms, competition law, and citizenship rights, and accords an extraordinary role to the European Court of Justice in policymaking. Constitutionalized European rules regarding freedom of movement and EU citizens' access to the welfare state drove the politicization of EU-membership in the UK. To understand why 'taking back control' found such resonance, it is important to reflect the core features of the UK polity.

Introduction

Analyses of the Brexit referendum abound.[1] Much of the Brexit literature has sought to explain political preference formation and politicization of EU membership (Hobolt, 2016), the lack of European identity (Curtice, 2017), or has connected the leave vote to low education and income, and high unemployment (Becker, Fetzer, & Novy, 2017; Colantone & Stanig, 2018). There has been less interest in exploring the underlying constitutional characteristics of the UK facilitating politicization, despite the distinct tradition of the UK vis-à-vis other EU member states (Lijphart, 1999). Following De Wilde (2011, p. 559) politicization can be defined as 'an increase in polarisation of opinions, interests or values' regarding policy formulation. The UK parliamentary system stands out with its electoral rules ('first past the post'), predominantly two-party system, its tradition of parliamentary sovereignty and of common law (Lijphart, 1999, pp. 10–21). These pronounced majoritarian traits can be regarded as in stark contrast to the political system of the EU. Integration in the EU is very much 'integration through law' with rulings of the European Court of Justice (ECJ) giving important impulses (Byberg, 2017; Cappelletti, Seccombe, & Weiler, 1986). Grimm (2017) argues that the EU is characterized by 'over-constitutionalization' imposing important limits for majoritarian decision-making. Such non-majoritarian decisions rooted in 'over-constitutionalization' create a significant institutional mismatch with the UK's strongly majoritarian polity. Moreover, as a common-law country, the UK has been particularly responsive to European case law. Frequent references to and good compliance with ECJ rulings in national policy brought significant political attention to the role of the ECJ in EU policies. Relying on case law implies weak input legitimacy, arguably facilitating politicization in the UK's majoritarian system. In this paper, I argue that these institutional traditions are central to our understanding the Brexit process.

Crucial for the Brexit decision was the politicization of inner-EU migration to the UK (Dennison & Geddes, 2018). After eschewing the possibility of a transitional arrangement for free movement, Premier Cameron could not realise his goals of ex-post exceptions and transitional arrangements at the European Council in February 2016. For the politicization of free movement, the UK's liberal labor market, moreover, according to Boräng (2018, p. 23), works to foster a 'perceived socio-economic threat' from migration. This political-economic dimension has to be kept in mind (though it cannot be developed here due to space constraints). Rather my focus will be to what extent EU rules on free-movement are driven by ECJ case law, and why this constitutes a mismatch to the UK's institutional traditions.

In the following, I start by analysing this mismatch between over-constitutionalized policymaking in the EU and parliamentary sovereignty in the UK. I then turn to intra-EU migration as the most politicized policy field in the context of Brexit (Goodwin & Milazzo, 2017; Parker, 2017, p. 480). I trace how the EU's legal regime is shaped by over-constitutionalization, and show how the UK's common-law tradition implies far-reaching attention to these non-majoritarian roots of European case law.

In sum, we can find a particular mismatch between the EU and the UK, where its tradition of parliamentary sovereignty led to high political sensitivity regarding the constraints of European case law, while the common-law tradition implied that the administration followed and implemented these constraints in a particularly detailed way. This institutional mismatch was important for the politicization of EU-membership, and it is necessary to understand why 'taking back control' could resonate so easily with British voters. With the study of a single case, the following analysis can only aspire to being a 'plausibility probe' in Eckstein's sense of inductively complementing existing theories, deriving hypotheses for subsequent large-scale research (Eckstein, 1975, pp. 108–111). However, the extent of institutional mismatch of the UK polity, it is argued, is an omitted variable in existing research (George & Bennett, 2005, p. 134).

A case of mismatch: institutional incompatibilities between the EU's over-constitutionalization and the UK's parliamentary sovereignty

The UK has always been a difficult member for the EU, demanding several special deals, such as the famous rebate, an exemption from joining the Euro or a special role in Justice and Home Affairs (Becker et al., 2017, p. 543). Membership in the European Union has lower than average support in the UK, and 'the British public has consistently been the most Eurosceptic electorate in the EU ever since the UK joined in 1973' (Hobolt, 2016, pp. 1259–60). What are the institutional roots of the UK's special role in the EU? In the following, I will first discuss the importance of the European Court of Justice in the EU's policymaking process. I then turn to the political system of the UK, given its tradition of common law and parliamentary sovereignty. Judicialized policymaking in the EU, I argue, brought particular problems to the UK.

Over-constitutionalization in the EU

Starting with the 'coup d'État' of declaring the Treaty's direct effect and supremacy in 1963/64 (Stone Sweet, 2007), case law interpreting the rules of the Treaties as quasi-constitutional requirements has pushed European integration beyond what legislative majorities could have achieved. The constitutionalization of the Treaties gives the European Court of Justice a unique power in the EU's political process. Early research noted its importance in the context of the 'integration through law' literature (Byberg, 2017; Cappelletti et al., 1986). Political science concentrates more on the ECJ as a neutral arbiter enforcing legislative compromises (Börzel & Sedelmeier, 2017), giving less attention to the importance of case law in policymaking, though its relevance in the single-market project has long been acknowledged (Alter & Meunier-Aitsahalia, 1994).

The former German constitutional judge Dieter Grimm coined the term 'over-constitutionalization' to point to the consequences of constitutionalising the Treaty. National constitutions, notwithstanding their heterogeneity, focus on state organization and fundamental individual rights (Grimm, 2017). Because of its origin as an international treaty, the Treaty of Rome and its successors describe many material policies as cooperation aims, namely the four freedoms, competition law, and later, introduced in Maastricht, EU citizenship. As Grimm warns, over-constitutionalization greatly reduces the scope for majoritarian decision-making. European secondary law arising from the EU's legislative process in the interplay of Commission, Council and European Parliament cannot simply overrule primary law (Schmidt, 2018).

To sum up, for the understanding of policymaking in the EU and the degree of integration, over-constitutionalization is an important explanation. Moreover, when we turn to the characteristics of the UK polity, we see that there is a significant institutional mismatch.

Parliamentary sovereignty and common law in the UK

National polities differ in the way that sovereignty is conceptualized, depending on historical trajectories. Abromeit (1995) compared different concepts of sovereignty regarding institutional fit or misfit to membership in the EU. Comparing German constitutional sovereignty, British parliamentary sovereignty, and Swiss sovereignty of the people, the German legally defined concept of sovereignty fits the EU best. For Germans, used to obey their constitutional court in Karlsruhe, it is a small step to accept that the ECJ rules instead. For Switzerland, acknowledging that the ECJ has the last word, violates the Swiss conception of the people being the sovereign. In fact, the ongoing 2018/20 Swiss discussions of the new bilateral treaty between the EU and Switzerland bears evidence to the difficulty of accepting jurisdiction of the ECJ (Bundesrat, 2018).

For the UK, the extent to which the ECJ defines the order of competence in the EU constitutes an institutional mismatch. The tradition of parliamentary sovereignty emphasizes the freedom to legislate in any area, with courts not being able to challenge parliament's decisions (Goldsworthy, 2015). Note that following from the majoritarian system, parliamentary sovereignty works in tandem with the unfettered prerogative of the executive, also termed 'elective dictatorship' (Lijphart, 1999, p. 12). Lord Justice Ryder points out that 'the idea that courts could embark upon the judicial review of legislation never became a feature of our constitutional settlement (…) the check on Parliamentary supremacy in the United Kingdom was Parliament itself through 'the power of a free public opinion represented by the Commons'.' (Ryder, 2017, p. 123). As Dicey termed it in the late nineteenth century, parliament has 'the right to make or unmake any law whatever'. But supreme EU law cannot be changed by parliament. With the UK's accession, the British parliament recognized the supremacy of EU law under the European Communities Act of 1972. Because this bound future parliaments as well, EU membership sits uneasily with the tradition of parliamentary sovereignty (Elliott, 2004). That later parliaments cannot undo this decision but have to accept the supremacy of EU law was settled for the UK only with the *Factortame* ruling (C-213/89) in 1990 (Barber, 2011). Parliamentary sovereignty also conflicts with a strong understanding of judicial review. 'The judiciary is seen as a potentially undemocratic force; therefore, no judicial review of legislation exists, or it is strongly limited' (Tabarelli, 2013, p. 342). This presents a stark contrast to the history of expansive interpretation of the four fundamental freedoms. As the former President of the ECJ, Skouris, argued, no area exists that can be seen as exempt from possible interference with the four market freedoms (Höpner, 2010, p. 145). To name a few examples, environmental policies on bottle deposits can be framed as interfering with the free movement of goods – as can be a prohibition of tobacco advertising; or the prohibition of abortion can be a restriction of the freedom to provide services. Because the EU legal order knows no exclusive domain that is reserved for member states (Börzel, 2005, p. 223), European judicial review has such a large impact on the order of competences between the European and the member-state level, restricting parliamentary sovereignty 'to make or unmake any law whatever'. In the context of Brexit, the tradition of parliamentary sovereignty has received some attention, in particular following the 2017 *Miller* judgment. *Miller* strengthened the rights of parliament in the Brexit process (Ewing, 2017; Reyes, 2017), in itself a break from the tradition of executive dominance.

Another important institutional characteristic of the UK has not been discussed in the Brexit context: It is a common-law country, meaning that legal principles set up by judges are treated as law, without necessary codification by the legislature (Dainow, 1966/1967). 'Case law (…) has been the key tenet of the common-law tradition, to the point that cases and precedents can be considered de facto if not *de iure* the main repositories of Anglo-American law' (Mattei & Pes, 2008, p. 273). While parliamentary sovereignty stands in opposition to the supremacy of EU law, the common-law tradition implies that the UK's administration is much attuned to implementing case law alongside legislation. Not only may the UK be particularly sensitive to the loss of sovereignty going via integration through law, it is also likely to implement these constraints with explicit reference to the ECJ. In fact, comparative research finds that the UK's compliance record is 'exemplary' (Börzel, Hofmann, Panke, & Sprungk, 2010, p. 1364), despite the low public support of membership.

The UK's struggle with constitutionalized free-movement rights

An important result of the European Council meeting in February 2016 dealing with Premier Cameron's requests was the amendment to Regulation 492/2011 that the UK government had negotiated. In times of extraordinary migration, a safeguard mechanism could be triggered, allowing a member state to restrict benefits for EU citizens for the first four years of residence.[2] The Commission stated that the UK met the pre-conditions of this safeguard. In a recent analysis, Beach and Smeets (2019, p. 2) characterise this deal as 'quite exceptional reforms in which the EU bent over backwards to accommodate the United Kingdom, perhaps even going beyond the bounds of the EU Treaties themselves in the issue of immigration.' In the following analysis, I show how these bounds of the Treaty were rather flexible bounds until recently, continuously expanded by the ECJ. Turning to intra-EU migration to the UK, we find that the common-law tradition made this judicial origin of European rights of access to welfare for EU citizens particularly transparent.

Free movement and the indivisibility of the four freedoms

The four freedoms, of goods, services, persons (comprising the freedom of establishment for companies and the free movement of workers), and capital go back to the Treaty of Rome. The Treaty of Rome states on the freedom of movement of workers in Article 48 (2): 'Such freedom of movement shall entail the abolition of any discrimination based on nationality between workers of the Member States as regards employment, remuneration and other conditions of work and employment.' (now Article 45 TFEU, Treaty on the Functioning of the European Union). The claim to equal treatment is backed by the general prohibition to discriminate on the grounds of nationality in Article 7: 'Within the scope of application of the Treaties, and without prejudice to any special provisions contained therein, any discrimination on grounds of nationality shall be prohibited.' (now Article 18 TFEU). As member states have kept their national welfare systems as their own responsibility, free movement and non-discrimination produce a potential conflict. Geddes and Hadj-Abdou even speak of 'a radical experiment in open borders', given that 'social solidarity and cohesion' (Geddes & Hadj-Abdou, 2016, p. 222) remains the responsibility of national welfare states.

In fact, member states did not embark into this 'experiment' light-heartedly. Among the original six, Italy pressured for free movement of labor, given its high unemployment. Italy had set itself the goal of a yearly net-emigration of 200.000. But its attempts to push for a European labor market in regional organisations like the ECSC and the OEEC did not succeed. Once economic development picked up, Italy secured bilateral treaties for labor migration, but these allowed host countries to define the conditions. Yearly net-emigration thus fell short of the self-set aim (Romero, 1993, p. 50). When negotiations on the EEC Treaty started in 1955, the other five continued to oppose the idea of a free circulation of labor, just having successfully coped with high unemployment in the years following the war, and profiting from the bilateral arrangements with Italy and other countries of the Mediterranean. The agreement on the free movement of workers in the Treaty of Rome settled for the twelve year transition period of gradual liberalisation and against a supranational employment policy. As member states retained control over their migration policy, the gradual opening for workers of other member states fell short of any privilege as Italy found out in the 1960s, when workers from Turkey and Portugal entered on a larger scale (Romero, 1993, pp. 53–55). The high growth rates of the 1960s de-escalated the conflict, but member states 'rebuffed any attempt to interfere with their full sovereignty on recruitment policies' (Romero, 1993, p. 55)). While the indivisibility of the four freedoms has been an important argument of the EU in negotiating the Brexit Treaty[3], historically it does not exist (Barnard & Fraser Butlin, 2018). Free movement was the result of intense bargaining. It is complemented by the coordination of national security systems for migrant workers that was agreed in regulations no. 3 and no. 4 in 1958 (currently set by regulations 884/2004 and 987/2009 (White, 2010)).

Important for our context is how much the free-movement regime has been shaped by case law of the ECJ, elucidating the constitutional requirements following directly from the Treaty, as well as the conditions resulting from secondary law. It was the Court which defined the status of worker under the Treaty, and therefore the precondition to the privileges of equal treatment. As Davies (2003, p. 195) shows, the Court set out the concept of 'worker' relatively broadly in a series of cases in the 1980s (C-53/81; C-139/85; C-196/87). Following *Levin* (C-53/81), work has to be 'genuine and effective' though not 'purely marginal and ancillary'. In C-14/09 *Genc*, the Court even regarded, under specific circumstances, a five hour contract per week as sufficient. Equal treatment under the free movement of workers also provides that those EU citizens not earning a living have a right to national social support without further preconditions (C-139/85).

An active Court furthermore helped to establish equal treatment of EU workers in member states' social security. Martinsen and Falkner have shown in some detail how the evolution of the secondary law of social-security coordination was shaped by case law of the Court, frequently referring to the constitutional demands of free movement. Revisions of the regulations partly codified and partly aimed to overrule this case law. The Court countered time and again attempts of member states to control their social-security spending into other member states with reference to the Treaty's prohibition of discrimination on the basis of nationality (Martinsen & Falkner, 2011).

The Treaty of Maastricht took a further step by introducing EU citizenship rights in Article 18 TEC: 'Every citizen of the Union shall have the right to move and reside freely within the territory of the Member States, subject to the limitations and conditions laid down in this Treaty and by the measures adopted to give it effect.' This was a last minute addition that was not accompanied by intensive discussions (Aziz, 2009), showing that governments did not accord high political importance to the status. The qualifications regarding 'limitations and conditions' as well as 'measures adopted' emphasized the continued sovereignty of member states in shaping citizenship regimes.

Notwithstanding the qualifications of the new Treaty addition, the Court embarked on a journey that appeared to promise equal rights to EU citizens, disregarding their financial means (Thym, 2017; Wind, 2009). 'In a sequence of judgments the Court in the meantime has considerably expanded its case law leading some commentators to the assumption that migrant citizens who are not economically active now have the right to claim all benefits available in the host State on the same terms as nationals' (Hailbronner, 2005, p. 1248). One notable ruling was C-184/99 *Grzelczyk*, in which the Court declared member states' duty to a 'certain degree of financial solidarity with nationals of other Member States' (No. 44). The ruling was passed in the middle of the negotiations on the citizenship rights directive 2004/38 (CRD). This Treaty interpretation strongly conditioned what the EU legislators could write into the directive (Wasserfallen, 2010). The interaction between case-law development and legislation resulted in some ambiguities of the CRD. On the one hand, following *Grzelczyk*, there is a duty of assistance, and EU citizens cannot automatically be expelled. On the other hand, member states can demand of EU citizens to be financially self-sufficient and to have a comprehensive health insurance (Article 7(1b)) until five years of legal residence.

Though the directive made clear that member states were keen to uphold differences in entitlements between economically active and inactive EU citizens (recitals 16, 19, 21, Articles 7 & 12), following the directive, the Court continued extending rights to equal treatment in member states' welfare systems until autumn 2014. With the case of *Dano* (C-333/13), the Court started to take the restrictions on equal treatment of the CRD seriously. Member states' rights to exclude economically inactive EU citizens from their welfare state were elucidated. Whether this amounts to an about-turn of the Court (Blauberger et al., 2018), or merely a clarification of existing limits being rooted in the Maastricht Treaty, remains contentious in the literature (Carter & Jesse, 2018; Davies, 2018). During the UK referendum campaign, these free movement rights were particularly politicized.

Before turning to the question, of how the UK dealt with intra-EU migration and the extent of judicially mandated equal treatment, we can summarize as follows: Over-constitutionalization implies that integration is driven to a considerable extent by case law of the Court, in a non-majoritarian way. The depth of European integration cannot be explained through political-preference aggregation alone. The UK's institutional traditions are in a relative mismatch to the EU's polity.

Intra-EU migration to the UK and its institutional preconditions

In opting against transitionally suspending the free movement rights for new member states in 2004, the UK both acted on wrong assumptions (that most other member states would open-up immediately) and wrong forecasts.

> However, even in the worst case scenario, migration to the UK as a result of Eastern enlargement of the EU is not likely to be overly large. The evidence brought together indicates that net migration from the AC-10 to the UK will be broadly in line with current migration movements. (Dustmann, Casanova, Fertig, Preston, & Schmidt, 2003, p. 8)

The Workers Registration Scheme (WRS) that was operated for the Eastern EU-8 member states in the transition period showed that about half a million workers registered in the first 2.5 years, while it was unclear for how long these persons stayed in the UK (Drew & Sriskandarajah, 2007). The non-British resident population grew in total from 5% in 2004–8.4% in 2014[4], and migration from Poland was described as possibly the largest movement between two countries in peace times (Okólski & Salt, 2014). The extent of migration was not only substantial; it also has to be seen in the context of several institutional characteristics of the UK.

To begin with, inhabitants in the UK are not obliged to register with the authorities. ONS (Office of National Statistics) data on migration therefore works with estimates. Only in 2019, it was found that data had underestimated by up to 16% the extent of EU-migration, a finding that downgraded the status of the official migration statistics to experimental: 'This means an increase in the estimate of EU migration from 178,000–207,000 for the year ending March 2016.'[5] Neither is there precise data as to claimants (and their nationality) of welfare state services (Sumption & Altorjai, 2016, p. 3).

The UK's welfare state relies in part on non-contributory welfare. In-work benefits complement a flexible labor market, giving incentives for taking up work, even if it is low-paid. Labor regulations are hardly enforced. This combination means a propensity to attract lower skilled migration, also lowering the overall benefits from labor migration (Ruhs, 2015, p. 19, 24). Estimates found higher in-work benefits but lower out-of-work benefits of EU migrants compared to the overall population (Ruhs, 2015, p. 22). Although analyses showed overall benefits from intra-EU migration (Dustmann & Frattini, 2014), the lack of data, and the political discussion on how to restrict early access to welfare benefits overshadowed the debate. Moreover, it has been shown for the UK that workers with lower wages come under pressure while higher wages profit from additional labor supply (Ruhs & Vargas-Silva, 2018). Boräng (2018) analyses, how labor market structure and wage formation influences the position and attitudes towards migrant workers. This interaction of labor market institutions and labor migration explains why liberal market economies are more closely linked with labor migration control (for instance via a grading system), which then leads to strong support for (highly contributing) migrants (Manow, 2018, p. 60).

Building on case law: the rights of EU citizens

Because a non-contributory, tax-financed welfare system is very open to claims by migrants, particularly when there is no registration requirement, the UK had introduced a habitual-residence test as early as 1994, under the Conservative Government. Previously, income support had been granted irrespective of length of residence in the UK. The term 'habitual residence' draws on the rules of the European regulation of social security. For the definition and determination of habitual residence, the UK government uses criteria established by the ECJ in its case law, taking into account the length of residence, prospects of employment, existing links to the UK, and the intention to settle there (Kennedy, 2011b). The common-law tradition becomes apparent here, and ECJ rulings figure prominently in administrative guidelines and political discussions.

In 2004, linked to Eastern enlargement, the government introduced a new right-to-reside test for EU-citizens, that needs to be passed before the habitual-residence test applies (O'Brien, 2015). This test is relevant for accessing different benefits (job-seeker allowance, child- and housing benefits) and was meant to ensure that EU citizens settling in the UK are either self-sufficient or economically active (Kennedy, 2011a, p. 4). The concomitant privileging of UK nationals, led the European Commission to initiate an infringement procedure in 2010 (Kennedy, 2011a, p. 15f). In defense, the responsible Secretary of State for Work and Pensions, Iain Duncan Smith, claimed that without the test the government might have spent up to £ 2.5 billion a year in additional benefits – a politically disputed estimate (Kennedy, 2011a, p. 18f). While the infringement procedure lingered on, the UK Supreme Court backed the government in mid-2011 in the *Patmalniece* case, agreeing that equal benefits to EU-citizens would result in an undue financial burden for the UK. This backing is in line with what we would expect from courts in the tradition of parliamentary sovereignty that defer to parliament (Tabarelli, 2013, p. 344). The Commission took the UK to the ECJ in 2013, which decided the infringement procedure (C-308/14) in favor of the UK just days before the June 2016 referendum.

Other UK reforms closely followed the evolving ECJ case law. It also has to be kept in mind that the reforms were part of the austerity program in the wake of the financial crisis (Hemerijck, 2013, p. 358, 370). A revised habitual-residence test with more individualized questions, guided by an intelligent IT system, including queries regarding efforts to get into work (Kennedy, 2015, p. 8f) mirrored the ECJ's requirement of individual assessments in its ruling of *Brey* (C-140/12). In mid-2014, the government introduced a Genuine Prospect of Work test (GPoW), drawing on the case *Antonissen* (C-292/89), and the Court's connection of the eligibility of EU citizens for jobseekers' allowance with their 'genuine chances of being engaged' (No. 21) (Kennedy, 2015, pp. 17–19). Because the ECJ accords worker status once employment is not only 'marginal and ancillary' but 'genuine and effective' (case 53/81 *Levin*), the UK government set a minimum earning threshold of £ 150/week, corresponding to 24 h a week at the National Minimum Wage, to meet the criteria. Those persons earning less, are individually assessed with detailed guidelines of the responsible Department of Work and Pensions (DWP) (Kennedy, 2015, p. 21). Internal data of the DWP showed that about 90% of claimants in 2015/16 did not pass the test.[6] The 2018 administrative guideline[7] that provides the details for applying these different rules is 142 pages long. The document gives 46 references to case law of the ECJ (automated search C-), four references to the citizenship directive, and two references each to regulations 883/2004 and 987/2009 – showing how much implementation draws on case law and rather than EU-legislation.

Given the extent of politicization and continuous reforms tackling spending on EU citizens, it is surprising that some legally possible restrictions were introduced rather late. Only in 2014, the UK restricted payment of unemployment support for EU jobseekers in the first three months (Harris, 2016, p. 147). However, the roll-out of universal credit since 2013, which includes jobseeker's allowance (JSA) and to which job-seeking EU citizens are not eligible, also made this question less relevant.[8] Moreover, in the British system, it is in-work benefits for the working EU-poor that make up the bulk of the cost. In 2013/14 about 551,000 working EEA received tax credits, but only about 24,000 EU nationals received JSA.[9] Thus, Harris (2016) refers to estimates of £37 million savings a year after the introduction of the habitual-residence test (p. 140), and £10 million over the next six years for restricting access to housing benefits for EU-job seekers, also from 2014 onwards (p. 150).

Institutional mismatch in practice

The case study elucidates how the institutional mismatch between the UK and the EU polities contributed to the politicization of inner-EU migration following Eastern enlargement in the UK. Bruzelius, Chase, and Seeleib-Kaiser (2016, p. 404) give support to my interpretation. They write: 'Nonetheless, recent debates on EU immigration and welfare access in Britain suggest that the idea of 'semi'-sovereignty is not widely recognised in political circles and conflicts strongly with traditional understandings of parliamentary sovereignty.'

Intra-EU migration was the single most important political issue leading to the politicization of EU-membership, resulting in the vote for leave. Once the decision against a transition period was taken, British flexible labor markets and the wage difference motivated significant and unexpected migration from new Eastern member states, leading to a noticeable rise of the EU-migrant population. Constitutionalized rights to EU equal treatment combined with a low threshold of the worker status as defined in ECJ case law. In the UK common law tradition, these judicial principles found a direct way into administrative practices, leaving the reference to the ECJ's interpretations intact. These frequent references to ECJ rulings substantiating claims to social rights highlighted the institutional conflict with UK parliamentary sovereignty, thereby undermining the legitimacy of EU migrants' social rights. Poor statistics on movement, claims, and economic contribution of EU migrants then added to politicization. That 'take back control' could find such resonance is rooted in the institutional mismatch between an EU that has constitutionalized and judicialized many policy choices, and the common-law tradition of the UK, that made the stark contrast with legitimacy rooted in parliamentary sovereignty so transparent.

Conclusion

In this article, I have argued that the abundant literature on the Brexit decision has paid insufficient attention to the long-standing institutional underpinnings of the Brexit decision. There is a notable mismatch between the UK polity with its strong majoritarian traits and its common-law tradition on the one hand, and an EU that is marked by over-constitutionalization on the other. The relevance of constitutionalized case law for EU policies was traced for the free-movement regime that became so politicized in the UK. The common-law tradition of the UK clearly highlighted the relevance of case law for EU policies at the same time. Institutional mismatch can thus contribute to explain why 'taking back control' became so important in the UK.

Drawing on a single case study, I could only argue in the sense of a 'plausibility probe'. Malta and Ireland, two other member states share institutional traits with the UK, might undermine my central argument. However, both Malta and Ireland are small states and are, importantly, non-net contributors to the EU budget. Thus, the benefits of EU-membership for both states are more directly apparent than they were for the UK. As we know from Scharpf's analysis, input- and output-legitimacy are interdependent (Scharpf, 2009). Institutionally, it is plausible that other member states struggle less with over-constitutionalized policymaking in the EU. This may be the case but need not necessarily imply that the UK remains the odd one out. As much as Brexit is connected with quite unique conditions of politicization of EU membership (as analyzed in much of the literature), embedded in institutionalized conditions (as I have argued), Brexit can also be read as a sign of warning about fundamental problems in the EU integration process. As heterogeneous as the Union has become with rounds of enlargement, it is plausible that European policies have to cater for greater diversity. Constitutionalising policy choices, accepting case law rather than political preferences to shape policy decisions, implies the danger of shifting political contestation to another level.[10]

Notes

1. I am most grateful for the excellent research assistance of Sofie Wißmann. Moreover, I would like to thank Jeremy Richardson, Berthold Rittberger, Michael Blauberger, Anita Heindlmeier, Philip Manow, Friederike Römer and Jakob Henninger for their helpful comments. The paper profited much from the critical comments of three anonymous reviewers. Research funding of the CRC 1342 (DFG project-no. 374666841) is gratefully acknowledged.
2. http://www.consilium.europa.eu/en/press/press-releases/2016/02/19-euco-conclusions/
3. European Council: Informal meeting at 27, Brussels, 29 June 2016 https://www.consilium.europa.eu/en/press/press-releases/2016/06/29/27ms-informal-meeting-statement/
4. https://www.ons.gov.uk/peoplepopulationandcommunity/populationandmigration/internationalmigration/articles/populationbycountryofbirthandnationalityreport/2015-09-27, Figure 2
5. BBC, 21.8.2019: 'EU migration to UK 'underestimated' by ONS', https://www.bbc.com/news/uk-49420730
6. Interview DWP 22 February 2017.
7. Part 3 - Habitual residence & right to reside - IS/JSA/SPC/ESA. Vol 2 Amendment 3 9 February 2018 https://www.gov.uk/government/uploads/system/uploads/attachment_data/file/572413/dmgch0703.pdf
8. Interview German Embassy, London 21 February 2017.
9. Interview DWP 22 February 2017.
10. I am grateful for discussion with Philip Manow that made this point clearer to me.

Disclosure statement

No potential conflict of interest was reported by the author(s).

Funding

This work was supported by Deutsche Forschungsgemeinschaft [Grant Number CRC 1342].

ORCID

Susanne K. Schmidt http://orcid.org/0000-0001-7931-9935

References

Abromeit, H. (1995). Volkssouveränität, Parlamentssouveränität, Verfassungssouveränität: Drei Realmodelle der Legitimation staatlichen Handelns. *Politische Vierteljahresschrift, 36*(1), 49–66.

Alter, K. J., & Meunier-Aitsahalia, S. (1994). Judicial politics in the European Community. European integration and the pathbreaking cassis de Dijon decision. *Comparative Political Studies, 26*(4), 535–561.

Aziz, M. (2009). Implementation as the test case of European Union citizenship. *Columbia Journal of European Law, 15*(2), 281–298.

Barber, N. W. (2011). The afterlife of parliamentary sovereignty. *International Journal of Constitutional Law, 9*(1), 144–154.

Barnard, C., & Fraser Butlin, S. (2018). Free movement vs. fair movement: Brexit and managed migration. *Common Market Law Review, 55*(2/3), 203–226.

Beach, D., & Smeets, S. (2019). The unseen hands: Collaborative instrumental leadership in the British renegotiation case. *European Journal of Political Research*. Early view. doi:10.1111/1475-6765.12354.

Becker, S. O., Fetzer, T., & Novy, D. (2017). Who voted for Brexit? A comprehensive district-level analysis. *Economic Policy, 32*(92), 601–650.

Blauberger, M., Heindlmaier, A., Kramer, D., Martinsen, D. S., Thierry, J. S., Schenk, A., & Werner, B. (2018). ECJ judges read the morning papers. Explaining the turnaround of European citizenship jurisprudence. *Journal of European Public Policy, 25*(10), 1422–1441.

Boräng, F. (2018). *National institutions - international migration. labour markets, welfare states and immigration policy*. Lanham: Rowman & Littlefield Publ.

Börzel, T. A. (2005). Mind the gap! European integration between level and scope. *Journal of European Public Policy, 12*(2), 217–236.

Börzel, T. A., Hofmann, T., Panke, D., & Sprungk, C. (2010). Obstinate and inefficient: Why member states do not comply with European law. *Comparative Political Studies, 43* (11), 1363–1390.

Börzel, T. A., & Sedelmeier, U. (2017). Larger and more law abiding? The impact of enlargement on compliance in the European Union. *Journal of European Public Policy, 24* (2), 197–215.

Bruzelius, C., Chase, E., & Seeleib-Kaiser, M. (2016). Social rights of EU migrant citizens: Britain and Germany compared. *Social Policy & Society, 15*(3), 403–416.

Bundesrat. (2018). Der Bundesrat schickt den Text zum institutionellen Abkommen in die Konsultation. Bern, 7.12.2018. Retrieved from https://www.admin.ch/gov/de/start/dokumentation/medienmitteilungen.msg-id-73292.html.

Byberg, R. B. (2017). The history of the integration through law project: Creating the academic expression of a constitutional legal vision for Europe. *German Law Journal, 18*(6), 1531–1556.

Cappelletti, M., Seccombe, M., & Weiler, J. H. H. (1986). *Integration through law. Europe and the American federal experience. Volume 1: Methods, tools and institutions*. Berlin: Walter de Gruyter.

Carter, D., & Jesse, M. (2018). The 'dano evolution': Assessing legal integration and access to social benefits for EU citizens. *European Papers, 3*(3), 1179–1208.

Colantone, I., & Stanig, P. (2018). Global competition and Brexit. *American Political Science Review, 112*(2), 201–218.

Curtice, J. (2017). Why leave won the UK's EU referendum. *Journal of Common Market Studies, 55*(S1), 19–37.

Dainow, J. (1966/1967). The civil law and the common law: Some points of comparison. *The American Journal of Comparative Law, 15*(3), 419–435.

Davies, G. (2003). *Nationality discrimination in the European internal market*. London/ New York: Kluwer Law International.

Davies, G. (2018). Has the court changed, or have the cases? The deservingness of litigants as an element in court of justice adjudication. *Journal of European Public Policy, 25*(10), 1442–1460.

Dennison, J., & Geddes, A. (2018). Brexit and the perils of 'Europeanised' Migration. *Journal of European Public Policy, 25*(8), 1137–1153.
De Wilde, P. (2011). No polity for old politics? A framework for analyzing the politicization of European integration. *Journal of European Integration, 33*(5), 559–575.
Drew, C., & Sriskandarajah, D. (2007). EU enlargement in 2007: No warm welcome for labor migrants. *The Online Journal of the Migration Policy Institute.*
Dustmann, C., Casanova, M., Fertig, M., Preston, I., & Schmidt, C. M. (2003). *The impact of EU enlargement on migration flows*. London: Research Development and Statistics Directorate, Home Office.
Dustmann, C., & Frattini, T. (2014). The fiscal effects of immigration to the UK. *The Economic Journal, 124*(580), F593–F643.
Eckstein, H. (1975). Case study and theory in political science. In I. G. Fred & N. W. Polsby (Eds.), *Handbook of political science volume 7* (pp. 79–137). Reading, MA: Addison-Wesley.
Elliott, M. (2004). United Kingdom: Parliamentary sovereignty under pressure. *International Journal of Constitutional Law, 2*(3), 545–627.
Ewing, K. (2017). Brexit and parliamentary sovereignty. *The Modern Law Review, 80*(4), 711–726.
Geddes, A., & Hadj-Abdou, L. (2016). An unstable equilibrium: Freedom of movement and the welfare state in the European Union. In G. P. Freeman & G. P. Mirilovic (Eds.), *Handbook on migration and social Policy* (pp. 222–238). Cheltenham: Edward Elgar.
George, A. L., & Bennett, A. (2005). *Case studies and theory development in the social sciences*. Cambridge: The MIT Press.
Goldsworthy, J. (2015). *Losing faith in democracy: why judicial supremacy is rising and what to do about it*. London: Manuscript. Retrieved from https://judicialpowerproject.org.uk/jeffrey-goldsworthy-losing-faith-in-democracy-why-judicial-supremacy-is-rising-and-what-to-do-about-it/.
Goodwin, M., & Milazzo, C. (2017). Taking back control? Investigating the role of immigration in the 2016 vote for Brexit. *The British Journal of Politics and International Relations, 19*(3), 450–464.
Grimm, D. (2017). *The constitution of European democracy*. Oxford: Oxford University Press.
Hailbronner, K. (2005). Union citizenship and access to social benefits. *Common Market Law Review, 42*(5), 1245–1267.
Harris, N. (2016). Demagnetisation of social security and health care for migrants to the UK. *European Journal of Social Security, 18*(2), 130–163.
Hemerijck, A. (2013). *Changing Welfare States*. Oxford: Oxford University Press.
Hobolt, S. B. (2016). The Brexit vote: A divided nation, a divided continent. *Journal of European Public Policy, 23*(9), 1259–1277.
Höpner, M. (2010). Warum betreibt der Europäische Gerichtshof Rechtsfortbildung? Die Politisierungshypothese. *Sozialer Fortschritt, 59*(5), 141–151.
Kennedy, S. (2011a). *EEA nationals: The 'right to reside' requirement for benefits*. London: House of Commons Library.
Kennedy, S. (2011b). *The habitual residence test*. London: House of Commons Library.
Kennedy, S. (2015). *People From abroad: What benefits can they claim?* London: House of Commons Library Briefing. Paper Number 06847.
Lijphart, A. (1999). *Patterns of democracy. Government forms and performance in thirty-six countries*. New Haven/ London: Yale University Press.
Manow, P. (2018). *Die Politische Ökonomie des Populismus*. Berlin: Suhrkamp Verlag.

Martinsen, D. S., & Falkner, G. (2011). Social policy: Problem-solving gaps, partial exits, and court-decision traps. In G. Falkner (Ed.), *The EU's decision traps* (pp. 128–144). New York: Oxford University Press.

Mattei, U., & Pes, L. G. (2008). Civil law and common law: Toward convergence? In K. E. Whittington, R. D. Kelemen, & G. A. Caldeira (Eds.), *The oxford handbook of law and politics* (pp. 267–281). Oxford: Oxford University Press.

O'Brien, C. (2015). The pillory, the precipice and the slippery slope: The profound effects of the UK's legal reform programme targeting EU migrants. *Journal of Social Welfare and Family Law, 37*(1), 111–136.

Okólski, M., & Salt, J. (2014). Polish emigration to the UK after 2004; Why did so many come? *Central and Eastern European Migration Review, 3*(2), 11–37.

Parker, O. (2017). Critical political economy, free movement and Brexit: Beyond the progressive's dilemma. *The British Journal of Politics and International Relations, 19*(3), 479–496.

Reyes, R. (2017). Legislative sovereignty, executive power, and judicial review: Comparative Insights from Brexit. *Michigan Law Review, 115*(1), 91–99.

Romero, F. (1993). Migration as an issue in European interdependence and integration: The case of Italy. In A. S. Milward, F. M. B. Lynch, F. Romero, & V. Sorenson (Eds.), *The frontier of national Sovereignty: History and theory 1945-1992* (pp. 33–58). London: Routledge.

Ruhs, M. (2015). *Is unrestricted immigration compatible with inclusive welfare states? The (Un)sustainability of EU exceptionalism*. Oxford: Compas, Centre on Migration, Policy and Society. Working Paper No. 125.

Ruhs, M., & Vargas-Silva, C. (2018). *The labour market effects of immigration*. Oxford: The Migration Observatory at the University of Oxford.

Ryder, L. J. (2017). Improving the delivery of justice in the shadow of magna carta. In J. Cooper (Ed.), *Being a Judge in the Modern World* (pp. 121–134). Oxford: Oxford University Press.

Scharpf, F. W. (2009). Legitimacy in the multilevel European polity. *European Political Science Review, 1*(2), 173–204.

Schmidt, S. K. (2018). *The European court of justice and the policy process: The shadow of case law*. Oxford: Oxford University Press.

Stone Sweet, A. (2007). The juridical coup d'état and the problem of authority. *German Law Journal, 8*(10), 915–927.

Sumption, M., & Altorjai, S. (2016). *EU migration, welfare benefits and EU membership*. Oxford: University of Oxford.

Tabarelli, M. (2013). The influence of the EU and the ECHR on 'parliamentary sovereignty regimes': Assessing the impact of European integration on the British and Swedish Judiciaries. *European Law Journal, 19*(3), 340–363.

Thym, D. (2017). The evolution of citizens' rights in light of the European Union's constitutional development. In D. Thym (Ed.), *Questioning EU citizenship. Judges and the limits of Free movement and solidarity in the EU* (pp. 111–134). Oxford/Portland: Hart Publishing.

Wasserfallen, F. (2010). The judiciary as legislator? How the European Court of Justice shapes policy-making in the European Union. *Journal of European Public Policy, 17*(8), 1128–1146.

White, R. C. A. (2010). The new European social security regulations in context. *Journal of Social Security Law, 17*(3), 144–163.

Wind, M. (2009). Post-national citizenship in Europe: The EU as a 'welfare rights generator'? *The Columbia Journal of European Law, 15*(2), 239–264.

Index

For Product Safety Concerns and Information please contact our EU representative GPSR@taylorandfrancis.com
Taylor & Francis Verlag GmbH, Kaufingerstraße 24, 80331 München, Germany

www.ingramcontent.com/pod-product-compliance
Ingram Content Group UK Ltd.
Pitfield, Milton Keynes, MK11 3LW, UK
UKHW022123190926
475702UK00013B/1605

* 9 7 8 0 3 6 7 7 4 8 9 4 4 *